The Diocese of
CLIFTON
1850–2000

Bishop Alexander is received in audience by Pope John Paul II.

The Diocese of
CLIFTON

1850–2000

J. A. Harding

Diocesan Archivist

CLIFTON CATHOLIC
DIOCESAN TRUSTEES

Dr. John Anthony Harding is a graduate of the Gregorian University, Rome, Bristol University and King's College, London. He has been parish priest of St. Bernadette, Whitchurch, Bristol for over twenty years and diocesan archivist since 1986.

ISBN 0 9536689 0 8

Published by Clifton Catholic Diocesan Trustees
© Clifton Catholic Diocesan Trustees 1999
Registered Charity No 233977
St. Ambrose, North Road, Leigh Woods, Bristol BS8 3PW

Design, typesetting and origination by Wyvern 21, Bristol
Printed and bound in Great Britain by J. W. Arrowsmith Ltd, Bristol

CONTENTS

Acknowledgements

Mrs. Beatrice Amblin
Mr. Desmond Anglin
Fr. Richard Barton
the late Miss Lillian Bell
Dom Aidan Bellenger O.S.B.
Fr. John Brennan
Mrs. Jane Butterworth
Mr. J. B. Chapman
Mrs. Christine Collins
Miss Teresa Cullis
Miss Sheila Dennison
Fr. Aelred Dobson S.D.S.
Fr. Anthony Fejer
Mr. George Hackett
Fr. James Halpin O.M.I.
Mr. Lez Hough
Sr. Julia Howard
Mrs. Valerie James
Canon Anthony Johnson
Mrs. Mary Jones

Fr. Michael Jones-Frank
Sr. Rosaria Kenny
Mr. and Mrs. M.J. Milout
Fr. Aidan Murray S.D.B.
the late Sr. Philomena Murray
Mr. Dennis O'Connor
Sr. Francis Agnes Onslow O.S.C.
Fr. George O'Sullivan M.S.F.S.
Mrs. Irene Pickford
Fr. Richard Randolph S.J.
Abbot Geoffrey Scott O.S.B.
Fr. Philip Smyth
Stone King,
    Solicitors, Bath
Mrs. Janette Strong
Fr. Damian Sturdy O.S.B.
Mr. J. Kenneth Vose
Mr. C. Whitmarsh-
    Everiss
Sr. Mary Wulstan

FOREWORD

by the Right Reverend Mervyn Alexander, D.D.

Christianity is certainly an historical religion. The Gospels link the events they relate with happenings in the secular world. St Luke starts his third chapter by referring to the Roman Emperor and the Jewish High Priests of the time.

It has been said that to be deep in history is to be a Catholic. Certainly Catholics attach great importance to historical continuity from New Testament times to the present day.

In Britain and Ireland we are still influenced by the memory of the struggle to keep the Faith alive in penal days and by the great awakening that followed Catholic Emancipation. A special milestone was the Restoration of the Catholic Hierarchy in 1850 when the Metropolitan See of Westminster was established with twelve suffragan sees, including the Diocese of Clifton. The 150th anniversary certainly calls for a celebration and what better celebration could there be than this fascinating account of the events and personalities in the Diocese during this important period?

We owe a great debt of gratitude to Rev Dr. Harding, the Diocesan Archivist, who inspired and led this project. His team included Dr. John Cashman, the Assistant Diocesan Archivist, as well as interested people from different parts of the Diocese. A great contribution to the work came from those who produced histories of their own parish. I am sure that for all who have shared in this project it has been a labour of love, but a labour all the same. So in your name I thank them.

✠Mervyn
Bishop of Clifton

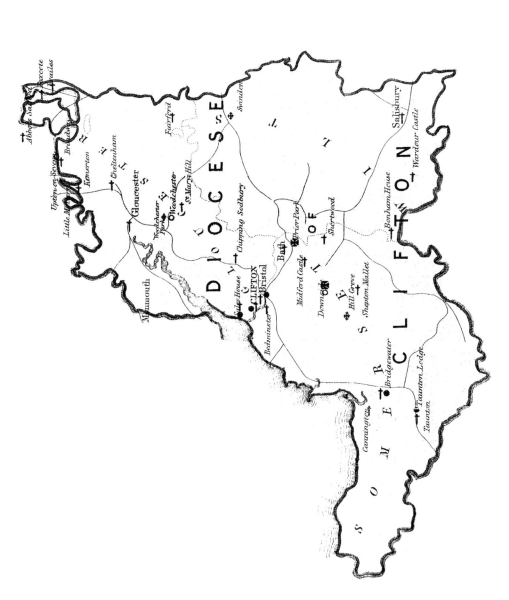

Map 1 Portion of the Ecclesiastical Map of England and Wales showing Churches, Colleges, Missions and Religious Houses, 1851

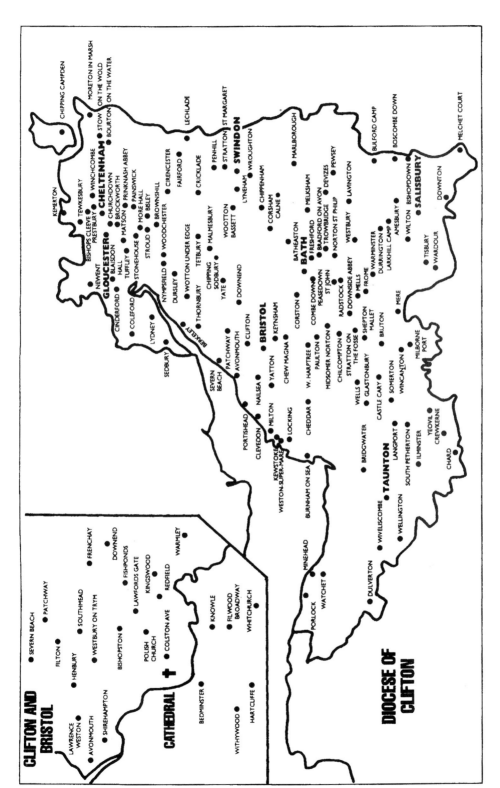

Map 2 The Diocese of Clifton, today

Preface

In the year 2000 people everywhere are commemorating the birth of Our Lord. In Clifton we are also celebrating the birth of our diocese. 150 years ago Pope Pius IX re-established the English and Welsh hierarchy by creating thirteen new dioceses, among them the diocese of Clifton. Since the Reformation this country had been regarded by Rome as missionary territory. Now, at a stroke, the eight vicariates including the Western District were swept away and ordinary episcopal government was restored to the Catholic community. So full of confidence was this gesture in the future of the English Catholic Church that John Henry Newman was moved to see in it the beginnings of a 'second spring'.

When, in 1950, the diocese celebrated its centenary, Fr. J.H. Darby composed a monograph entitled *The Diocese of Clifton 1850–1950*. Half a century later a totally new record is called for, and that is why in 1995, I initiated the production of a volume to mark the sesquicentenary.

This work has drawn on archival sources and on the publications listed in the appendices. Individual items, each identified by its author's initials, were written by Valerie Anglin, John Cashman, John Fendley, Madge McCarthy, Kevin McGarry and myself. Authors made use of much unpublished material and of inputs from many correspondents, some of whom wrote substantial contributions to the history of the diocese in response to our approaches. These sources are duly acknowledged; apologies are made for any inadvertent omissions. Editorial considerations and limitations of space have meant that they have only rarely been incorporated in their original form into this work. Responsibility now rests with the individuals identified above and with myself. Chapter One on the Western District includes extracts from a pamphlet I wrote in 1988 to mark the tercentenary of its foundation.

Parishes have been listed in alphabetical order with defunct missions included under the title of the parish which now serves the area concerned (e.g. *MIDFORD CASTLE:* See Bath: SS. Peter and Paul, Combe Down). Present day Mass centres have their own heading, again with a cross reference (e.g. STOCKWOOD: See Bristol: St Bernadette).

Clearly it would have been tedious to try to identify every priest associated with each parish. Our policy therefore has been to mention only those whose contribution has significantly helped to mould the parish life that we see today. This, however, should not be seen as in any way devaluing the memory of those whose names have been omitted.

Buildings have their own intrinsic interest and it has been our endeavour to identify as many places as possible which at one time or another have seen the celebration of Mass or have other Catholic associations. A wide variety of architectural styles can be found in our diocese and it is hoped that readers will use this book as an excuse to explore and discover them.

The work of the Good Shepherd sisters, carried out in a variety of locations in and around Bristol, has been described under one heading: **Bristol: St. Gerard Majella, Knowle.** *Arnos Court.*

Apart from Downside and Prinknash the work of the religious orders has been treated in the section on parishes and in the article on education.

Many of the photographs reproduced here come from a splendid private collection built up over a number of years by Fr. Richard Barton. The process of selection has been difficult but on balance it was felt that the reader would prefer to see a building recorded as it used to be rather than how it stands today. I should like to thank B.A. Tunbridge and Co. for permission to reproduce photographs of the Bishops of Clifton, and Mr. J.C.D. Smith for his early photograph of Bridgwater.

There are major contributions telling the story of the Cathedral and the Pro-Cathedral, and of education in the diocese, and I should like to thank Mrs. Maureen Smith who has allowed me to re-print in edited form some items which have appeared in past editions of the *Clifton Catholic Directory*.

Finally I am indebted to Bishop Alexander for his unfailing support of this project from the time I first suggested it to him.

This volume is the work of many hands and to all concerned in its production I express my sincere thanks. Like living the Faith itself, its preparation has been both a joy and a challenge. May it prove a fitting tribute to those who have gone before and an inspiration to those still to come.

J.A. Harding

INTRODUCTION

The diocese of Clifton, which covers Gloucestershire, Somerset and Wiltshire and has Bristol as its centre, is particularly rich in Catholic history. Glastonbury, for example, predates the arrival of St. Augustine in A.D. 597 by possibly some two hundred years and is generally regarded as the oldest shrine to Our Lady north of the Alps.

Another indication of the presence of Christianity in this region long before the time of Augustine is the amulet found in Shepton Mallet in 1991 and which has been ascribed by experts to the fourth or early fifth century A.D. It is in the shape of a cross about two inches long with the symbol Chi Rho (Greek letters referring to Christ) inscribed on it and was discovered in a grave in the Roman settlement near the town. The present Archbishop of Canterbury, Dr. George Carey, wears a replica as his pectoral cross.

From these two examples it must be reasonable to infer that the Christians then living in these parts shared the same faith as the three British bishops who attended the Council at Arles in France in A.D. 314 and not least when they joined their brother bishops in sending a letter of filial homage and obedience to the Pope.

Monastic foundations dating from Saxon times or the Middle Ages are numerous, with men like Aldhelm of Malmesbury and Dunstan of Glastonbury, and later of Canterbury, emerging as leaders during a period of considerable religious and cultural achievement. Over the centuries the three counties have seen the Carthusians at Hinton and Witham, the Cistercians at Hailes and Cleeve, the Benedictines at Glastonbury, Gloucester, Winchcombe and Malmesbury, and the Augustinians at Longleat, Bristol and Keynsham. These are but some of the places which maintained a tradition of Monasticism, unbroken until the Reformation. The sick and needy were ministered to in such religious foundations as the leper hospitals of

St. Lawrence, Bristol (hence Lawrence Hill) and, for women, of Maiden Bradley on the border of Wiltshire and Somerset. Similar institutions were to be found at Gloucester, Bridgwater, Taunton, Salisbury and elsewhere. Cathedrals, abbeys and parish churches all witnessed the celebration of Mass and the seven sacraments, and were settings for devotion to Mary and the saints. Priests and people alike gave spiritual allegiance to the Bishop of Rome, the successor of St. Peter.

At the time of the Reformation the authority of the see of Rome was repudiated. With a change of Faith and Order the Church of England came into being. Indeed, the flame of the old Faith was very nearly extinguished. However, of those who were prepared to suffer death rather than compromise their conscience many have since been officially recognised as martyrs by the Church. Some of the executions were carried out at places now within the existing diocese of Clifton.

Blessed Richard Whiting and his two companions were put to death on Glastonbury Tor overlooking the Abbey church (1539) while Blessed John Hambley and Blessed William Lampley were hanged at Salisbury (1587) and Gloucester (1588) respectively. In 1546 Father Robert Persons S.J., another figure in the Reformation story, was born at Nether Stowey, near Bridgwater.

Catholic families like the Stourtons and the Arundells persevered despite the threat of fines or the offer of temporal inducements. Ralph Buckland of West Harptree in Somerset, and the brothers Edward and Henry Mayhew of Dinton in Wiltshire, and other young men went abroad to study for the priesthood while the daughters of a number of the wealthier families made their way to the continent to be educated. Some entered the religious life.

The Catholics, formerly of the Western District (1688–1850) and now of the diocese of Clifton, are the inheritors of this same Faith. The present volume aims briefly to tell their story.

J.A.H.

CHAPTER ONE

The Western District
1688–1850

The rupture between England and Rome under Henry VIII (1509–1547)
and renewed after the Marian reconciliation by vigorous force of law
under Elizabeth I (1558–1603), necessitated a reappraisal by the Catholic
Church of its pastoral provision for its members in this country. Deprived
of the ministry of bishops for many years – the last of the Marian bishops,
Thomas Goldwell of St. Asaph, died in exile in Rome in 1585 – the Catholic
community was entirely dependent on the spiritual succour provided in
secret by the missionary priests ordained abroad.

By 1625 all the priests ordained during the reign of the Catholic Queen
Mary (1553–1558) must be assumed to have died. The remaining body of
clergy, for the most part brave and energetic, was nevertheless divided in
loyalty between religious superiors (often resident in Rome) and the priest
appointed by the Pope to exercise a limited overall jurisdiction in the conduct of the English Mission. This superior, appointed in 1598, was given
the title of Archpriest and he was helped in the exercise of his responsibilities by twelve assistants who represented the interests of the various
regions. The plan, however, was far from being a success, this being due
mainly to the controversies which often flared up between the Jesuits and
the secular clergy.

In 1623 Pope Gregory XI appointed a Vicar Apostolic, William Bishop.
Although possessing episcopal orders, such a prelate does not enjoy the
authority of a diocesan bishop as enacted by the 'ordinary' laws of the
Church. For the next 225 years – until 1850 – the English Catholic community was to remain in the charge of Vicars Apostolic. This underlined
the fact that in Rome England was regarded as missionary territory and in
consequence was given bishops who in their decision making were very

much subject to the Congregation of Propaganda Fide. This is a body (now known as the Congregation for the Evangelisation of the Peoples) composed of cardinals, bishops and other advisers whose responsibility it is to govern Catholics in those parts of the world where a properly constituted hierarchy has yet to be established.

The hopes of English Catholics were heightened with the accession of a Catholic King, James II, in 1685. All the Stuart Queens had been Catholics and there were well-founded rumours that Charles II had been reconciled to the Church on his death-bed. Anti-Catholic tensions were somewhat eased and these factors, together with the virtual impossibility of any bishop, alone, adequately ministering to a flock which extended from one end of the country to the other, persuaded the Pope, Blessed Innocent XI, to increase the number of Vicars Apostolic to four. The Districts were to be designated London, Midland, Northern and Western.

Of these, the last-named was by far the largest embracing the whole of Wales and the present-day dioceses of Clifton and Plymouth – some twenty counties in all. However, before the end of the year (1688) James had lost his throne, William of Orange was King and the hopes of the Catholics had been dashed.

The departure of James II did not signify a loss of royal influence over English Catholic affairs. For many years nominations to vacant Vicariates were channelled to Rome via the Old Pretender's residence in France and it was he and his son, the Young Pretender, who exercised a hidden but very real influence over the course of ecclesiastical affairs in England. Indeed, with English Catholics so determinedly giving allegiance to the Jacobite cause, they became their own worst enemies, giving credence well into the eighteenth century to Elizabeth's contention that to be a Catholic was to be a traitor. This, at least, was the popular perception, and it is to the great credit of Bishop John Stonor (Vicar Apostolic of the Midland District 1716–1756) that he successfully weaned his fellow bishops away from this highly damaging attachment to a more sober and realistic loyalty to the *de facto* succession of the House of Hanover.

1688–1800

The first of the Vicars Apostolic of the Western District was Philip Michael Ellis O.S.B. Born into a clerical family which was to produce a number of distinguished sons, the future bishop, not unlike William Brownlow two centuries later, was a convert to the Faith. After his consecration in 1688 he officiated in London at a small confirmation ceremony but before the end of the year, with the arrival of King William, he was in Newgate prison.

D · O · M ·
P·M·I·MYLORD·ELLI
EPISCOPO
PROTECTORI BENIGNISSIMO
ELEONORVS CIMINELLVS I·V·D·
HERES
MONVMENTVM IAM POSITV̄
RENOVAVIT
ET
DIVI FRANCISCI SACELLVM
A FVNDAMENTIS
ERECTV̄ ORNATVM ET DOTATV̄
A CANONICO
FRANCISCO CIMINELLO
IN HANC NOBILIOREM FORMAM
REDVXIT
ANNO MDCCXIII

Segni Cathedral: one of
several Latin
inscriptions referring to
'My Lord Ellis' ('Elli' is
an attempt to put his
name in the dative
case)

However, he may well have visited his District on one occasion. On his
release he went to the Court of James II at St. Germains and then to Italy.
It was not until 1705 that he was able to resign his Vicariate during which
time the affairs of the District were in the hands of Bishop Bonaventure
Giffard of the Midland District.

In 1708 Pope Clement XI appointed Ellis Bishop of Segni in the Vol-
scians. This was a very poor diocese but Ellis made such a success of his
ministry there – including holding a Synod, conducting visitations and car-
rying out repairs and improvements to the cathedral – that even today he
is regarded as one of the more outstanding bishops of a see which reaches
back to the year 499. He died in November 1726. The parish priest in
1993 of the cathedral at Segni has written a biography of their illustrious

bishop. Furthermore, he has actually seen him, lying in periwig and vestments in a tomb which mercifully has now been permanently sealed.

Meanwhile in the Western District the struggle continued to minister
to the community of Catholics scattered throughout the countryside. A
contemporary account graphically describes the difficulties being experienced by the Jesuits working here in 1690:

> Some of them were compelled to live for many days in huts or half-ruined
> cottages and during the severest cold of winter they were unable to kindle a
> fire lest the smoke should betray their hiding place. Nor could those who lived
> in Catholic families, though their position was of greater quiet and safety,
> venture for many months to go out of doors, except under cover of night, to
> visit the sick or the dying, in which charitable duty they often incurred the
> risk of life.
>
> On returning home at midnight, half dead with fatigue and cold, they were
> compelled to retire without a fire or candle for fear of discovery. They were
> induced to seek concealment, not on their personal account, but lest the flock
> should be scattered by the smiting and imprisonment of the shepherds.

(The Arundells, part II. Article by Nicholas Fitzherbert in *The Catholic Herald*
31 January 1986. Source not given.)

Ellis was a Benedictine and so were five of his successors. Three others
were Franciscans and only one (Baggs) was a secular. The reason for this
is twofold. The Western District, with its scattered rural communities, was
notoriously poor and it was felt that the bishop should not have to rely on
the meagre offerings of the faithful but be supported by the more reliable
resources of his religious order. Furthermore there was the question of
'balance'. The religious orders shouldered a great deal of the pastoral work
of the English Mission. Because relations with the secular clergy were not
always good, Rome thought it not only just but also politic to arrange that
de facto, if not *de jure*, the Regulars should have at least one representative
on the bench of bishops.

Bonaventure Giffard's brother, Andrew, was in 1705 appointed Vicar
Apostolic of the Western District but flatly refused to be consecrated and
to take office. The result was another vacancy, this time of eight years, until
the appointment of a Franciscan, Matthew Prichard (V.A. 1713–1750). He
was a Welshman who on his appointment endeavoured to work for the good
of the whole District surmounting the all too obvious difficulties which
arose because of poverty and distance.

Prichard shared a loyalty to the Jacobite cause with many of the Catholics of the time. Indeed he had strong scruples about siding with Bishop
Stonor in his desire to transfer Catholic allegiance to the Hanoverian succession. With Bishop Bonaventure Giffard (Vicar Apostolic of the London
District 1703–1734) he wrote to Propaganda Fide asking *inter alia* whether

by swearing fidelity to King George they were not thereby denying that anyone else had a right to the throne. (Catholics based their loyalty to the Jacobites on the theory of the Divine Right of Kings, a view strongly propagated by both James I and Charles I and which implied 'once a King always a King'.) Stonor's view, however, prevailed and Catholic Jacobitism, at least officially, was at an end.

Throughout his episcopal ministry Bishop Prichard lived in Monmouthshire. As time went by he saw the increasing need of a coadjutor. In 1714 Rome appointed a Benedictine, Dom Laurence York, who since 1729 had been in charge of the Benedictine Mission in Bath. He continued to reside in the city and was there at the time of the Jacobite Rebellion of 1745. At such a period it is not surprising to find examples of the rekindling of anti-Catholic bigotry. While in Bath York received a letter purporting to come from Prince Charles in which he (the Prince) thanked the bishop for his support of the rebels and promising him the Bishopric of Carlisle should he ever be restored to the English throne. The letter was a forgery and was recognised to be such by the authorities in Bath. Nevertheless it was thought prudent that the Bishop should absent himself from the city until things returned to normal.

In 1756 Charles Walmesley was appointed coadjutor with right of succession to Bishop York. Eight years later, on the resignation of his superior, he assumed full responsibility and remained in charge of the Western District until his death in 1792. Walmesley, a Benedictine, was a noted mathematician and astronomer and was consulted by the British Government when at last it decided to discard the Julian in favour of the Gregorian Calendar. This was in 1752 although most of Catholic Europe had already adopted the new calendar as far back as 1582. For Protestant England it had smelt too much of papal intrusion.

Bishop Walmesley lived, as did most of his successors, in Bath. The archives too were housed there. In 1780 a mob – no doubt inspired by the Gordon Riots in other parts of the country – attacked and destroyed a newly-built chapel in the city, and with it perished the records of the Western Vicariate. It was while Walmesley was bishop in 1778 and 1791, that the *Catholic Relief Acts* were passed, each in its own way helping forward the civic recognition of Catholics and so, albeit unwittingly, preparing the way for two Catholic immigrations of the next half century resulting from the French Revolution and the Irish Potato Famine (in the mid 1840s).

Catholic Missions in the Eighteenth Century

Between the years 1767 and 1780 there was actually a decrease in the number of Catholics living in the area now designated the diocese of Clif-

Church of England Diocese	1767 Census	1780 Census
Gloucester	316	291
Bristol	1018	767
Bath & Wells	383	548
Salisbury	1197	1019
TOTAL	2914	2625

ton. A picture, though not rigorously accurate, is available from the *Returns of Papists*, a census taken in both years on the orders of Parliament under the pretext of investigating the claim that there had been 'a dangerous increase of Popery'. That there had been *some* growth in the country as a whole – in fact, from 67,916 in 1767 to 69,373 in 1780 – clearly emerged from the evidence, and yet in the south west (Gloucestershire, Somerset, and Wiltshire) the trend had been in the opposite direction, in fact a fall of 10 per cent.

In the rural areas of what was to become our diocese, these Catholics were seen to gravitate around the houses of the better-off families who were able to support both a chapel and a chaplain. Lord Stourton at Bonham and Lord Clifford at Cannington may be cited out of a handful of examples. Most celebrated of all was the Arundell family at Wardour which attracted some 500 into its orbit of religious influence with Tisbury alone, in 1767, housing 188 Catholics. At Stourton, served from Bonham, there were 107.

The 1767 *Returns of Papists* also help us to build up a fairly accurate picture of the Catholic community in Bristol, a town which was still, but not for much longer, the second largest in England. In the city's twelve Anglican parishes there were 487 Catholics, to which may be added Clifton (10), Westbury (2), and Winterbourne (1) making a total of 500 in the deanery. A further point of interest is that the priest, at the age of sixty-six, was its third oldest member with only three men at seventy and one woman at seventy-five his senior.

The nascent tolerance of the period is well illustrated by Sketchley's *Bristol Directory of 1775* which, despite public Catholic worship being still illegal, has the entry:

SKUDAMORE (*sic*) John, rev. R. priest, 29 Montague Street.

The Society of Jesus, of which he was a member, had been suppressed in 1773 and later restored in 1814. Fr. Scudamore, who ministered at Baptist Mills, died in 1778 and lies buried 'in St. James churchyard opposite the church porch' (Dr. Oliver). Today many Catholics walk past his unmarked grave on their way to Mass in the Priory church.

Mention should be made of the clergy, mostly religious, who served the Catholic congregations during this period. The list of **English Benedictine** missions, for example, shows a predominantly rural ministry. (*Note* Many of the places and dates in the following lists are tentative, and the years given do not necessarily imply an unbroken ministry.)

Gloucestershire

Bourton-on-the-Water	1711–1744
Farmcote	1700–1725
Hartpury Court	1767–1778
Horton	1772–1777

Somerset

Bath	1685–1932
Leighland	1624–1767

Wiltshire

Bonham	1714–1719
	1785–1850
Easton Grey	1738–*c*.1755
Fonthill	1710–1721
Marlborough	1754–1794
Merevale	*c*.1721
Stourton	1652–1714
Sutton Mandeville	*c*.1721

(*Source*: Geoffrey Scott, OSB, *Gothic Rage Undone*, 1992, pages 278, 279.)

Jesuit chaplaincies and missions, in the main, show a similar rural preference.

BRISTOL	from 1740s or earlier

Gloucestershire

Beckford	from 1766
Cherry Orchard (House of Lord Gage)	from 1748
Leighland or Leigh	from 1767
Norton	*c*.1730 (very temporary)

Somerset

Bath	from 1765
Shepton Mallet	from 1765

Wiltshire

Ashcombe-Deane's Lease-Salisbury	from 1765

Bonham   *c*.1724–1785
Odstock   from 1748
Wardour   from the 17th century

Jesuit residence at these places, or some of them, may not have been continuous. Patrons could change and so could chaplains. During the suppression of the Society from 1773 till 1814 some places were given up for lack of priests. Missions no doubt often developed from chaplaincies.
(I am indebted to Fr. T.G. Holt, S.J. for the above.)

There were 143 Jesuits in England and Wales at the time of the suppression. Their vow of obedience, hitherto to a religious superior, was now to their local Vicar Apostolic.

Catholics and the Law in the Eighteenth Century

The penal laws against Catholics, many of which had been enacted during the reign of Elizabeth I, were not enforced in a uniform manner across the country. In other words, although in theory penalties could be quite severe – for example, the forfeiture of goods for non-attendance at services of the Established Church – in practice flexibility even amounting on occasions to leniency was in fact the practice of the time. The reason is not hard to find. In the shires, for example, where two local squires enjoyed a long-standing friendship, it was hardly likely that the one who was the local magistrate, and a Protestant, would invoke the full rigour of the law on his Catholic neighbour with whom he was in the habit of sharing a glass of port.

Popular sympathies, too, played their part. In 1700 a ferocious Act against Catholics was enacted which promised a reward of one hundred pounds to any informer who was able to bring about the conviction of a priest. Priests themselves, if found guilty, were liable to life imprisonment. This seductive piece of legislation led even some poor Catholics, on receiving the sacraments, then to betray their priests to the authorities. In 1719 Bishop Giffard of the London District reported to Rome three such cases, one of which involved a priest then languishing in Gloucester Jail. As the eighteenth century progressed no one was regarded with greater odium than these common informers. Eventually a systematic campaign culminating in a succession of convictions led Lord Mansfield in 1769 to deliver a celebrated judgement in which he ruled that, to prove a man was a priest, it was not sufficient to have seen him going through the motions of saying Mass. Evidence of ordination must be forthcoming. There were no further successful prosecutions and the law, by falling into desuetude, at last caught up with a more sympathetic public opinion.

Toleration came by stages and this is best illustrated on the issue of the erection of Catholic churches and chapels. The First Catholic Relief Act (1778) gave a guarded permission but insisted that they should not be free-standing. This explains why the chapel at Wardour is but part of a larger structure. That fact may even have saved it at the time of the Gordon Riots. Rioters who were on their way to destroy the chapel were possibly fooled by not being able to find anything that resembled a chapel. The point was that it did not *look* like an ecclesiastical building and it was this line of thinking that allegedly George III (1760–1820) adopted when, during one of his visits to Lulworth, he was asked by his friend Thomas Weld for permission to build a Catholic chapel. In effect the monarch's reply was, 'Alright, but make sure that it does not look like one'. Today the resulting edifice still has all the cold grace of a mausoleum. Later concessions allowed churches to stand alone but there were still restrictions – no steeple and no bells. In practice, however, this mattered little as Catholics for the most part were too stretched financially to provide them anyway.

The situation in England with regard to Catholics getting married was a delicate one. Because the law recognised clandestine marriages, Catholics took advantage of the situation and married before their own priests. Abuses, however, – not only amongst Catholics – became so serious that in 1753 Lord Hardwicke secured the passing of a Marriage Act which decreed that in future only those marriages would be recognised as valid which were contracted according to the Anglican rite. Although the primary intention of the Act had been to regularise the somewhat chaotic situation with regard to rights of inheritance it nevertheless created turmoil in the conscience of many Catholic couples who, because their vows had not been exchanged in the presence of a Catholic priest, felt that the Church would not regard them as being properly married. Leaders of the Catholic community were put in a very difficult position but decided to tolerate what in the end became the general practice in England, namely, that the Anglican ceremony preceded the Catholic. Rome, wisely, did not intervene. In 1836 this provision of Hardwicke's bill was repealed and Catholics were free to marry without needing the presence of an Anglican clergyman. A civil registrar, however, was required to attend.

The issue of Catholic burials also presented difficulties. As far back as 1689 – ironically shortly after the arrival of William of Orange – it became legal to provide cemeteries specifically for Catholics, although by an equal irony it was not until the forty-fourth year of the reign of Queen Victoria (1880) that the Burials Law Amendment Act allowed a Catholic priest publicly to officiate, robed, at a burial service even though he could already legally conduct such a service in a Catholic graveyard.

Finally and, as it were, placing all these matters in sobering context, there was an issue which concerned human rights at their most fundamental level, namely, the slave trade. Statistics presented to Parliament convey vividly the flood of black humanity transported by Bristol merchants as recently as the late eighteenth century – a trade in which the port was second only to Liverpool.

1789	15 voyages	2,691 slaves
1790	27 voyages	4,968 slaves
1791	22 voyages	4,069 slaves

(*Source*: Peter Marshall, *The Anti-Slave Trade Movement in Bristol*, 1968, p. 22.)

The almost universal acceptance of this iniquitous practice is reflected in the archives of the Western District where there appears to be a total absence of any reference to anyone wishing to combat it. Sadly, the local Catholic conscience had not yet been awakened.

1800–1850

Yet another Benedictine, Gregory William Sharrock, came to the Western District as Vicar Apostolic. Wardour Chapel was the setting for the splendid ceremony of his consecration (1780) as coadjutor to Bishop Walmesley whom he succeeded in 1797. For years Sharrock, a Lancastrian, suffered from ill health and towards the end of his life much of the burden of office was shouldered by his coadjutor. Even so in 1808 – the year before he died – we find Bishop Sharrock and the other Vicars Apostolic supporting the Earl of Shrewsbury, Lord Clifford and other leading Catholics who called a meeting 'in consequence of the state of the public mind respecting the Roman Catholics, and the numerous calumnies widely and industriously spread against them'. An Association was founded, supported by a very substantial Fund made up of subscriptions amounting initially to some £1,400. Catholics, only slightly helped by the Relief Acts, were now 'on the move' and the question of their civil rights could no longer be ignored. Under the next Vicar Apostolic Emancipation was to become a reality.

Bishop Sharrock died on October 7th, 1809. His coadjutor was a Franciscan, Bernardine Peter Collingridge, who had been consecrated some two years before. He now assumed responsibility and it was during his time in the Western District that the Benedictines came to Downside (1814). Like Prichard before him Bishop Collingridge's attitude to the seculars and other religious orders was invariably fair despite an unfortunate dispute with the Jesuit Fr. Robert Plowden, in Bristol.

But the Bishop is probably best remembered for his contribution to the debate prior to the passing of the *Catholic Emancipation Act* in 1829. The grievances felt by Catholics had now been before the public eye for several years and in the early part of the century the Vicars Apostolic had issued a pastoral letter in which they argued that their co-religionists, while maintaining their spiritual independence, would nevertheless not be found wanting in that temporal allegiance which all good citizens 'owe to Caesar'.

Collingridge died in 1829 and initially was buried at Cannington, near Bridgwater, in the grounds of what is now the Somerset College of Agriculture and Horticulture. Today the spot is known as 'The Bishop's Garden' although his body was re-interred in 1914 in the north choir of Downside Abbey.

Before Collingridge's death – and not without a considerable period of searching – Peter Augustine Baines (a secularised Benedictine from Ampleforth) was named coadjutor. Like Bishop York he had been in charge of the Benedictine Mission at Bath; even so, unlike his predecessors, he was not always as sympathetic as he might have been to the religious of his Vicariate.

While still coadjutor he suffered from ill health, and it seems that it was during a period of convalescence in Rome that he acquired a love of classical architecture which led him when he eventually took charge of the District, to undertake several grandiose schemes at Prior Park. This establishment he saw not only as a seminary but also as a centre of Catholic culture and learning for the West of England. But in financial matters Bishop Baines was unwise in the extreme. Indeed for some years to come the Western District and its offspring, the infant Diocese of Clifton, were to teeter on the verge of bankruptcy as a result of the debts which he had incurred at Prior Park.

In 1840 Pope Gregory XVI increased the number of Vicariates from four to eight. Wales was taken from the Western District and made a Vicariate in its own right.

When Bishop Baines died in 1843 – just hours after the opening of St. Mary-on-the-Quay, Bristol – Rome appointed the only member of the secular clergy to take charge of the Western District. Although a man of great promise Charles Michael Baggs was destined to be bishop for less than two years, and before he was forty he was dead. Like Pope John Paul I he is one of the might-have-beens of Catholic history for had he lived there is every chance that he would have become the first Bishop of Clifton.

The ninth Vicar Apostolic was yet another Benedictine, William

Bernard Ullathorne. He had worked among the convicts in Australia before returning to England to minister in Coventry. Known as a strong, forthright character he was the very embodiment of a sturdy Yorkshireman and it was doubtless this practical turn of mind which led him, despite the financial obstacles involved, to get a roof put on the Church of the Twelve Apostles in Clifton thus making it available for worship at a time when it had long remained unfinished and so unusable. In 1850 it became the Pro-Cathedral and Ullathorne's 'temporary' roof lasted almost a hundred years.

Bishop Ullathorne in 1848 was transferred to the Central District and on the Restoration of the Hierarchy in 1850 he became the first Bishop of Birmingham. Until his death in 1889 he exercised an enormous personal influence on the fortunes of the Church in this country. The last Vicar Apostolic of the Western District was a Franciscan, Joseph William Hendren. He was appointed in 1848 and became the first Bishop of Clifton in 1850.

Pope Pius IX restored normal ecclesiastical government to the English Catholic Church on September 29th 1850. The bull *Universalis Ecclesiae* established a metropolitan see at Westminster and twelve other dioceses, one of which was Clifton. In later years some of these have been subdivided: e.g. Beverley became two dioceses, Leeds and Middlesborough, and Southwark became three, Southwark, Portsmouth, and Arundel & Brighton.

With prudent foresight Rome chose not to assume the titles, by now held by the Anglicans, of the Pre-Reformation sees (like London) nor even of those (like Bristol) created by Henry VIII. The titles chosen for the bishopric to be based at Bristol was 'Clifton', at that time a fashionable suburb of the city. Similarly at Manchester the title taken was that of one of its suburbs, Salford. It is important to recall that the Ecclesiastical Titles Assumption Bill forbidding the taking of Anglican titles had not yet been passed. This did not take place until August 1st 1851. In the meantime – and apparently in order to meet even an apparent legal deadline – no fewer than five Catholic bishops (including Thomas Burgess, second Bishop of Clifton) were consecrated in the previous three weeks. Clearly the Act was not intended to prevent the Church of England at a later date taking titles already held by Catholics (eg. Liverpool, Birmingham and Portsmouth).

The newly-created diocese of Clifton extended as far as the boundaries *as they then existed* of Gloucestershire, Somerset and Wiltshire. It was also to prove to be an entity of considerable national, cultural and sociological interest, comprising in general several quite disparate groups of people. First there were the old Catholic families who continued to hold sway, though by now to a lesser degree, in the rural areas of the three counties. It was here, too, that the yeoman stock which formed the backbone of agriculture and farming in the south west was to be found. For example, one of the earliest missions of the diocese is at Frome where the names in the baptism registers show quite clearly the almost exclusively indigenous origins of the people there. Thirdly, the French exiles at the time of the Revolution – not only welcomed but even financially assisted by His Majesty's Government for whom the great upheaval had been anathema – also made their mark with clergy giving an early impetus over the next decades to missions at Burnham-on-Sea, Bridgwater and elsewhere. Fourthly, at Clifton and in Bath there were enclaves of Oxford converts, many of them influential people who, like Manning, saw in the Gorham judgment (1850) which rejected baptismal regeneration an abdication by the Church of England of its theological independence of the State. But more numerous than all these groupings combined was the massive immigration from Ireland. This theme will be taken up in Chapter Six.

J.A. HARDING

CHAPTER TWO

The Bishops of the Diocese of Clifton

William Joseph Hendren Vicar Apostolic 1848–1850 and First Bishop of Clifton 1850–1851

The future bishop was born in Birmingham on 19 October 1791. He joined the Franciscan novitiate at Abergavenny in June 1806 and was ordained on 28 September 1815. He taught at the Francisan novitiate at Perthyr in the Monnow valley until 1818 when he moved to Aston. In 1826 he was appointed missioner at Abergavenny and served there until he was sent to the Franciscan convent at Taunton. Here he was chaplain from 1839 until 1848. In that year he was appointed Vicar Apostolic of the Western District in succession to Bishop Ullathorne. He was consecrated bishop by his predecessor in the church of St Mary-on-the-Quay in Bristol on 10 September 1848.

When the English Hierarchy was restored in 1850 Bishop Hendren was appointed first bishop of the new diocese of Clifton and later in that year he was enthroned at the Pro-Cathedral. In June 1851 he was transferred to the new diocese of Nottingham, but ill-health forced him to resign, and he retired on 23 February 1853. He returned to the Franciscan convent at Taunton where he died on 14 November 1866.

Bishop Hendren is remembered at Clifton for his efforts in completing the building of the Pro-Cathedral, establishing the parish school, organising the building of the presbytery and purchasing the site of the Catholic cemetery at Arno's Vale and the adjacent Catholic Reformatory for girls. These were not inconsiderable achievements in his three years of office.

Thomas Burgess Second Bishop of Clifton 1851–1854

Thomas Burgess was born at Clayton-le-Woods, Lancashire on 1 October 1791. He was educated at Ampleforth where he became a professed monk

William Hendren

of the Order of St. Benedict on 13 October 1807. He was ordained priest in 1814 and elected Prior of Ampleforth in 1826. In 1830, with his sub-prior, Fr. Thomas Rooker and the Procurator, Fr. Edward Metcalfe, he left Ampleforth and the Benedictine Order to join two other former members of the Order, Bishop Peter Baines, Vicar Apostolic of the Western District, and Fr. Thomas Brindle, the missioner at Bath, in the task of establishing the new school and seminary at Prior Park.

A difference of opinion with Bishop Baines in 1831 caused Fr. Burgess to leave Prior Park. He served as missioner at Cannington and later in the new chapel at Brunswick Place in Bath. From 1835 until his appointment at Bishop of Clifton he was missioner at Monmouth. He was consecrated at Southwark on 17 July 1851. On returning to his diocese, he set himself the task of putting the financial affairs of Prior Park in order, but this proved to be beyond his ability and, indeed, beyond the ability of anyone. In spite of his failing health he made several 'begging missions', as he called them, in the dioceses in the north of England to raise funds to keep the college in being. Shortly after one such mission, in October 1854, he

Thomas Burgess

became seriously ill and died at the convent at Westbury-on-Trym on 27 November 1854.

William Clifford Third Bishop of Clifton 1857–1893

The future bishop was born in Irnham, Lincolnshire on 24 December 1823, the second son of the seventh Baron Clifford of Chudleigh. He received his early education at Hodder Place, near Stonyhurst, and at the age of fifteen he went to live in Rome where his father had a house. In Rome he studied at the Collegio di Nobili and later at the Collegio Pio. He left Rome in 1848 to continue his studies at the Jesuit College in Louvain. On 26 July 1849 he received the Diaconate at Bruges and returned to complete his studies at St Bueno's College in North Wales. He was ordained priest by Bishop Hendren at the Church of the Twelve Apostles in Clifton on 25 August 1850. After his ordination he returned to Rome where, in 1852, he was awarded the degree of Doctor of Divinity. He served as a priest in the new diocese of Plymouth but returned to Rome to study canon law. On 15 February 1857 he was consecrated Bishop of Clifton by Pope Pius IX in

Rome. He was enthroned in his diocese at the Pro-Cathedral on 17 March 1857. At the age of thirty-three he was the youngest English bishop to be appointed since the Reformation.

During the next thirty-six years at Clifton Bishop Clifford succeeded in laying the foundation of the modern diocese. The early years saw the diocesan finances restored, often with the bishop's private means. In 1867 he re-purchased the Prior Park estate to re-open the school and seminary there. Between 1871 and 1874 he undertook a massive refurbishment of the Pro-Cathedral under the guidance of Charles Hansom, a Catholic architect who was also responsible for the original buildings at Clifton College. Bishop Clifford, at his personal expense, provided the new premises for the boys' school to comply with the requirements of the 1870 Education Act. In 1882, to celebrate the Silver Jubilee of his consecration as a Bishop, he had the church at Prior Park completed. The church, originally intended

William Clifford

William Brownlow

to be a memorial for Bishop Baines, had been left unfinished through lack of funds since 1845.

Nationally Bishop Clifford came into prominence for the part he played during the deliberations of the Vatican Council of 1870.

In spite of failing health Bishop Clifford made his last *Ad Limina* visit to Rome in June 1893. He died at Prior Park on 14 August of the same year and is buried there.

William Robert Brownlow Fourth Bishop of Clifton 1894–1901

William Brownlow was born at Wilmslow, Cheshire on 4 July 1830. His father, Canon William Brownlow, was vicar of the parish church. Robert was educated at Cambridge and, after graduating, was ordained in the Anglican church. He served at the parish church in Torquay for four years but resigned in 1861. He was received into the Catholic church in 1863 by Newman, and was ordained priest in Rome in 1866. As a priest of the diocese of Plymouth Fr. Brownlow became well known for his writing in defence of the Catholic Faith. He was consecrated Bishop of Clifton by Cardinal Vaughan at the Pro-Cathedral on 1 May 1894.

Bishop Brownlow, lacking the wealth of his predecessor, was unable to give Prior Park the financial support the college had received from Bishop Clifford. Accordingly, he invited the Irish Christian Brothers, who had recently opened a grammar school for Catholic boys in Clifton (St. Brendan's), to be responsible for Prior Park. The Brothers agreed to take the college for a trial period of seven years. At the end of that time the college had proved to be a success with, at the end of the century, over one hundred boarders.

In addition to the many new churches which he opened in the diocese Bishop Brownlow had a special care for the spiritual well-being of the many Irish labourers who came to Avonmouth to work on the construction of the new dock. For this reason St. Bernard's Church in Shirehampton is dedicated to his memory. For many years, both during his time as an Anglican and after his conversion, the Bishop exchanged letters with Newman, many of which are preserved in the diocesan archives. Among the Bishop's other works are his *History of the Catholic Church in England* and, in collaboration with Dr. Northcote, a priest of the Diocese of Birmingham, *Roma Sottoranea* a history of the Roman catacombs.

Bishop Brownlow died at Clifton on 9 November 1901 and is buried in the chapel of Holy Souls Cemetery, Arnos Vale.

George Ambrose Burton Fifth Bishop of Clifton 1902–1931

The future bishop was born at Kingston-on-Hull on 28 April 1852. After education at Ratcliffe College he taught there until 1884, when, at the age of thirty-two, he went to the Venerable English College in Rome to study for the priesthood. He was ordained at St. John Lateran in 1890 and in the same year gained his Doctorate. He returned to England and for two years served as curate at St. Mary's Cathedral, Newcastle-on-Tyne. He was then appointed to the church of St. Bede in South Shields, where he served first as curate and later as parish priest until 1902 when he was appointed Bishop of Clifton. He was consecrated at the Pro-Cathedral by Bishop Riddell of Northampton on 1 May 1902. The finances of Prior Park, the college which the diocese had taken over from the Irish Christian Brothers in 1903, soon began to cause the bishop serious problems and, at Easter 1904, he had no alternative but to close it. Bishop Burton had been living at the college, but following the closure, he took up residence at St. Ambrose, Leigh Woods, which remains the present residence of the Bishops of Clifton.

George Ambrose Burton

The outbreak of war in 1914 brought many problems for the diocese and its bishop. The influx of Belgian refugees and the vast army camps around Salisbury Plain caused serious difficulties in the provision of chaplains and Mass centres. However the bishop's Pastoral Letters of the war years were particularly inspiring and were often quoted in the local press.

After the Armistice there were further troubles for the bishop. The large number of Irish Catholics in the diocese seemed divided in their views on the political difficulties of their country. Unemployment, too, was a social problem and the bishop earned the admiration of many by addressing mass meetings of the unemployed in the city. He also took great pleasure in the church-building programme which went on in the diocese in the 1920s. In addition, he improved the Pro-Cathedral by installing a new high altar and several stained-glass windows. But towards the end of the decade, the bishop's health began to fail and his vicar general, Mgr. (later Bishop) Lee deputised for him at many ceremonies during his last years. Bishop Burton died on 8 February 1931.

William Lee Sixth Bishop of Clifton 1931–1948

William Lee was born at Mitchelstown, County Cork, on 27 September 1875. He was educated at St Colman's College, Fermoy, St. John's College, Waterford, and the seminary at Oscott, where he was ordained on 2 March 1901. His first appointment in the diocese was at Holy Cross church, then in Victoria Street. He was appointed bishop's secretary and diocesan treasurer in 1903. In 1910 he became Administrator of the Pro-Cathedral and in 1920 was awarded the M.B.E. for his welfare work among the Belgian refugees who had come to the country during the war years.

During the years between the wars the future of Catholic schools was much to the fore. As a co-opted member of the Bristol Education Committee, the future bishop was familiar with the debates which raged in the committee over the question of grants for the new Catholic schools which would be required as a consequence of the re-organisation of the school system. When the new bishop was consecrated at the Pro-Cathedral on 26

William Lee

January 1932 he knew only too well the difficulties which lay ahead for the Diocesan Schools Committee.

The outbreak of war in 1939 added to the bishop's problems as there were many Catholic children among the evacuees who came into the diocese, and the bishop took a personal interest in their welfare. The onset of the air-raids in 1940–1942 and the consequent damage to Catholic churches and schools created a host of new problems. It was not surprising that the bishop's health deteriorated under the strain of the war years. Nevertheless, he persevered in the great desire of his priesthood, to bring the Mass to the people. In spite of all the difficulties, seventy-two new missions and Mass centres were established in the diocese during his years as bishop.

Bishop Lee had done much to improve the interior of the Pro-Cathedral, including the installation of several stained-glass windows, during his time as Administrator, but to the end of his life his main concern was the preservation of Catholic schools. He died suddenly on 21 September 1948.

Joseph Rudderham Seventh Bishop of Clifton 1949–1974

The future bishop was born at Norwich on 17 June 1899. He was educated at St Bede's School, Manchester, St Edmund's College, Ware, Christ's College, Cambridge and the Venerable English College, Rome, where he was ordained in 1926. He served at All Saints' Church, Peterborough from 1927 until 1943, as curate until 1932 and later as parish priest. From 1943 until his appointment to Clifton, he was Administrator of Northampton Cathedral. He also served as diocesan Inspector of Schools from 1941 until 1949. He was consecrated Bishop of Clifton by Archbishop Masterson of Birmingham at the Pro-Cathedral on 26 July 1949.

The new bishop soon found himself enmeshed in the many difficulties created by the 1944 Education Act and the raising of the School-leaving Age Act which came into effect in 1948. As a means of raising the funds to provide the Catholic schools made necessary by the 1944 Act, the bishop was forced to raise a financial levy on each parish in the diocese to inaugurate the Diocesan Development Fund. In the 1960s and 1970s other tasks faced the bishop. Between 1962 and 1965 he was required to spend lengthy periods in Rome to attend the various sessions of the Second Vatican Council. Putting into effect the recommendations of the Council caused much controversy among the older generation of Catholics. Then came the debates over the controversial Papal Encyclical, *Humanae Vitae*. On a more mundane level came the problem about what

Joseph Rudderham

to do about the deteriorating condition of the Pro-Cathedral building. Surveys by experts all agreed that little could be done to guarantee a long life to the building, but expensive work on the foundations would provide a short-term alternative which seemed to be a false economy. When a generous donation of half a million pounds was made specifically for the building of a new Cathedral this was readily accepted. Before a vast gathering of church and civic dignitaries the bishop took possession of the new Cathedral on the feast of SS. Peter and Paul 1973. In 1975 Bishop Rudderham retired to Nazareth House at Cheltenham where he died on 24 February 1979.

Mervyn Alban Alexander Eighth Bishop of Clifton 1974–

Mervyn Alexander was born in London on 29 June 1925, his parents being William and Grace Alexander (née Newman). Having been educated at Bishop Wordsworth School, Salisbury and Prior Park College, Bath he was sent by Bishop Lee to the Venerable English College, first at Stonyhurst and then (1946) Rome where he was ordained priest at the Leonine College by the Vice-Gerent, Archbishop (later Cardinal) Luigi Traglia on 18 July 1948. He continued his studies at the Gregorian University where, in 1951, he took his Doctorate in Theology.

On his return to England he spent twelve years as assistant priest at the Pro-Cathedral, Clifton. From 1953 he was also part-time chaplain to Bristol University. Having served from 1963 to 1967 as full-time chaplain he was then appointed to Our Lady of Lourdes, Weston-super-Mare as parish priest.

After a process of consultation among clergy and some laity, the Holy Father in 1972 nominated him titular Bishop of Pinhel (in Portugal) and auxiliary to Bishop Rudderham. His episcopal ordination took place on 25 April 1972. When he succeeded to the see of Clifton in 1974 his main task was the further implementation of the decrees of the Second Vatican Council. These included the greater involvement of the clergy and laity in decision making, the continued reorganisation of education throughout the diocese, and the fostering of the still nascent spirit of ecumenism among his flock. (Since 1976 Bishop Alexander has been co-chairman of the Ecumenical Society of the Blessed Virgin Mary.) Much attention was given to liturgical reforms, including the re-ordering of churches.

The needs of the Third World assumed a higher profile with priests again being encouraged to spend a period of service in South America. The diocese saw an emergence of parish projects to help the world's poor, the establishment of a Justice and Peace Commission, and an ongoing programme to combat racism at home and generally to promote social justice and harmony.

An engaging relaxed style has won him many friends and no doubt eased the passage of former Anglican clergy, both married and celibate, seeking to be ordained for the diocese.

His Episcopal Silver Jubilee in 1997 was marked in splendid fashion with a Mass in the presence of Cardinal Basil Hume, the Papal Nuncio and other church and civic dignitaries.

J.C.

CHAPTER THREE

The Clifton Mission:
Origins 1830–1850

The story starts in the 1820s when the missioner at St. Joseph's church in Trenchard Street, then the only Catholic church in Bristol, Fr. Francis Edgeworth, suggested to the Vicar Apostolic of the Western District, Bishop Collingridge, that he should be allowed to build a new church at Clifton. He suggested a church capable of accommodating 2,500 persons which could be seen from all parts of the city. If the bishop gave his permission, Fr. Edgeworth felt that the church could be built in three years. Bishop Collingridge gave permission but before much of the preliminary work was done he died and the scheme was held up until the new Vicar Apostolic sanctioned it.

Overleaf is an artist's impression of the large Catholic church which was to be built at Clifton in the nineteenth century. Although the building was started and, indeed, half finished, it was never completed in the way that the architect had planned it. Older parishioners, when looking at the drawing, will notice some familiar details such as the massive pillars in the side walls which formed part of the church of the Twelve Apostles which, in 1850, became the provisional or Pro-Cathedral of the new diocese of Clifton.

On 4 October 1834, the feast of St. Francis of Assisi, the two Franciscan priests from St Joseph's, Frs. Francis Edgeworth and Patrick O'Farrell, laid the foundation stone, with a minimum of ceremony, at a site called Stony Fields in Clifton. The site had been purchased in 1831 at a cost of £2,250 by a Catholic gentleman named John Tilladam who lived in Park Street. The money had been raised by local Catholics and Fr. Edgeworth's plan was to build houses along the boundaries of the site whose rents would help to support the mission. The Bath architect, Goodridge, who was also engaged in work on Bishop Baines' new buildings at Prior Park, prepared

Architect Goodridge's original design (1833) for the Catholic Church of the Twelve Apostles at Stony Fields, Clifton. The project was abandoned in 1843 when the foundations failed for the second time

the plans for the new church and work on the houses in Meridian Place and Berkeley Place was started.

The architect proposed a massive construction in the classical style, crowned by a huge stone lantern, the windows of which were designed to flood the sanctuary area with light leaving the remainder of the building in half-light. It was the weight of this stone lantern, carried by four massive stone pillars rising from the floor of the crypt, which was to cause trouble with the building. The combined weight of these pillars, together with those supporting the roof, caused the edge of the site to slip down to the base of the nearby disused quarry. Any further work was out of the question until this had been corrected but, by the end of 1838 the site and half-completed building were derelict.

Fr. Edgeworth, conscious of the disappointment felt by those who had supported him, built a small chapel half-way down the slope on the Berkeley Place side. This chapel, dedicated to St. Augustine of Canterbury, was opened in November 1842, and it was here that the Clifton Mission came into being. (The building, formerly known as St. Catherine's Hall, is still in existence as part of the Waldorf School complex.) Assured by the architect that it would be possible to secure the foundations, Fr. Edgeworth raised £4,000 by selling some of the completed houses, and a further £3,500 by mortgaging the site, and in 1843 work on the original building re-started. Within six months, however, the foundation had again slipped, causing all work to cease. The building, now almost up to roof level, had to be abandoned. Fr. Edgeworth, now bankrupt and in failing health, retired to the Franciscan monastery at Antwerp where he died in 1850.

Bishop Ullathorne O.S.B. Vicar Apostolic of the Western District 1846–1848 set himself the task of roofing the building and having windows cut in the walls so that it could be used as a church. He refused to live at Prior Park, choosing to live in Bristol, first in King Square, and as soon as work on the building began, at 22 Meridian Place, adjacent to the site. Part of the Bishop's autobiography, preserved in the diocesan archives, describes

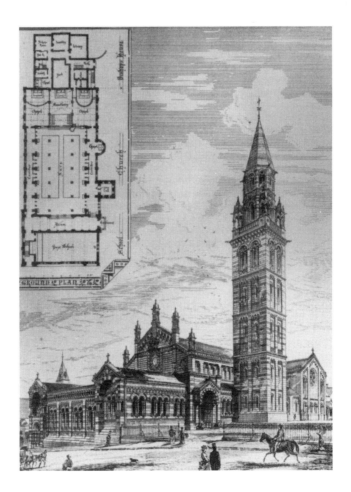

Clifton: Pro-Cathedral, proposed design by Charles Francis Hansom, 1870

the directions he gave to Charles Hansom, a Catholic architect living in Arlington Villas. He wrote

> we must run two beams the whole length of the building on the crowns of the crypt vaultings, like the keels of two ships, join the separate pieces together on the sub-walls, mortice them into the end walls and step wooden pillars upon them, and raise wooden semi-circular arches above them so as to receive an open roof.

The bishop's plan was clear enough. The roof, kept as light as possible, was to be supported by the wooden pillars and not by the side walls. Three windows of plain glass were cut in each side wall, the pillars intended to form the portico at the Park Place end were demolished and a plain stone wall built. The main door was in the centre of this wall and there were two smaller doors, one at each corner. In the south corner a circular staircase gave access to a gallery which extended across the width of the building. Gas lighting was installed and the interior was heated by gas fires placed at the foot of each pillar. A local contractor named Brooks carried out the work under the supervision of Charles Hansom. The new church was 140 feet long, 70 feet wide, had seating for 700 and standing room for a further 300. It had cost £6,600 which included the redemption of the mortgage, the building work and the gas-fitting. It was hoped that the church would be ready for the consecration of Bishop Hendren, Bishop Ullathorne's successor, but this was not possible, so Bishop Hendren was consecrated on 10 September 1848 in St Mary-on-the-Quay. The Church of the Twelve Apostles was finally opened on 21 September 1848 by Bishop Ullathorne.

The first task of the new parish priest, Fr. (later Bishop) Vaughan, was to convert part of the crypt area into a parish school. Another part of the crypt was set aside for the burial of parishioners. Between the opening of the church and the passing of the Burial Grounds Act in 1855, 145 persons were buried in the crypt, including Bishop Thomas Burgess. (When the Pro-Cathedral ceased to be used as a place of worship in 1973 these bodies had to be re-interred.) With the restoration of the hierarchy in 1850 the church became the provisional Cathedral of the diocese of Clifton with Bishop Hendren as its first bishop. To mark this occasion a parishioner, William Maskell, presented the church with the Stations of the Cross, which, it was claimed, was the first time since the reign of Queen Mary Tudor that Stations had been erected in any English cathedral.

The Pro-Cathedral 1850–1973

In 1850 Bishop Hendren consulted Charles Hansom with regard to the building of a presbytery adjoining the east end of the church. This was achieved by setting the foundations at the base of the old quarry and building a wall up to the required level before building the house. Some of the stone which had been used in the half-completed portico and left on the site was used. The presbytery cost £1,850.

In June 1851 Bishop Hendren was transferred to the new diocese of Nottingham and was succeeded by Bishop Burgess, the Vicar General of the Welsh diocese of Menevia. In 1830 the future bishop, who was then Prior to Ampleforth, left the Benedictine Order to join Bishop Baines in the ill-fated Prior Park venture. During his three short years as bishop of Clifton his time was almost entirely occupied by trying to save the college from bankruptcy. He died in Westbury-on-Trym convent on 27 November 1854 and was laid to rest in the crypt of his cathedral.

In eleven years five bishops had tried and failed to find a solution to the problem of Prior Park, so it was no surprise when the Pope refused to appoint a successor to Bishop Burgess until a satisfactory solution was reached. Cardinal Wiseman's coadjutor, Archbishop Errington was appointed as administrator of the Clifton diocese. It was during this period that Canon Vaughan, who was administrator of the Pro-Cathedral, was named as the new bishop of Plymouth. He was consecrated at Clifton on 16 September 1855. The Prior Park problem was solved in December 1855 when bailiffs occupied the college and impounded the property for non payment of rent. The sale of the college treasures was completed by 11 March 1856 and the premises vacated. Fortunately the college organ was not included in the sale and it was removed and installed in the Pro-Cathedral. The third bishop of Clifton, William Clifford, who had been consecrated in Rome by Pope Pius IX on 15 February 1857 was enthroned in his cathedral on St. Patrick's Day that year.

The new bishop, only thirty-three years old, immediately set himself the task of clearing the debt on the building, which at that time stood at £3,600. In three years this had been cleared, thanks largely to the generosity of the bishop's family. When the library of the Franciscan house at Baddesley Clinton in Warwickshire closed, the missioner at St. Mary-on-the-Quay, Fr. O'Farrell, asked that the books be given to Clifton. These included an ancient Hereford Missal which was sold to the Bodleian Library at Oxford for £400. The money enabled Bishop Clifford to found the Pro-Cathedral Library, which remained in existence for over a century.

As a result of the closure of Prior Park the diocese had no seminary for training its priests and no grammar school for educating young Catholic students. In February 1860 the bishop established a Catholic Grammar School for boys in the basement at 22 Meridian Place, but by 1864 this had increased so much that a larger house was purchased in St Edward's Road, Clifton Wood to accommodate the school. The bishop had plans to buy Goldney House in Clifton as a seminary and site for a future cathedral, but this did not materialise and a temporary seminary was set up in 10 Berkeley Square, receiving its first students in July 1865.

In December 1866 the bishop announced that he would be re-purchasing Prior Park in order to site the grammar school and seminary there. At Easter 1867 the school in St. Edward's Road was closed and the house became a home for retired priests in the care of the Sisters of the Temple. The seminary at Prior Park opened in July 1870 during the bishop's absence at the Vatican Council. On his return he set about building a new school to relieve the overcrowding at the school in the crypt. It was built at the Park Place end of the church with access through an atrium on the north side. By 1876 the whole of the west end of the building had been transformed. The upper part of the rebuilt façade was decorated with sculptures representing Our Lord seated in the centre with SS. Matthew and John on the south side and SS. Luke and Mark on the north side. In September 1898 the contractors Kemp Brothers of Union Street installed a striking clock with a fourteen feet square decorated clock face with a niche either side intended for mechanical striking figures, but these were never installed. The motto on the clock was *Umbrae transitus est tempus nostrum* (time is but a shadow that fades).

The elaborate plans which Charles Hansom submitted for a complete re-furbishment of the Pro-Cathedral are still preserved but lack of money prevented them from becoming a reality. However it is still possible to decipher the carving of the Papal Arms on the west gable of the boys' school, although the carving of the Clifford family arms has almost disappeared. The main changes made inside the church were the erection of wrought iron screens around the altars, the reversal of the positions of the Lady altar and the Blessed Sacrament altar and the installation of a new carved oak pulpit on the south side of the nave. Mr. O'Bryan of Torquay gave an altar dedicated to St. Joseph, the Dominican nuns who had lived in the convent in Park Place from 1850–1876 presented a large 'pieta' and a parishioner Miss Barry had the oak canopy over the pieta carved in Bruges by the Flemish woodcarver Charles Bayart. Possibly the most welcome improvement at this time was the installation of a central heating system which replaced the old gas fires.

Although in failing health Bishop Clifford could often be seen in his place in the church in the early months of 1893. Shortly before his death in August of that year he had the plain glass in the three windows on the south side of the church replaced with stained glass. His Requiem took place at Prior Park on 18 August 1893 and he was buried at the college.

The consecration of Bishop William Brownlow took place on 1 May

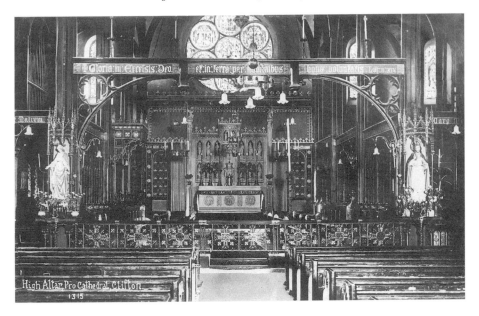

Clifton: Pro-Cathedral, high altar, pre-1927

1894, the consecrating bishop being Cardinal Vaughan assisted by his uncle, Bishop Vaughan of Plymouth who had himself been consecrated bishop at the Pro-Cathedral almost forty years before. In 1895 Bishop Brownlow installed three stained glass windows on the north side of the church to match those which Bishop Clifford had installed two years earlier. An anonymous donor presented a copy of a painting by Rubens of the Holy Family and a new baptismal font was installed in 1898. In July 1899 Bishop Brownlow blessed and dedicated twelve statues of the apostles in memory of his predecessor, William Clifford. This was highly appropriate in that during the debate on Papal Infallibility at the First Vatican Council, it was Clifford who had advised caution, urging that nothing should be done which might seem to minimise the authority of the college of bishops, the successors of the apostles.

In 1896 the Irish Christian Brothers had established a grammar school for boys but the departure of the community from Park Place meant that the parish was without a grammar school for girls. The Sisters of St. Joseph of Cluny, who had a convent at Westbury-on-Trym, opened a school at 17 Meridian Place but this soon became too small and was moved to larger premises on the corner of Manilla Road. This was followed by a further move to Cornwallis Grove where St Joseph's Academy flourished for many years until the school was taken over by the Sisters of La Retraite in 1924 and renamed.

Bishop Brownlow died on 9 November 1901 and his Requiem Mass was celebrated at Prior Park. A funeral Mass was celebrated at the Pro-Cathedral on 14 November by Bishop Graham of Plymouth in the presence of four other bishops.

Bishop Brownlow's successor was Bishop George Ambrose Burton who was consecrated on 1 May 1902. As a memorial to his predecessors he installed three stained glass windows dedicated to St. Hugh, St. William and St. Ambrose. In 1924 another window dedicated to six West-Country saints was installed as a War Memorial to the men of the parish who had been killed on active service during the 1914–1918 war. Bishop Burton died in February 1931 and was succeeded by Mgr. Canon William Lee, a priest of the Clifton diocese. Bishop Lee's years in office were to prove extremely difficult as he had to cope with the reorganisation of the Catholic schools and the many problems of the war. It is a tribute to his steadfastness that, in spite of all these, eighty-one new churches and chapels were founded in the diocese during these years as bishop from 1931 to 1948.

Bishop Lee's successor, Bishop Joseph Rudderham, was consecrated on 26 July 1949 and he presided over the celebrations in 1950 to mark the centenary of the restoration of the hierarchy. In this same year the roof of the church was renewed, making good the damage caused by the air-raids of 1940–1942. It was while these repairs were in progress that fears were expressed by the builders about the general stability of the building. It was generally agreed that some large-scale works would, sooner or later, be necessary if the future of the building was to be assured. In 1964 Bishop Rudderham called for an architect's report on the work necessary to stabilise the foundations. This suggested that for an outlay of between £80,000 and £100,000 it would be possible to guarantee the safety of the structure for twenty years. A long-term guarantee could not be given because of the nature of the site. In 1965, a most generous donation made it possible to build a new cathedral on a more suitable site.

The Cathedral Church of SS. Peter and Paul

When Cardinal Heenan preached at the opening of the new Clifton Cathedral on Friday 29 June 1973 he referred to a newspaper headline: 'Bargain Cathedral to be consecrated'. The article described the new cathedral as 'the ecclesiastical bargain of the century'. The Cardinal commented on the fact that the building of the new cathedral appeared to be not quite so important as the success in building it for such a low price. That was its real importance. Contemporary newspapers are often reliable mirrors of public opinion.

Many of the wonderful cathedrals which still grace our cities were built by members of religious orders, assisted by local craftsmen who were proud to demonstrate their skills in praise of God. Time and expense were of little consequence to them. Yet, on the morning of 29 June 1973 there was a demonstration outside the new cathedral by a group which protested against so much money being spent on a church when there were so many families in the city who were without homes. Presumably, new hotels, cinemas and clubs did not call for such protests commented the Cardinal.

The architect, Frederick Jennett, departed from the old principle of using local stone for the building of such a large cathedral. His use of reinforced concrete and pre-cast concrete slabs was both admired and criticised. Many local residents mourned the loss of the fine old house, St. Vincent's Lodge, for many years the residence of Dame Monica Wills, which had been demolished to clear the site for the new building. The most frequent comment heard as the building took shape was 'but it does not look like a cathedral'. To generations used to seeing cathedrals as oblong cruciform buildings with a nave and transept, the new building must have seemed very strange indeed. But, on entering, the immediate impression was of a stately and dignified arena. The baptistery, close to the door, with its large font, provision for running water, and the Paschal candle close by, left no doubt that this was a parish church as well as a cathedral. It was here that young and old received the Sacrament of Baptism, and the Paschal candle brought the promise of the joy of Easter.

The high altar, visible from all parts of the cathedral, might appear rather stark when compared with the decorated altars of other earlier churches. But, at Mass, with the congregation gathered around the altar, the true worth of the cathedral design becomes obvious.

High behind the altar is the bishop's 'cathedra' or chair, a symbol of every cathedral. We have become accustomed to hearing of professors at universities who occupy 'the chair of Modern History' or 'the chair of Philosophy'. The rank is a sign that the professor is the acknowledged leader in the teaching of his subject. So, too, is the bishop, occupying his 'cathedra' or chair by the high altar of his cathedral, recognised as the teacher of his flock.

Catholics, accustomed to seeing the high altar in a church flanked by two 'side altars' usually dedicated to Our Lady and the Sacred Heart, will have noticed that there is only one side altar and that it is in the Blessed

Sacrament chapel, where the Sacrament is reserved at all times. It is here that daily Mass is offered and people make private visits. Our Lady's shrine does not have an altar and is at the back of the cathedral.

The fourteen Stations of the Cross, moulded in the concrete of the cathedral walls, have aroused much comment. The Stations have always been a feature of Catholic churches and chapels. At one period there were as many as thirty-six Stations in some churches, but since the sixteenth century there have invariably been fourteen. (It may be of interest to know that in 1850, when the diocese of Clifton was established a parishioner of the Pro-Cathedral, William Maskell, presented the church with a beautiful set of Stations of the Cross, carved in plaster. At the time it was claimed that this was the first occasion since the reign of Queen Mary Tudor that the Stations of the Cross had been erected in a Catholic cathedral in this country.) The Stations in the new cathedral were designed and executed by William Mitchell.

The bell on the new cathedral is the bell which was bought from Park Place when the old Pro-Cathedral was vacated, and it is fitting that on 4 October 1984 a special Mass was celebrated at the new cathedral to mark the 150th. anniversary of the day when the two Franciscan priests, Frs. Francis Edgeworth O.F.M. and Patrick O'Farrell O.F.M., without any ceremony, placed in position the foundation stone of what was to be the new church of the Holy Apostles at Park Place – the beginning of the Clifton Catholic mission.

J.C.

*   *   *   *   *

The Bishop's Chair

The word 'cathedral' comes from the latin word *cathedra* meaning a chair. A church becomes a cathedral when the Bishop chooses to have his episcopal chair (throne) in that particular church, thereby making it the mother church of his diocese. Incidentally, the Pope's Cathedral as Bishop of Rome is not St. Peter but St. John Lateran. The throne of the Archbishop of Westminster in London is a replica of the Pope's throne in Rome. It is at his episcopal chair that the bishop presides at the Eucharistic liturgy. When seated there, surrounded by his priests, he is seen to be the shepherd and teacher of his flock. The Pope, when speaking infallibly as shepherd of the whole flock on a matter of faith or morals, is said to be speaking *ex cathedra* (i.e. from the chair).

From the Reformation until 1850 England and Wales were regarded as missionary territory. True, there were bishops known as Vicars Apostolic, but they did not have cathedrals. They settled wherever circumstances allowed. For the most part the Vicars Apostolic of the Western District lived in Bath – which is where the story of the Bishop's Chair begins.

Naturally these early bishop celebrated Mass and administered Confirmation, and on these occasions a special chair would have been used. As far as we know the original chair was destroyed at the time of the Gordon Riots in Bath when, according to a contemporary newspaper account of the events on 9/10 June 1780, the rioters: 'entering the Chapel, threw everything that was moveable into the street, and burnt them'. There is no mention of a chair in Bishop Walmesley's Inventory of 1781.

The present chair was placed in Clifton Cathedral in December 1987, just in time for the Diocesan Synod. It had been in use in Prior Park for many years and, according to tradition, was used by the late Vicars Apostolic in the period after 1780. Among these was Bishop Baines (1829–1843) who was responsible for many of the additions to Prior Park and the financial troubles which resulted from those undertakings. The chair was later discarded and found its way to the organ loft at St. Mary, Bath. A former curate remembers it being there in the 1940s. A curate from a later generation, Fr. Mervin Havard-Brown, recognising its history, had it restored and re-upholstered in flame-coloured woven silk – it had previously been green Italian velvet with gold talon fringes – and took it with him to St. Joseph, Wroughton in 1985 on his appointment as parish priest. However, he was more than happy to return it to Clifton Cathedral where it could be restored to its rightful place as the Bishop's chair.

But what had served as the Bishop's throne during the intervening period? In the Pro-Cathedral there was an oak chair on which most of the Bishops of Clifton had sat. Given that it was specially covered for the occasion, it is likely that this was the throne alluded to in the following news item, which appeared in *The Bristol Mercury and Western Counties Advertiser*: 'We understand that the throne used at the enthronement of the new Roman Catholic Bishop of Clifton (Dr. Clifford) . . . was the gift of William Maskell, Esq. It was carved and illuminated in crimson, purple and gold'. (21 March, 1857).

Maskell, a convert, had been domestic chaplain to Bishop Phillpotts of Exeter, of Gorham Judgement fame, and was a close friend of Clifford. Sadly, this was disposed of at the auction of church furnishings held on 15 August 1973, just a matter of weeks after the consecration of the new Cathedral Church of SS. Peter and Paul. The chair, listed in the catalogue as Lot 131, was described as follows: 'A late nineteenth century carved oak Bishops elbow chair with Grecian key pattern border and acanthus and florette carved decoration, having seat, back and arms upholstered in American cloth'. It was sold for £44, but as the auctioneers' records have long since been destroyed, we have no idea who bought it.

From 1973 until the re-emergence of the present chair, the bishop's cathedra was a chair in no way different from the others in the cathedral.

Report on the Bishop's Chair by Miss Karin M. Walton, Curator of Applied Art at the City of Bristol Museum and Art Gallery. Reprinted by kind permission of the author

In my opinion it is a nineteenth century version of the X-frame chair which was used as a chair of state in the late sixteenth and early seventeenth centuries. The X-form of the legs derived from a type of folding chair in the medieval period, but by c.1700 the frame was usually fixed. Similar chairs can be seen in portraits of monarchs and popes which gives some indication of their status. These early chairs, however, were always highly decorative. The frame was made of cheap wood and was usually covered in rich velvet or brocade, although I know of examples with painted frames. The fact that the Clifton chair is of oak, and the style of the carving are indicative of a nineteenth century date. Whoever made the chair had obviously seen an original example because he has copied in carving the brass studs that held the fabric in place on the frame; he has also copied the fringing that was often around the feet, and the 'pommels' surmounting the back uprights. The carving is somewhat mechanical and lacks the spirited exuberance of much seventeenth century carving. Also the 'guilloche' motif on the legs and arms would not have been used like this in the seventeenth century, whereas in the nineteenth century it was common to cover every available surface with decoration. I would think that the chair dates from after 1840 and was a conscious effort to copy a throne chair of the sixteenth/seventeenth centuries. It might just be earlier; there was an antiquarian revival in the 1820s and 1830s, when antique furniture was avidly collected and copied, but my instinct places it later.

The above article first appeared in the Clifton Diocesan Directory 1989. It is reprinted here by kind permission of the editor.

*   *   *   *   *

The cathedral is, of course, a normal working parish and as such houses the usual parochial institutions such as a primary school. The original infants' school was housed in the crypt of the Pro-Cathedral, but a new school, built on the site of the Old Park Place Convent, was opened by Bishop Brownlow in August 1899. It cost £2,300 and was named Park Place School. When the new Cathedral of SS. Peter and Paul was built in 1973 it was decided that the school should also move, and a site on Aberdeen Road, Cotham was acquired. The new school, called SS. Peter and Paul Primary School was opened in 1976.

The parish also has four congregations of religious sisters.

Sisters of La Retraite, Emmaus House, Clifton Hill

In 1977, when the La Retraite Preparatory School moved back into the main building, the sisters decided to set up Emmaus House as a Pastoral Retreat Centre, remaining there after the closure of the school in 1982. The sisters host residential workshops and retreats, and provide personal spiritual development based on Jung's theories. The building provides a chapel, hall, meeting rooms, a counselling room and art room. It also has a bookshop, various landscaped gardens and a restaurant which is open to the public every day.

Little Sisters of the Poor, Cotham Hill. (St. Joseph's Home for the Elderly)

In 1862 the Little Sisters of the Poor arrived in Bristol from Brittany, France, where they had been founded in 1839 by Blessed Jeanne Jugan to care for the elderly poor. They began their work in a rented house in Tortworth Villa, Coronation Road, Bedminster, but this house quickly became too small and they moved to 20 Trinity Street, College Green in 1863. A further move was necessary in 1864 to accommodate the increasing numbers of elderly poor seeking admission, so a property was acquired in Park Row.

In 1869 the present site in Cotham Hill was bought and work commenced on the existing building. The new chapel was blessed and opened in July 1899. On 24 November 1940 the home was partly destroyed by enemy action. The building was restored in 1951, by which time the sisters were caring for over 100 residents of all denominations. In 1986 a modernisation programme was begun to provide single room accommodation. In 1990 the roof was raised and another floor added to one of the wings. In 1999 the sisters are seeking to raise over two million pounds as work begins to complete the entire refurbishment of the house in order to comply with current legislation and enhance the quality of life of the residents.

The Poor Servants of the Mother of God

The sisters first came to Bristol in 1920 where they lived at 4 Pembroke Road, visiting the poor in their own homes and teaching in the Pro-Cathedral School.

When the boarders from St. Brendan's College moved to Prior Park in

1922 the sisters purchased 3, 4 and 5 Upper Byron Place from the Irish Christian Brothers, but it was a further two years before they were able to take possession of the property and start the reconstruction needed to turn it into a thirty-bed hospital. St. Mary's Hospital was officially opened on 6 July 1926.

Between 1941 and 1944 all the patients and sisters were evacuated to Chew Magna. Since their return to Upper Byron Place many improvements and additions have been made over the years, including the five-bed Frances Taylor Hospice Unit which opened in 1993.

The unit is named after the foundress of the Congregation of the Poor Servants of the Mother of God who joined Florence Nightingale's band of volunteer nurses in the Crimea in 1855.

The Sisters of Jesus in the Temple (The Blue Nuns)

Moved by the desire to foster vocations to the priesthood in England, a group of sisters from Seez in Normandy arrived in England and received ecclesiastical approval on 15 August 1862. Cardinal Wiseman became the Father Founder of the new congregation to be known as the Congregation of the Child Jesus in the Temple. Its special mission is the service of the priesthood, and by praying for priestly vocations, caring for students in the seminaries, or nursing sick and retired priests, the congregation has remained faithful to this.

On 29 June 1867 Bishop Clifford welcomed the community to the diocese and asked it to continue the work for which it had been founded, in particular the care of the young students to the priesthood at Prior Park, and to open a house for priests of the diocese who were ill or retired. The first house opened in Bristol was at Clifton Wood, on the present site of St Edward's Road. Retired priests found the hill to the shops tough going from Clifton Wood, and in December 1900 the community moved to No 1 Rodney Place. In 1920 the sisters moved again, this time to Litfield Place where, at St Angela's the work for priests and elderly ladies continues.

V.A.

Park Place Convent

When the newly-appointed Vicar Apostolic of the Western District, Bishop Ullathorne, presented a Pastoral Letter to the Catholics of his district in November 1847, he outlined his plans for completing the near-derelict building at Park Place in Clifton. He explained that if this large structure were to be completed to a state where it could be used, 'the present small and inadequate chapel would be devoted to the purpose for which it was intended, forming part of a convent . . . the Sisters of Penance are prepared to purchase it at its value in part payment of the purchase money of the whole property, and would hope, in time, to form the site of their convent'.

The community of nuns to which the bishop referred, the Dominican Sisters of Penance, had been invited to come to Bristol from their convent near Coventry where the new vicar apostolic had been a missioner. The little community's first home in Bristol, in 1846, was a rented house in King Square, from where they moved to a larger house in Queen Square in 1847, and finally in 1848 to the newly-built convent in Park Place. The missioner at the new church of the Holy Apostles, soon to become the Pro-Cathedral, Fr. Frederick Neve, gave the community a gift of £2,000 to help pay for the convent. The building, traces of which still remain, occupied the space between the new church at the top of the site and St. Augustine's chapel situated further down the slope. The convent cloister was adjacent to the north side of the chapel. The Pope appointed Bishop Ullathorne as Canonical Superior of the community for the duration of his life.

It soon became necessary to enlarge the convent chapel, as St. Augustine's now became, and this could only be done by demolishing the end wall at the rear of the chapel and creating a gallery space on which the nuns' stalls could be erected. It now became possible for the nuns to enter their stalls by a private door at the back of the gallery. Before the work on the chapel was completed, Bishop Ullathorne was translated to the Central (formerly Midland) District as Vicar Apostolic, and his successor in the Western District was his Grand Vicar (or deputy) Joseph William Hendren O.S.F. who, for many years, had been chaplain to the Franciscan Convent at Taunton. It was Bishop Hendren who, on 27 December 1850, formally opened the newly-enlarged convent chapel and dedicated it to St. Catherine of Siena. (It is of interest to note that when the refurbished building was re-opened as a parish centre in 1934, it was named St. Catherine's Hall.)

The translation of Bishop Hendren to Nottingham in 1851, and the early death of his successor, Bishop Burgess, in 1854, left the diocese without a bishop. The Pope refused to appoint another bishop until its financial affairs had been put in a satisfactory state. (The main cause of the problem was the cost of supporting the college and seminary at Prior Park, which had been established by Bishop Baines in 1830. Archbishop Errington, who was Co-adjutor Archbishop to Cardinal Wiseman at Westminster, came to Clifton as Diocesan Administrator in order to sort out the problem.)

Archbishop Errington, well known for his strict adherence to the instructions of Canon Law, soon made known his views about the arrangements of the convent chapel. Many parishioners preferred to attend services there rather than in the vast empty spaces of the new Pro-Cathedral, but, in spite of Archbishop Errington's complaints, Bishop Ullathorne, as Canonical Superior of the convent, refused to prohibit the parishioners from attending services at the chapel. The Archbishop also expressed his dislike of the nuns' stalls being situated in the gallery at the back of the chapel. He insisted that they should be at the front so that the priest would not have to carry the Blessed Sacrament through the chapel when the nuns were receiving Holy Communion. Again, Bishop Ullathorne would not agree to the change, and his defiant attitude caused the Archbishop to refer the question to Rome. However, nothing appears to have come of the matter, as the Pope appointed a new bishop to the diocese and Archbishop Errington returned to Westminster.

The new bishop, William Clifford, who, according to Cardinal Wiseman had been chosen for, among other things, his ability 'to get on with Mother Hallahan', wisely decided that so long as the nuns were willing to allow the laity to attend their chapel there was no reason why they should not do so. Indeed, in 1874, the convent chapel became the mission church for several months. At the end of that year, the architect, Charles Hansom, at the bishop's request, designed the new school-room, atrium and end wall to the Pro-Cathedral. The blank wall, which had been hurriedly built in 1848 to enclose the end of the building, and the gallery inside it, were demolished and replaced with the Italianate wall and figures.

The Sisters of Penance remained at Park Place until 1876. In that year the community moved to Stone, in Staffordshire. Bishop Clifford bought the site, the convent buildings and the chapel for £2,000. The low price took account of the fact that the community had excluded several of the fittings in the chapel from the purchase. These included the three altars, the stained glass window over the high altar and the nuns' stalls. As a temporary measure, the bishop let the convent buildings, excluding the chapel, the priest's house and the yard at the bottom of the site to Mrs. Mathews, who, with the assistance of her daughter, ran a very successful boarding house for gentlemen at Park House, as the buildings were now named.

In 1881 Bishop Clifford offered the use of the convent and chapel to a community of Franciscan friars who had been expelled from France. The Franciscans assisted at the services in the Pro-Cathedral, and at the convents in Clifton Wood and Cotham. For a period they also served the short-lived Catholic mission at Sharpness.

In 1884 the Franciscans left Park Place to establish the mission at Portishead, and Bishop Clifford was again faced with the problem of what to do with the buildings. He invited the Sisters of St. Rose of Lima, who had a convent at Stroud, in Gloucestershire, to take over the convent at Park Place and provide the teachers for the girls' and infants' school which, in 1884, was still part of the crypt of the Pro-Cathedral.

The community agreed, and in addition to their work in the parish school, established a higher grade school for girls in part of the convent buildings. They remained at Park Place until December 1898, when the Superiors decided to close the convent at Park Place and concentrate resources at their other establishments at Erdington, Birmingham and Cheadle, Staffordshire. It so happened that when H. M. Inspectors carried out their annual inspection in the summer of 1898, they raised the issue of the suitability of the church crypt as accommodation for a school. Although it was not exactly condemned, the Administrator of the Pro-Cathedral, Canon Eustace Barron, realised that it was only a matter of time before this would happen. Bishop Brownlow agreed and so it became necessary to demolish most of the empty buildings of the former convent to built the new school. The site was cleared down the slope to the cloister, leaving the chapel, the small tower and tower room and the bishop's robing room intact. On 28 August 1899 Bishop Brownlow formally opened the new school which had been built at a cost of £2,300.

In 1904 the High Altar was removed from the chapel and re-erected in the new church then being built in Swindon. At one time the main altar in Holy Rood, it now serves as the altar of the Blessed Sacrament chapel. The stained glass window was removed and installed at the Dominican convent at Hawick in Scotland. The two side altars, dedicated to St. Dominic and to the Holy Rosary, were removed and re-erected in the chapel at the convent in Stone, Staffordshire. The nuns' stalls, about which there had been so much controversy in Archbishop Errington's time, were also removed. Some went to the convent at Erdington and the remainder to St. Mary's church in Julian Road, Bath. Thus stripped of the last vestiges of its past, St. Catherine's was leased to a local furniture business as a store. It was not until 1934 that, as St. Catherine's Hall, it again became a part of the Pro-Cathedral parish and remained so until 1973. It is now part of the Waldorf School complex.

J.C.

The Clifton Boys' Grammar Schools

The closure of Prior Park in 1856 left the area without any form of grammar school for boys, although the Benedictine school at Downside was available for those who could afford the fees.

On 1 February 1860 Bishop Clifford established a grammar school for Catholic boys in the basement of a house at 22 Meridian Place, close to the Pro-Cathedral. By making a gateway in the wall at the end of the garden the boys had access to a strip of land adjoining the church which could be used for recreation. The school was under the direction of Fr. Walter Buckle, a convert Anglican clergyman. All the expenses of the school were guaranteed by the bishop and the numbers attending increased rapidly. The *Catholic Directory* for 1863 gives the address of the school as 21 and 22 Meridian Place. The same directory shows that by 1863 Fr. Buckle was no longer at the school which was now in the charge of two brothers, Frs. Edward and James Williams, who were destined to play an important part in the later history of Prior Park.

In 1864 Bishop Clifford purchased a large house in St. Edward's Road, Clifton Wood, and the Catholic Grammar School, now known as St. Edward's, was transferred there from Meridian Place. But the stay in St. Edward's Road was destined to be a brief one. After Easter 1867, the school was again transferred to new quarters, this time to the splendour of Prior Park, where it took the name of the former school there, St. Peter's. (The house in St. Edward's Road became the first home for retired and infirm priests of the diocese under the care of the Sisters of Jesus in the Temple). Although there was accommodation for 120 boys at Prior Park, Br. J. S. Roche in his *History of Prior Park College* suggests that between 1867 and 1895 there were never more than eighty boys at the college. Financial problems caused its closure in 1904.

The Irish Christian Brothers, who lived at 9 Priory Road, Clifton in a house then called Terra Felix, had established their grammar school, St. Brendan's College, at 9 Berkeley Square in 1896. Two years later the adjoining house, 10 Berkeley Square, the home of the former diocesan seminary, was in use to cope with the increased number of students, and shortly before the outbreak of the First World War in 1914 a new school building was erected in the gardens of the two houses. Lack of space meant that the roof of the new building had to be strengthened so that it could be used for recreation purposes. The boarders lived nearby in a large house in Upper Byron Place which is now part of the St. Mary's Hospital complex. In 1925 the boarders were transferred to Prior Park and St. Brendan's served as the Catholic grammar school until the new premises were built at Brislington. These were blessed in November 1961 by a former pupil, Archbishop Grimshaw of Birmingham.

For later history see St. Brendan's Sixth Form College entry in Chapter 4.

J.C.

Girls' Grammar Schools

In 1882, before the departure of the Sisters of St. Rose of Lima from their convent and higher grade school for girls at Park Place in 1898, a community of nuns from France, the Order of Dames de la Mère, had established a day school for girls at College Road in Clifton. The number of pupils seeking admission to the school caused it to transfer to Manilla Hall, a larger house on the edge of Clifton Down, in the following year 1883. Although the order continued to live at Manilla Hall until 1900, it is not clear when the school closed. Advertisements ceased to appear in the *Catholic Directory* after 1894.

St. Gabriel's

An account of this school, established by the Sisters of Mercy at their convent in Dighton Street, can be found under the parish of St. Mary-on-the-Quay, Bristol.

St. Ursula's

An account of this school can be found under the parish of Bristol: Sacred Heart.

St. Joseph's Academy for Young Ladies

In 1903 the Sisters of St. Joseph of Annecy established a boarding and day school for girls at 17 Meridian Place, close to the Pro-Cathedral and a few doors away from the house at 22 Meridian Place where Bishop Clifford had established the Catholic grammar school in 1860. Increasing numbers soon caused the sisters to seek larger accommodation, and St. Joseph's Academy for Young Ladies, as the school was named, moved to Tottenham House in Gordon Road, Clifton, the following year, 1904. The school, ever increasing in size, was again forced to move, this time to a large detached house in Cornwallis Grove, Clifton. Here the school remained until 1924.

La Retraite High School for Girls

In 1924 the La Retraite Congregation took over the direction of St. Joseph's and changed the name to La Retraite High School for Girls. The first headmistress was Mother St. Paul and under her direction the school grew. During the next twenty years a hall and gymnasium were added, together with tennis courts and the new west wing housing laboratories, music room and classrooms. The school escaped serious damage during the Second World War, although, in fact, the boarders had already moved to La Retraite, Burnham-on-Sea, where the sisters had another school.

In 1944 the school obtained Direct Grant status under the Education Act and in 1953 acquired the property on the opposite side of Hensmans Hill to serve as a Preparatory School. During the 1960s the debate on the comprehensive reorganisation of Bristol's Catholic secondary schools began and plans to replace the hall, gallery and dining hall were put aside. The sudden collapse of the southern boundary wall in 1966 meant that over £20,000 had to be raised to rebuild it. In 1977 the preparatory school moved back into the main building, and the Emmaus House Retreat centre was established. (*see* Cathedral Church of SS. Peter and Paul).

In 1982 the school closed when all the remaining pupils transferred to the newly-formed Sixth Form College of St. Brendan's at Brislington. The convent building now houses the Bristol Cancer Help Centre and the west wing has been converted into residential accommodation.

V.A.

CHAPTER FOUR

The Parishes and Defunct Missions of the Diocese

Amesbury, Wiltshire: Christ the King

The Catholic parish of Christ the King was established in 1933. Prior to that time priests visited the area from St. Osmond, Salisbury to say Mass. At one time there was a monthly Mass in the British Legion Hall, and at other times the people made their way to the army camps at Larkhill and Bulford. During the same period Mass was offered occasionally at Ludgershall for the few scattered Catholics of that area. It soon became obvious to the diocesan authorities that an area which covered two hundred square miles of the plain required the services of a resident priest to serve the expanding population.

In 1933 this became possible through the efforts of Mr. J. Cockle, and premises were purchased in what was then called London Road, in the form of a piano shop with a bungalow attached. These premises were purchased for £857. After the necessary adaptations had been made these buildings became the parish church and the presbytery. Fr. (later Canon) Joseph Dolan was appointed the first parish priest and the first Mass was offered in the church on 17 December 1933 by Bishop Lee. In 1934 a parish hall was added – originally an army hut – at the rear of the church. This hall occupied almost all of the ground that the parish then owned. For many years it served as a place for social gatherings and as a source of revenue for the parish.

In November 1944 a strip of ground was purchased from the 'Popular Café' in Amesbury with the intention of building a new church. This ground was added to in 1945 by the acquisition of an area of adjoining woodland, but the hopes of a new building receded owing to the restrictions of the postwar years. To add to these difficulties the parish hall was destroyed in a fire. However, with the determined help of parishioners this building was quickly restored – a task that seemed impossible at the time.

During the postwar years, with the rapid growth of the population, a small church was opened at **Ludgershall**, and a new church built at **Durrington**. A primary school was added in 1963. About this time it was decided that the passing years were taking their toll on the existing Amesbury church. After a detailed inspection of the fabric the parish had to balance the costs of repair against the building of a new church. Eventually it was decided to convert the large club complex at the rear into a new church and social facility. This work was completed in 1985 and the new church was consecrated by Bishop Alexander on 16 November that year.

K.McG.

Ammerdown, Somerset: See Radstock

Ashwicke Hall, Wiltshire: See Bristol St. Gerard Majella

Avonmouth, Bristol: St. Brendan and the Port Chaplaincy

The Catholic population of Avonmouth was served for many years by the clergy of St. Bernard Shirehampton where a mission had been established in 1901. The Avonmouth Old Dock had been opened in 1887 and many Irish and other Catholic seamen had passed through the port. In 1924 the National Smelting Corporation built a new plant at Avonmouth and many craftsmen were transferred from Swansea, so the management arranged for a hut at the works to be used as a Mass centre.

In 1946 a site was purchased in St. Andrews Road, Avonmouth, where a wooden church dedicated to St. Brendan was constructed. It was blessed by Bishop Lee later that year. Fund raising was now a priority for the parish of Shirehampton who needed to pay for the site at Avonmouth and also for another new church at Lawrence Weston. Weekly bingo sessions and football pools raised thousands of pounds and in 1955 the wooden church at Avonmouth was dismantled and transferred to Lawrence Weston to serve as the scout hut, and a new permanent St. Brendan was built and blessed by Bishop Rudderham in January 1956.

Fr. Patrick Ryan was appointed the first resident port chaplain and he was succeeded by Fr. Thomas Keane who became the first parish priest when St. Brendan was established as a separate parish in 1973. Fr. John Yiend arrived in 1979. The original altar rails depicted the church's connection with the port and with St. Brendan the navigator. However, the decline of Avonmouth and the advent of the new dock at Portbury resulted

Bath: Orchard Street Chapel (1809–63)

in diminishing congregations, now served by Canon Anthony Cotter, whilst Fr. Yiend remained as port chaplain until his death in 1998.

V.A.

Bath: Our Lady and St. Alphege

With the development and growth of the south western area of Bath, and an increase in the number of Catholics, it became necessary in the 1920s to build a church to accommodate those who were obliged to walk long distances either to St. John the Evangelist or St. Mary. The Father Prior of St. John, Dom Anselm Rutherford, purchased a site in Oldfield Lane in 1925. The architect chosen to design the new church was Sir Giles Gilbert Scott, the architect of the Anglican Cathedral in Liverpool. The church, of the Roman basilica type, was completed and opened in 1929 and was dedicated to Our Lady and St Alphege. The latter was a monk at Deerhurst in Gloucestershire in the tenth century and eventually became Abbot of Bath.

St. Alphege was at first used as a chapel-of-ease being served from St. John both under the Benedictines and, after the transfer in 1932, by the secular clergy. In 1937, the debt for its construction having been paid, it was constituted as a separate parish by Bishop Lee. The church was consecrated by Bishop Rudderham in October 1954, the year appropriately marking the Silver Jubilee of the opening of the church (the one thousandth anniversary of the birth of the patron St. Alphege) and the completion of the Lady Chapel and sacristy. Four years later the presbytery and the linking passage to the church were completed.

In 1958 the modified campanile, also designed by Sir Giles Gilbert Scott, was completed but only to half the planned height. The ground floor of this tower served as the baptistery for many years. In 1960 a parish hall was opened and a new organ installed in the church. This was originally built in 1915 by Rushworth and Dreaper and is regarded as a superb instrument for a church the size of St. Alphege. A second smaller church to accommodate the increase in the number of Catholics was built at **Southdown** and dedicated to **St. Joseph** when it was completed in 1969 and opened by Bishop Rudderham.

Alterations were subsequently made to the sanctuary of St. Alphege and in 1986 a new lighting system was installed. However, the unusual pendant lampholders designed by Scott were retained.

From 1934 to 1996 the Irish Sisters of Charity were at 27 Oldfield Road with a nursing home at No. 30.

M.McC.

Bath: St. Joseph Served from Our Lady and St. Alphege

Bath: St. John the Evangelist

The records of the Jesuit priests, then based at the College of St. Francis Xavier, near Hereford, suggest that in 1632 the Jesuits celebrated Mass in Bath from time to time as they made the circuit of the district. In 1685 a Benedictine priest, Dom Anselm Williams, was sent from the Jesuit college at Cambrai to establish a mission in the city of Bath. However, little seems to have been recorded of his progress.

By 1713 the Benedictines were established in a large house, 'Bell Tree House' situated at the corner of Beau Street and the Lower Borough Walls. In that year Dom Bernard Quyne carried out some repairs and alterations to 'Bell Tree House' which apparently served as a chapel, presbytery and guest house. In 1778, after the passing of the first Catholic Relief Act, a site for a new church and presbytery between St. James Parade and the Lower Borough Walls was purchased. By 1780 the church was completed.

Bath: St. John the Evangelist

Sadly, in that same year, the followers of Lord George Gordon destroyed the church and its contents in the notorious riots against the Catholics. (In passing, it may be observed that there are no documents dating from before 1781–82 in the Clifton Diocesan Archives as the earlier ones were destroyed in these riots.)

With the compensation paid by the City of Bath, Fr. Michael Pembridge bought another site in Corn Street and built a small church, connected by the garden at the rear, to the presbytery at 12 St James Square. This church proved to be too small and in 1805 Fr. Ainsworth bought an old theatre in Orchard Street and converted it into a chapel. The congregation worshipped here until 1861 when the building of the present St. John's church was completed. The spire – which at 202 feet is half the height of Salisbury, the highest spire in England – was not finished until 1863. It contains a bell inscribed 'Long live Pius IX Pope and King'.

There is a letter in the Archives of the Venerable English College in Rome, written by Bishop Clifford to Mgr. Talbot, the Pope's secretary at the Vatican, on 10 October 1863 describing the opening of the new church of St. John:

> 'This has been a glorious week in Bath . . . and the impression made in the city is great notwithstanding the great efforts made by the parsons and the evangelical alliance to counteract it. The town was placarded all over with abusive placards – all in vain – the respectable people were with us. After High Mass there was a grand luncheon in the Assembly Rooms – upwards of 300 people. The only drawback there has been to this happy event is the illness of Cardinal Wiseman. Still there is no doubt that religion is making steady progress in this part of England'.

On the night of 26 April 1942 the wall on the south side of the church and the presbytery were destroyed in an air-raid. Fr. Timothy Sheridan, an assistant priest at St. John was killed in the raid. It was not until Whit-Sunday 1943 that Mass could again be celebrated at St. John. In the interval services were held in the convent chapel in Pulteney Road. Permanent repairs to the church were completed in 1953. As part of the War Memorial to the citizens of Bath a Book of Remembrance is preserved in St. John, and each year during the Mass on Remembrance Sunday this is brought to the altar.

Perrymead Cemetery

Bishop Clifford consecrated the cemetery on 1 June 1858 and the chapel on 28 April 1859.

J.A.H.

St. John's Flats and Oratory

When St. John's primary school in South Parade, Bath had to close down for lack of playground space in the early 1980s, the vacant Victorian buildings presented a problem for St. John's parish. The school moved to new premises which had been the Bath Convent School from which the pupils and staff had transferred to the newly-established St. Gregory's Comprehensive School in Odd Down, the former Cardinal Newman Secondary Modern School. It was decided that the redundant buildings at St. John's could usefully be converted into flats for retired diocesan priests. The conversion was done in a couple of years providing four flats and three suites of offices.

On Christmas Day 1997 the first Mass was concelebrated in the small chapel which will be a domestic oratory for retired priests living in St. John's flats. Work had begun in October. The old plaster was removed from the walls to uncover original stonework of high quality. Ashlars from the dividing walls were used to make a permanent square altar. The tabernacle is sited on an end wall and a beautiful statue of Our Lady is enshrined in the sanctuary area. The furnishings, chairs, carpet and other fittings have been donated by the present residents, parishes of the deanery, benefactors and Downside Abbey. The work, under the supervision and advice of Martin Fisher, who painted the mural of the Presentation in the Temple, was carried out by Kevin Donohue and his team.

Matthew Hayes

Bath: St. Mary

A mission existed to the north of the city of Bath from the setting up of a Mass centre at 3 Brunswick Place in 1823 up to the opening of the church of St. Mary in 1881, with the exception of a few years in the 1840s. The second, and larger, Chapel of St. Augustine at 5 Portland Place was opened in 1832 but it had to be sold in 1841 because the numbers attending services were not sufficient for it to survive. For a few years there appears to have been no mission in the northern part of the city, but by 1848 Mass was once again celebrated at 3 Brunswick Place. In 1852 the mission moved to St. Mary Chapel, Montpelier, a building which originally formed part of a riding school, with seating accommodation for 250 parishioners. In 1870 a new altar designed by a Roman artist, Leonardo, and constructed entirely of sixteen varieties of marble was built for the chapel. This altar stands today in the Lady Chapel of St. Mary church.

By 1877 the Montpelier chapel was proving inadequate for the increasingly populous northern section of Bath, and so the diocese purchased the present site of St. Mary only 300 yards away. In May 1881 the church was consecrated by Cardinal Manning and dedicated to Our Lady, Help of Christians. The founder of the church, Canon Francis Loughnan, who also purchased 5 Harley Street, which is currently the parish rectory, was succeeded by Fr. Arnold Matthew.

The whole vicinity of the church was altered by the Baedeker Raids in April 1942, but the building itself suffered only minor damage with the shattering of the original windows and damage to the roof. Major restoration and refurbishment took place in the interior of the church as part of the plan for celebrating the centenary of the consecration in 1981. One of the alterations was the removal of the High Altar from the reredos to place it nearer the congregation. The reredos formerly contained fabric panels and when it was cleared it was found that the fabric had disintegrated and had to be removed. In 1985 John Armstrong, a member of the International Society of Christian Artists, was asked to fill the eight niches with paintings of sants and martyrs. Four of those portrayed had local connections: St. Dunstan, St. Alphege and the two Glastonbury martyrs, Blessed Richard Whiting and Blessed John Thorne. The project was painted in oil colour and gold metallic paint and was designed to harmonise in style, colour and tone with the Victorian church. It was formally blessed by Bishop Alexander in October 1986.

In the original plans for the church by the architects Dunn and Hansom, the north wall contained five stone panels which were to be filled at a later date with frescoes. In 1997 these panels, painted by the artist Fleur Kelly, depicting the Annunciation, the Visitation, the Nativity, the Marriage Feast at Cana and the Deposition from the Cross were donated by the artist and the parishioners.

Batheaston: The Good Shepherd

Ironically it was a stick of bombs falling on a building some twelve miles away that determined the dedication of this parish.

On the night of 2 January 1941 both the convent of the Good Shepherd and the adjoining reformatory at Arnos Vale were severely damaged, and the Home Office insisted on a move to a safer area. On 3 March two sisters and twenty girls moved to Eagle House, Bathford, to be followed three days later by four more sisters and the remaining sixty girls. Bishop Lee offered the first Mass there on 7 March and consecrated the Home to the Sacred Heart. Conditions were cramped and the Home Office inspector agreed that, as a concession, the registered number be reduced from eighty to seventy-two. In December 1947 the sisters moved from Eagle House to Ashwicke Hall, near Chippenham. Bishop Lee promised that one day a parish church would be built in the district and that, appropriately, it would be dedicated to the foundress of the Good Shepherd order, St. Euphrasia Pelletier (1796–1868) who had recently (1940) been canonised.

A temporary church bearing this dedication was erected at Batheaston in 1947. It was replaced by the present church, opened by Bishop Rudderham on Ascension Day, 1967, and dedicated to the Good Shepherd. It was one of the first churches in the diocese to be planned according to the new liturgical requirements, with a freestanding altar that can be served from either side. Seating is arranged radially with a capacity of 200. A church hall is provided under part of the main building. The church was served from St. Mary, Bath until 1978 when Fr. John Fairfoot became the first resident priest.

After his death in 1992 the parish was served for some time from SS. Peter and Paul until Fr. (now Canon) Matthew Hayes retired and for a time came to live in the parish. In 1998 it was taken under the pastoral care of St. Mary's, Bath.

The statues of St. Thomas More and St. John Fisher were donated to the church by the Army when the chapel at **Azimgher Barracks, Colerne**, which the parish had served for many years, closed in 1985. The fine brass eagle lectern which graced the Good Shepherd for some time now stands in St. Mary.

M.McC.

Bath: SS. Peter and Paul, Combe Down

The present church of SS. Peter and Paul was opened in the summer of 1965 but the history of the Combe Down parish is much older. It can be seen from the meticulously recorded parish registers that Mass was celebrated at Midford House, the home of the Parfitt family, between 1820 and 1837 and from 1837 to 1901 at Midford Castle, when the owner, Mr. Conolly, added a chapel* for the use of his wife, an Italian noblewoman, Louisa Brancaccio. Up to 1841 the monks of Downside Abbey served this chapel, dedicated to the Immaculate Conception, and after that Prior Park provided a chaplain.

Midford Castle

A member of the Parfitt family, Charles, was ordained by Bishop Baines in 1842. He was a convert, and an amusing anecdote, recalled by Bishop Burton and quoted by Brother Roche in his *History of Prior Park College*, relates how as a young priest Parfitt went into Bishop Bagg's study at Prior Park, found the sermon he was due to preach at the evening service, memorised it and proceeded to deliver it himself at the morning Mass. When at the end of Mass the procession returned to the sacristy Baggs, without any further ado, said to Parfitt: 'I suspend you'. In 1846 Parfitt retired and undertook the post of missioner at Midford, returning there in 1876 after

---

* An important treasure, possibly purchased by Mgr. Charles Parfitt, and once housed in the castle chapel is a Trinity Altar (probably fifteenth century). It is described as having 'eight medieval alabaster panels and a fine alabaster statue of the Trinity'. The chapel at Midford Castle closed in 1901 and for many years the altar was set against the wall in the north aisle of the Pro-Cathedral. In July 1973 it was presented as a gift to the St. Nicholas Church Museum, Baldwin Street, Bristol.

Because it was a consecrated building the chapel was pulled down when it ceased to be a place of worship. This was in accordance with the canon law of the day. The pointed arch of the entrance leading to the chapel may still be seen in the perimeter wall at the side of the road.

a period at Cottles, near Melksham, the original home of the Conolly family. The records for 1855 show that there were 62 Catholics in the Midford area and there was also a Poor School, but over the years the numbers went into decline.

Charles Conolly died at Midford Castle in 1850, but when his wife died some twenty years later, Fr. Parfitt again became the centre of controversy. In her will she left a substantial amount of her property, valued at £7,000, to her chaplain. However, in 1871 this was disputed by the family in the probate court on the grounds that it was obtained 'by undue influence'. The jury found in favour of Parfitt as did a subsequent hearing (1872) when Lord Penzance said that he had been 'unable to find in the evidence any act or word to show that the testatrix has ever subordinated her own to that of the plaintiff'. After Mgr. Parfitt's death in 1886, Midford was served from Prior Park. These facilities for Catholics ceased to exist at the Castle in 1901 when it was no longer in the possession of the Conolly family. When the mission at Midford closed, the bodies of Bishop Baggs, who was Vicar Apostolic of the Western District from 1844 to 1845, Mgr. Charles Parfitt and others were re-interred in the crypt of the chapel at Holy Souls Cemetery, Arno's Vale, Bristol. After 1901 the local parishioners attended the chapel at Prior Park, which was then a junior seminary and a college. The Irish Christian Brothers were invited by Bishop Burton to return to Prior Park in 1919 after the occupation by the British Army, and in 1920 the Catholic Industrial School was transferred there from Cannington. Fr. Michael O'Sullivan, the chaplain to the school, became the first parish priest, and the chapel, dedicated to Our Lady of the Snows, was shared by the college and the parish.

The new housing at Foxhill increased the number of Catholics in the area, and Fr. John McReynolds, the chaplain of Prior Park in the 1950s, initiated the idea of creating a new parish church which was more centrally situated. In 1954 he moved the presbytery to a Georgian property at 112 Entry Hill, donated by a convert, Miss Dorothy Spear. Fr. Graham Langford was largely responsible for the building of the church in the grounds some eleven years later. It was one of the first churches in the diocese to be built in accordance with the liturgical requirements of the Second Vatican Council. The church, opened in the summer of 1965, was consecrated by Bishop Alexander on 1 June 1976. In 1999 the parish took over the pastoral care of the parish of Peasedown St. John, formerly served from Downside.

M.McC. and J.A.H.

Beachley Camp, Gloucestershire: St. Joseph Served from Coleford

Berkeley, Gloucestershire: Berkeley Castle Served from Thornbury

Bishop's Cleeve, Gloucestershire: St. John Fisher Served from Winchcombe

Bishops Lydeard, Somerset: Parish Church Served from Taunton

Bishopdown, Wiltshire: Served from Salisbury St. Gregory

Bishopston: See Bristol St. Bonaventure

Bishopsworth: See Bristol St. Pius X

Bisley, Gloucestershire: St. Mary of the Angels Served from Stroud

Blaisdon, Gloucestershire: See Newent

Bonham, Wiltshire See Wincanton

Bourton-on-the-Water, Gloucestershire: Served from Stow-on-the-Wold

Bradford-on-Avon, Wiltshire: St. Thomas More

A century ago Bradford-on-Avon was a town with a very small population. The few, if any, Catholics who lived there would have attended Mass at Trowbridge or Bath. We know very little of these early days for, unlike many other parishes, there seemed to have been no prominent individual or individuals to organise the local Catholic community and arrange for Mass to be said. This changed for a time when a convert named Roger Kynaston moved into the town with his wife and six children. He soon became an organising force within the area and had part of his property converted into a fine chapel.

This was opened in 1929 in Church Street and dedicated to Blessed Thomas More who was canonised six years later. In 1945 the Mass centre was transferred to Trowbridge Road School. (During the Second World War Mass was also being said in the assembly hall of an underground factory at Westwood.)

In 1955 Bishop Rudderham purchased the Town Hall and had the upper

The old Catholic chapel in Gordon Terrace, Bridgwater

floor converted into a church dedicated to St. Thomas More. At the time it was thought that this was to be a temporary measure but plans to buy land on Congre Hill encountered difficulties. By 1960 the numbers of Catholics in Bradford-on-Avon had increased and a move was made to set up a choir for Sunday Mass. The parish was finally separated from Trowbridge in 1968 when Fr. Thomas Aherne, who had been looking after St. Thomas More from his base in Trowbridge became the first parish priest in residence.

K. McG.

Bradley Stoke: See Bristol Holy Family

Bramshaw, Wiltshire: See Salisbury St. Osmund

Bridgwater, Somerset: St. Joseph

When Lord Clifford allowed his house in Cannington to be used as a convent for refugee Benedictine nuns in 1807, there were only five Catholic missions in Somerset for the public celebration of Mass. The convent chapel was eventually declared 'Cannington Mission of the Holy Name' in June 1831 with Fr. William O'Meara as priest-in-charge.

In 1845 the population of Bridgwater was over 10,000 when a Church of England clergyman, the Rev. J. Moore Capes, built St. John the Baptist church and preached the opening sermon there in April of that year. Two months later he announced his intention of becoming a Catholic and several parishioners of St. John followed his example. Now a Catholic layman, Mr. Moore Capes undertook the responsibility of establishing the first Catholic mission in Bridgwater since the Reformation. With the agreement of Bishop Baggs a fund was opened to raise £850 to build a church. The main contributors were Moore Capes, the Knight family of Cannington and Dr. (later Cardinal) Wiseman.

The new church site, which is now part of Gordon Terrace and St. John Street, was purchased, and it included the land then known as St. John's Close and two cottages. The foundation stone was laid on 2 October 1845 and the church of St. Joseph was opened on 14 February 1846 with sung Mass. This little chapel was only fifty feet by twenty-five feet and the organ was one previously used in St. John's church. Whilst the chapel was being built Mr. Moore Capes allowed his drawing-room to be used, and it was there that the first public Mass since the Reformation was celebrated in Bridgwater.

At first the little chapel was served by the priest from Holy Name, Cannington, Fr. Jacob Illingworth, who travelled into Bridgwater on horseback until 4 June 1852 when Fr. Thomas Rooker was appointed first resident priest. After thirty-six years the attendance at this little chapel had reached 200, and it became necessary to build a new church.

Built on the west bank of the river Parrett, the church was opened by Bishop Clifford on 22 June 1882. Fr. (later Canon) A. J. C. Scoles was both the rector and the architect. Nine months later, on 27 March, a school was opened with eighteen pupils arriving on the first day. In 1885 the Sisters of Charity came to live in a house in King Street near the church and some of the sisters took up teaching posts in the school. Three years later they opened a laundry, employing about twenty local girls.

1891 saw the departure of both the sisters and Fr. Scoles, who went to Yeovil. Fr. Thomas O'Meara served the parish for two years and, after a gap, Fr. Robert Wadman was appointed. Bishop Burton consecrated the church on the occasion of its silver jubilee (1907).

In 1914 Canon Wadman died and the 200 parishioners at St. Joseph welcomed a new priest, Dr. George Brown, whose brief ministry was cut short when he succumbed to the flu epidemic which raged at the end of the Great War. He was only forty-one years old. The Calvary on the north wall of the church was erected as a memorial to him.

The 1920s saw the closure of the Holy Name mission at Cannington (1921), the ordination in Rome of one of the parishioners, the future Archbishop Grimshaw (1926), and the departure to Taunton of Fr. (later Mgr. Provost) Richard Iles.

Fr. (later Canon) Michael Cashman served the parish for five years during which he installed electric light in the church, doing most of the work himself. At the time unemployment in the town was at a high level and money was scarce.

After the outbreak of the Second World War numbers in the parish began to increase, many of the new faces being those of evacuees. Canon (later Mgr. Provost) Davey went to the Franciscan nuns at Taunton, Fr. Michael Byrne arrived as parish priest to be followed shortly by the Sisters of the Holy Rosary who opened a new convent in Durleigh Road. October 1939 saw the opening of both the convent chapel and of a school. In 1940 a curate was appointed to St. Joseph and the two priests, with men of the parish, began work renovating the old school buildings. The school, with fifty-nine children, re-opened with staff from the convent.

Fr. Timothy O'Connell, Fr. (now Canon) William Ryan and Fr. (later Canon) Thomas Morrissey came in succession as parish priests. In 1963 Fr. John McReynolds took charge of the parish and on 2 September the new primary school of St. Joseph was opened. Mass began to be said the following year at the **Sydenham Community Centre** and in 1966 in the **Cannington Village Hall**.

In 1979 the Co-operative building adjacent to the church was purchased for £20,000. It was demolished and work on building an extension to the church was commenced in May 1981. The new extension to the church was used for the first time for Christmas midnight Mass the same year.

The present parish priest Fr. Thomas Aherne, was curate at St. Joseph from 1952 to 1954.

Acknowledgements to Bridgwater's Catholic Past by
Wilf Drumm and to the Centenary Booklet

Cannington, Somerset

After the restoration of the monarchy in 1660, Thomas Clifford, who became a member of King Charles' cabinet, the famous 'Cabal', was richly rewarded for his services. He became Lord High Treasurer and was created Lord Clifford of Chudleigh (in Devonshire). He also received the manor of

Bridgwater: Cannington, former chapel (now Clifford Hall, Somerset College of Agriculture and Horticulture), window depicting Perpetual Adoration

Cannington, near Bridgwater, where he built an imposing house, the Court House. Clifford was a strongly pro-Catholic member of the Cabal and may have died a Catholic. His family maintained a priest and chapel there until 1768 when they moved to Chudleigh, and the mission closed.

In 1795 a community of Benedictine nuns, driven out of France after the Revolution, settled at Marnhull in Dorset, in accommodation provided by the Hussey family. By 1807 the community had increased, making it necessary for them to find larger accommodation. Hearing of their plight, Lord Clifford offered to refurbish part of the Court House at Cannington. The offer was accepted and the nuns and their chaplain came to Cannington, thus opening the mission for the convenience of local Catholics. The Vicar Apostolic of the Western District, Bishop Collingridge, was invited to make his home at the convent and resided there from 1812 until his death in 1829.

Bishop Collingridge's successor, Bishop Baines, purchased the Prior Park estate in 1830 and lived there. The mission at Cannington thrived, and Bishop Baines appointed a missioner who would be responsible for the mission, while the nuns' chaplain cared for the community. (One of the missioners was Fr. Thomas Burgess, who, in June 1851, became the second Bishop of Clifton). In July 1831 Bishop Baines dedicated an impressive new chapel provided by the nuns. When the Bishop sent his returns to Rome in 1838, they showed that there were 160 Catholics at Cannington.

When in 1836 the community left Cannington for more convenient premises at Colwich in Staffordshire, the nuns left to the local Anglican parish church, where it is now on permanent display, the beautiful stone altar frontal from their chapel. The subject is 'The Lamb of God in Glory'. The mission itself remained under the care of a succession of missioners, although in the 1850s, some members of the Clifford family returned to live in part of the Court House.

On 15 June 1863, the nuns of the Order of Perpetual Adoration of the Blessed Sacrament established a convent at the Court House (now the Somerset College of Agriculture and Horticulture). The order, (also known as the Sacramentines) was founded about the middle of the seventeenth century by the Ven. Antoine Lequien. The members who came to Somerset belonged to the house at Bollène (Vaucluse), a community which at the time of the Revolution suffered greviously when thirteen of its members were guillotined for fidelity to their religious profession.

Although the sisters remained only four years – they moved to more spacious accommodation in Taunton in 1867 – there is still one outstanding relic of their sojourn at Cannington: a stained glass window in the Clifford Hall of the College depicting the adoration of the Blessed Sacrament exposed in a monstrance.

Further use was made of some of the buildings at Cannington when the Catholic Industrial School was opened there as a result of the legislation passed between the years 1854 and 1868. The newly-restored hierarchy issued a directive to each diocese to provide establishments where 'youthful delinquents can be reformed without danger to their faith'. The Clifton diocese responded by opening a reformatory for girls at Arno's Court in 1861 while in 1868 an Industrial School for boys serving the dioceses of Clifton, Newport and Plymouth, was commenced at Cannington. The latter remained in use until 1921 when it was transferred to the buildings at Prior Park, then recently released by the War Department. However, the Industrial School closed shortly after the move.

In 1913 Bishop Collingridge's body was exhumed at Cannington and transferred to the Abbey at Downside where it now rests in the north aisle next to that of his successor Bishop Baines. There was a resident priest at Cannington until 1921, when the mission was closed. Mass continued to be offered in the village hall until as recently as 1990, served from Bridgwater.

J.C. and J.A.H.

Bristol: St. Mary-on-the-Quay

St. Mary-on-the-Quay, in the heart of the city, is, apart from the pre-Reformation St. James Priory, Bristol's oldest Catholic church. It was built in 1840 by the Irvingites at a cost of £15,000, but they found it difficult to maintain, and three years later it was bought for the Catholic community for £5,000 by the Franciscan, Fr. Patrick O'Farrell, St. Mary's first priest. With its neo-classical façade it must have seemed particularly handsome amongst the utilitarian buildings and clutter of the harbourside, and Bishop Bernard Ward, the historian, considered it to be the most impressive Catholic church in England outside London when Bishop Baines opened it in 1843.

Until Fr. O'Farrell's retirement from St. Mary in 1857, raising money to pay off the debt incurred in its purchase was a constant worry and a task that continually engaged his attention. There was another problem. Scarcely two hundred yards away there existed St. Joseph's Chapel in Trenchard Street, Bristol's first post-Reformation Catholic church, built in 1790 by the Jesuits. It was clearly unsatisfactory that there should be two Catholic places of worship in the city centre in such close proximity, with their own priests and congregations. Bishop Clifford determined to rationalise the situation, and in 1861 St. Mary was made the parish church under the care of the Jesuits, whilst St. Joseph was adapted for use as St. Mary's schools. Until their convent closed in 1967, the Sisters of Mercy, who came to Bristol in 1846, played a prominent part in the educational and general life of the parish. Towards the end of the 1860s negotiations took place for the Society of Jesus to buy St. Mary's for £2,700, and by 3 August 1871 the purchase was complete. The Jesuits once again had their own church in Bristol.

As the years passed, the narrow, busy drawbridge across the harbour in the centre of Bristol proved less and less capable of coping with the heavy traffic. By 1893, the fiftieth anniversary of St. Mary's, a solution had been found. Until then the Frome flowed, an open river, past the frontage of St. Mary-on-the-Quay, hence its name, but in 1891 the authorities set work in hand to cover the area. By 6 May 1893 the Frome was no longer to be seen: the metamorphosis was complete. So today, St. Mary faces not the waters of the harbour but the swirling traffic of Colston Avenue and the city's Cenotaph, now standing where boats once plied.

St. Joseph's Chapel, Trenchard Street

In the final year of the century there were four priests serving the church. The number of Catholics in the parish, which was becoming more and more a commercial and business area, gradually dwindled as they looked for homes elsewhere, but the congregation itself continued to increase thanks to an efficient and cheap tram service, an effective choir though in 1877 its members ceased to be paid, and what the parish priest called 'the adoption of a more general system of congregational singing'.

The twentieth century saw St. Mary's grow as a city-centre church, and the boys' and girls' schools on the old St. Joseph's site behind the Colston Hall were enlarged. In the First World War 545 men of the parish joined the forces, many from the same family; sixty-seven lost their lives and their names are recorded on a fine brass memorial tablet fixed to the wall outside the church. The first name is that of George Archer-Shee. He had served as an altar boy at St. Mary's and become a naval cadet, and when in 1908, he was falsely implicated in the theft of a five-shilling postal order, he had been expelled from his college in disgrace. His father, firmly believing in his son's innocence, secured the services of a famous advocate and he was finally exonerated. At the time, the episode was something of a *cause célèbre* and the case was discussed in Parliament. In 1946 Terrence Rattigan wrote a play based on it, *The Winslow Boy*. It became hugely popular and was later seen on film and television. Today, passers-by who read the first entry on St. Mary's War Memorial – Archer-Shee G. – are looking at the name of the real Winslow Boy.

For a few months in 1933 and 1934 the Society of Jesus had difficulty in finding younger priests for St. Mary's, and Bishop Lee, growing impatient, offered to staff the church with his own diocesan clergy. But the Provincial, reluctant to see the parish pass from Jesuit control, replied, 'our Fr. General has given the matter careful consideration and ... it has seemed to him not altogether wise that we should leave so promising a field as Bristol'. In time the Provincial was able to resolve things satisfactorily.

During the Second World War Bristol was heavily bombed, but, although its central position made it so vulnerable, St. Mary's remained virtually untouched. On one occasion an incendiary bomb crashed through the skylight of the sacristy, landing on the vestment press. A Jesuit temporarily assisting at the church, and a fellow fire-watcher, manoeuvred the bomb on to the floor where they extinguished it. All was saved it seemed, but the priest's biretta perished in the attack. They then dealt with more incendiaries in the clubroom before taking refuge in the school shelter.

In the late 1960s St. Mary's entertained ambitious plans for the redevelopment of its site, to include an eighteen-storey office block and a modern church building with the entrance from a pedestrian walkway above the shops at street level. But in 1959 the church had been made a Grade 2 listed building, and various schemes for change were ultimately rejected by the city's planning authority. But there were matters of greater concern. The development of new housing estates on the outskirts of the city resulted in an exodus of Catholic families from the parish. By 1971 St. Mary's schools had been closed and the pupils accommodated in modern Catholic schools elsewhere. Eventually the church was unable to meet the heavy cost of maintenance and on Sunday 3 February 1980, after consultation with the Jesuits, Bishop Alexander announced that St. Mary-on-the-Quay was to close. One Bristol newspaper encapsulated the story with the headline: 'Famous church closed by rising repair bill'. For a year the fate of St. Mary's was in the balance, but determined fund-raising by many supporters and a grant from the Society of Jesus of £10,000 secured the church's continuance. In 1993 it celebrated its one hundred and fiftieth anniversary.

'St. Mary-on-the-Quay is central to the history of the Catholic Church in Bristol.' The words are those of Bishop Alexander. It is descended directly from the first post-Reformation Catholic missions established by the Jesuit Fathers in the eighteenth century and Bristol's early churches in St. James Back and Trenchard Street. Through family associations with its historic past, many people have an affection for St. Mary's and many who live outside the parish, indeed outside the city, choose to make it their regular place of worship. This continuity of support enables St. Mary's to perform its function as a Catholic church available to the workers and visitors, who throng the city centre. During the hours of daylight the church is never closed.

In the past it has been usual for teams of three priests to serve the parish, and on occasions there have been as many as five or six, though by 1996 the numbers had fallen to one. It seemed ironic, therefore, that on 7 July 1996 the Provincial of the Jesuits, Fr. James Crampsey, should announce at all Masses that owing to staffing difficulties the Society would be withdrawing from Bristol, and that by agreement with Bishop Alexander, the parish would be handed over to the administration of the Clifton diocese. On 19 September 1996 Fr. Claudio Rossi, the last Jesuit to serve as parish priest, handed over the church to the care of the Clifton diocese. So the Jesuit mission in Bristol came to an end.

In June 1999 a font, weighing two tonnes, designed in 1860 by G. E. Street (d. 1881), the architect responsible for the Law Courts in London and the nave of the restored Bristol Cathedral, was brought from its original place in St. George's, Brandon Hill, by agreement with the Anglican diocese of Bristol, and installed in the baptistery in the Sacred Heart chapel.

Kenneth Hankins

Convent of the Sisters of Mercy, Dighton Street

The Congregation of the Sisters of Mercy were founded in the early nineteenth century by Catherine McAuley of Dublin. The establishment of the convent in Bristol was due mainly to the Rev. Dr. Brindle and the Hon. Miss Crewe. Four ladies entered the novitiate at Bermondsey in 1843 for the Bristol foundation and on 20 February 1846 moved into a temporary home in Pritchard Street, St. Paul's. In their first week they were admitted to the Enclosure of the Visitation Convent at Westbury-on-Trym: a stable and a coach house were adapted for school purposes, and there the sisters opened the first free school for Catholic girls.

This soon became too small, and in September 1846 the sisters purchased Harwood House in Dighton Street at a cost of £3,000. Over a decade later they bought two adjoining houses which Bishop Clifford suggested might be used as an orphanage for girls. For many years the sisters taught in the poor schools of St. Mary-on-the-Quay and they also carried out other charitable work among the sick in the Infirmary and the Workhouse. On 19 June 1857 the foundation stone of the chapel was laid. The carved stone altar was given by Mrs. Maisland, a friend of the sisters, and the completed chapel was blessed on 10 December by Bishop Clifford. The chapel was open to the public, and even today, the outline of a cross can still be seen over the entrance. Attached to the convent was a higher grade school for girls, and towards the end of the nineteenth century a laundry was established which gave employment to a number of Catholics in the St. Mary mission.

In 1895 the sisters moved their orphanage to Brockley Hall (now Bradley Court Home), eight miles from Bristol. The property, with its extensive grounds and capacity to accommodate nearly one hundred children, had been placed at the disposal of the sisters by Mrs. Smyth Pigott.

In 1896 the Visitation nuns moved to Harrow-on-the-Hill, London, and the Sisters of Mercy bought the Westbury-on-Trym convent, which became their Mother House.

By 1909 their higher grade school had become an independent all-age school (St. Gabriel's), attended by many pupils from all areas of the city. The orphanage closed in 1950, and in 1951 they started a hostel for young women. The hostel, school and convent closed in 1967, when the Sisters of Mercy left Dighton Street after 121 years service in the parish of St. Mary-on-the-Quay.

Sister Cecilia

Bristol: St. Nicholas of Tolentino

By the 1840s there were some 4,000 Catholics in Bristol: perhaps one-third of all in the Western District. There were then only two churches to serve them, St. Joseph's chapel in Trenchard Street and St. Mary-on-the-Quay. Bishop Ullathorne, then the Vicar Apostolic, had plans for establishing a mission in each of the five districts into which he divided the city. For one of them he acquired, at the cost of £4,000, 'a very eligible site for a church (the future St. Nicholas of Tolentino) and a school'.

Ullathorne had previously arranged with the Prior of the Irish Augustinian community in Rome for three priests 'fully competent to take care of any mission' to come to Bristol. He now proposed that they should come to start this mission. He would let them have the site for £500 and would give them £250 towards the cost of building. In the spring of 1848 an Augustinian, Fr. Nicholas O'Donnell, arrived to start work. It was intended that a cottage and stable on the site should serve as a chapel until the church was built. These plans were aborted when the Augustinians withdrew six months later. However, Hendren, Ullathorne's successor as Vicar Apostolic, was able to borrow £1,600 and the nave of the present parish church was opened in 1850 – unobtrusively, in order, in the words of the

Bristol Times, 'not to give umbrage to the Protestants of this most bigoted city'.

Fr. O'Donnell left in 1852. He had found the income from a congregation consisting largely of the occupants of two workhouses inadequate even to service the debt of £2,000. By 1854 a parish school had been built for £450. The congregation now numbered about 1,000 but the income was still very small: £170 in the year 1856, while the school was running at a loss. Subsequently the church was enlarged, first by the addition of one aisle, then by a second aisle, the chancel and the Lady Altar. A presbytery was also built. Finally, free of debt, the church, with a new high altar, was consecrated in 1895. On the following day Cardinal Vaughan of Westminster gave the homily at Pontifical High Mass, as his uncle, the future Bishop Vaughan, had done at its opening in 1850.

In the early twentieth century a convent of the Sisters of Charity of St. Vincent de Paul was established in Stapleton Road and ministered to a parish which the continuing influx of population had made into a slum area. Between the wars many parishioners were moved in clearance schemes, but the problem remained. The extensive damage by bombing in the 1939–45 war stimulated a radical plan for redevelopment, with the eventual loss of St. Nicholas's parish hall, by then seriously dilapidated. With the help of the Van Neste fund a new hall was built on a site made available near the church.

The changes in government education policy made the old all-age school built in 1854 redundant. The seniors transferred to the first Catholic comprehensive school in Bristol, St. Thomas More, which was built on land acquired by Canon Joseph Dolan off Muller Road. The school opened in 1954 and its first headmaster was William Mitchell. The school cadet force built a wooden hut nearby for their meetings but when the cadet force was disbanded this was transformed into a Mass centre dedicated to **St. Maximilian Kolbe**, who had been canonised that year (1982). There had been provision for a new church on the site but the expected development of the area had not occurred so a church was not needed. Mass which had been celebrated in the school hall since the opening now transferred to this Mass centre which continues to be served from St. Nicholas. A new primary school was opened in 1971 and the old school buildings, now called St. Nicholas House provide accommodation for the Diocesan Finance Offices.

In 1982 Canon Jeremiah O'Brien took on the responsibility of Chaplain at Horfield Prison which had previously been carried out by the Franciscan Friars of St. Bonaventure, Bishopston. When the diocesan priests took over the parish after the friars' withdrawal in 1981 it was no longer possible for them to carry on this task.

In 1993 a Rosary Garden was opened on a former waste area near the school. It had been developed under the direction of Canon O'Brien to commemorate the devoted service of three former teachers, Patricia Shore, William Underwood and John Bryan. Fifteen plaques are installed there, each representing a mystery of the Rosary. They were made by the Design Centre at Kilkenny.

In 1988 the former parish social club was converted into the Dunstan Centre, the diocesan Religious Education Centre, which provides accommodation for meetings of various groups, and runs a variety of academic, catechetical, training and in-service courses.

J.A.H.

Bristol: Holy Cross, Bedminster

When William of Wyrcester made his journey from Tintern Abbey to Bristol in the fifteenth century, he mentioned the shrine of 'the Hospital of the Brightbow at Bedminster'. This famous shrine, dedicated to St. Katherine of Alexandria, stood at the junction of the present Lombard Street and East Street. The last vestiges of the shrine were demolished in 1887 when a site was cleared to make way for the offices of the Imperial Tobacco Company.

By then a new Catholic church had appeared in Bedminster, a short distance from the site of St. Katherine. Since 1845 Fr. Prendergast and Fr. Cullinan had said Mass on Sundays at a house in Somerset Square, Redcliffe, for the few local Catholics. The congregation increased so rapidly that in 1850 Fr. Cullinan rented a house at 11 Redcliffe Parade West, and adapted two rooms on the first floor as a chapel where up to eighty Catholics met to hear Mass on Sunday mornings. Jeremiah Maher and his two daughters, Agnes and Jane, formed the nucleus of the choir. The first Holy Cross School was opened in the large conservatory in the garden, where Jane Maher taught her thirty pupils.

By 1854 Fr. Vaughan (later Bishop of Plymouth), who had succeeded Fr. Cullinan, bought a site for a new Catholic church and schoolroom a short distance away, at the junction of Regent Road and East Street. The new building cost £518. Part of this building, designed by the Catholic architect Charles Hansom, is still in use as the Bedminster Library. Until 1863 the *Catholic Directory* refers to the church as 'the Bedminster mission'

Bristol: Bedminster,
former Holy Cross
Church, Victoria Street,
exterior (in use until
1914)

but after that date refers to 'Holy Cross, Bedminster'. By 1870 it was clear
that neither the church nor the school was large enough. Bishop Clifford
asked Charles Hansom to look for a suitable site for a new Catholic church
nearer the centre of the city. The architect suggested a site on the new
Victoria Street, and it was here that the new Holy Cross school and a
temporary church were built and opened in 1874. The site was very
cramped and there was no room for a presbytery. Priests from the Pro-
Cathedral and the Catholic Reformatory at Arno's Court served the mission. It was not until 1885 that Mgr. Edgar English was appointed parish
priest and rented a house in nearby Clarence Road. Canon David O'Brien

was parish priest from 1890–1895 and lived first in Angers Road, Totterdown and later at York Road.

The passing of the 1902 Education Act and the abolition of the School Boards gave great advantage to the voluntary schools, teachers' salaries, capitation grants, and cleaning, lighting and heating costs now becoming the responsibility of the Local Education Authority. But these authorities were empowered to refuse to accept any school which did not conform to its required standards. Holy Cross School failed to reach such standards because of the lack of playing space. However, the grant was paid to the school on condition that it transferred to a site with adequate playing space.

The site chosen was in Dean Lane, on wasteland adjacent to St. Paul's Church of England School, and close to the disused Dean Lane coal mine. A presbytery and a 'school chapel', consisting of a building on two floors with four classrooms on each floor, was constructed on the site. Folding partitions made it possible for the rooms on the ground floor to be used as a chapel at weekends, although daily Mass was celebrated in one room on weekdays before school hours. The parish priest was Canon (later Mgr. Provost) Charles Davey, a Bristolian who had formerly been an Anglican priest. Bishop Burton opened the new school on 4 July 1912. For the convenience of some parishioners, Mass was said at the 'old Holy Cross' in Victoria Street every Sunday until the outbreak of war in 1914.

During the war years sufficient money was raised to start building the present Holy Cross church as soon as the building restrictions were eased.

Bristol: former Holy Cross (interior)

Bristol: Bedminster; Holy Cross, school chapel, Dean Lane, destroyed in air-raid, 1941

The first part of the building was completed and additional work was done in 1926–27, but the planned tower which the architect had proposed for the southwest corner of the building was never built. The final stages of the building were not completed until 1968.

The school chapel was destroyed in an air raid on the night of 3 January 1941, but the school was given the use of some spare classrooms in the adjacent St. Paul's School. In 1946 part of the former Windmill Hill Council School was refurbished for the use of Holy Cross, now reorganised as a Primary school. The school was rebuilt in Dean Lane and reopened in 1966. The complex of Holy Cross church school, presbytery and parish centre is close to the end of Catherine Mead Street, which leads down to the site of the original St. Katherine and serves as a reminder of the origins of the church in this ancient parish.

Sisters of St. Joseph of Annecy

Captain Dewell, a convert serving in the British army in India, had been much impressed by the work of the Catholic missionaries working there. On his return to his home town of Malmesbury he planned to open a convent, but when the Sisters of St. Joseph, whom he had invited, arrived, the house was not ready. Bishop Clifford stepped in and arranged for them to stay with the

Sisters of the Visitation (an enclosed convent) at Westbury-on-Trym, Bristol. They arrived in 1864, but their stay was brief, although they did return to teach at St. Joseph's School, Westbury from 1865 to 1868 and again from 1880 to 1895. In the next few years the sisters were invited to work not only in Holy Cross but also in the area served by the Pro-Cathedral. In 1898 Sister Alphonse was appointed head teacher in Holy Cross and the sisters continued to teach in the school until 1997. The first convent was in Somerset Square near Holy Cross church in Victoria Street. In 1922 the sisters moved to Bermuda Lodge, 68 Coronation Street near the present church. Some sisters taught for a while in the Pro-Cathedral primary school.

J.C.

Bristol: St. Bonaventure, Bishopston

In 1889 Bishop Clifford invited the Franciscans to come to the Clifton diocese to establish a foundation of Friars Minor, Fr. Thaddeus Hermans O.F.M. came from Forest Gate, London in November 1889 and in December of that year purchased, on behalf of the Order, the land which now includes the church, presbytery, club, school and playing fields. During the early months of 1890 a small community of two priests and a lay

St. Bonaventure's Sanctuary, *c.* 1910

brother took up residence at 120 Egerton Road and Mass was celebrated there for the first time on 19 March. The first building to be erected was the old school: work commenced in January 1890 and the first Mass was celebrated by Bishop Clifford on Passion Sunday, 23 March, in the chapel which was included as part of the school. William Slim (later to become commander of the legendary XIV Army in Burma and Governor General of Australia) was baptised here in September 1893. The Friary, now the presbytery, was started in 1891 when Bishop Clifford laid the foundation stone on 12 September of that year.

In 1900 work was started on the new church which was opened by Bishop Brownlow on 14 March 1901. A further extension was added in 1907 and two years later, a baptistery, another bay to the nave and aisles and a porch with an organ loft was ready for opening. In 1923 a *Pietà* was installed and blessed as a memorial to those parishioners who had died in the First World War. The parish hall was erected and opened by Bishop Lee in 1932 and he returned on 13 June 1936 to consecrate the completed church.

During the Second World War the Friary became an ARP Warden's post and the cellars were used as an air raid shelter, but the building only received one direct hit with an incendiary bomb in 1941, and this was soon dealt with. The school, however, evacuated to Glastonbury from 1941–1945. In 1963 a new club, 'Greyfriars' was built to replace the original. 1972 saw the arrival of the Sisters of Mercy who opened a convent in Kings Drive and served the parish until their departure in 1994. The new school which had been planned since the 1950s was opened in 1973 and the next year the stone High Altar, built during the 1930s, was replaced by the present altar which was designed to meet the changes in the liturgy brought about by the Second Vatican Council.

Possibly the most significant change in the history of the parish occurred in 1980 with the departure of the Franciscans and their replacement by secular clergy appointed by Bishop Alexander. The first diocesan parish priest was Fr. (now Canon) Martin Fitzpatrick assisted by Fr. Alan Finley, who later became an Army chaplain in the Gulf War. Fr. Michael McAndrew succeeded them.

In 1982 the chaplaincy at Horfield Prison, which had previously been carried out by the Franciscan Friars, was transferred to St. Nicholas of Tolentino parish.

In 1997 an ambitious redecorating and re-lighting project was carried out at a cost of £45,000, and a crypt chapel for silent prayer, dedicated to St. Thérèse of Lisieux, was opened. Parish returns at this time show an estimated congregation on Sundays of 1100.

V.A.

Bristol: St. Bernard, Shirehampton

A Mass centre was established at Shirehampton in 1901 with Fr. (later Bishop) William Lee celebrating the first Mass. Prior to that Catholics living in the Shirehampton and Avonmouth areas were obliged to walk to the chapel of St. Ursula's Convent, Westbury-on-Trym to hear Sunday Mass.

The opening of Avonmouth Old Dock in 1887 gradually led to an increase in the number of Irish and other Catholic seamen in the area and in the same year as the opening of the Mass centre (1901) a plot of land was purchased as a site for a church at the corner of Pembroke Avenue and Station Road, Shirehampton. Bishop Burton laid the foundation stone of the church in September 1902 and it was completed a year later with seating for sixty-five people. The church was intended as a memorial to the late Bishop Brownlow who had won a special place with the public due to his work for the National Society for the Protection of Cruelty to Children. The Carmelites served the church until 1909, and the Franciscans until 1928, when the parish was taken over by diocesan clergy.

In 1913 it was estimated that there were 112 Catholics in the parish. With the opening of the National Smelting Corporation at Avonmouth in 1924 the numbers increased to the extent that a hut at the plant was used as a Mass centre for the overflow. In 1925 the present presbytery was purchased and the priest moved from his former residence in Springfield Avenue. By the late 1920s the building of a substantial number of new homes in the Shirehampton area led to yet another increase in parish numbers and to priority being given for an extension of St. Bernard and the completion of the nave. The building work started in 1928 and was finished in 1929 when the High Altar was consecrated. A small wooden porch was added to the nave as a temporary measure but it was 1973 before sufficient funds were available for the present porch to be built.

The parish was partly responsible for raising the necessary funds to build two further churches, St. Brendan, Avonmouth and Our Lady of the Rosary, Lawrence Weston, in the 1950s. It was not until 1982 that the parish had cleared all its debts to enable Bishop Alexander to consecrate the church.

St. Bernard's School opened in 1935 with 100 pupils, and numbers continued to increase throughout the years until in 1950 it reached 250. Penlea House in the High Street was purchased to accommodate 100 infants and in 1951 the forty boys from Nazareth House who had been attending St. Bernard's were transferred to St. Mary-on-the-Quay. In September 1955 the opening of the new school of Our Lady of the Rosary at

Lawrence Weston caused a drop in numbers. In 1996 the Local Education Authority attempted to merge St. Bernard with Our Lady of the Rosary but this action was successfully resisted and numbers are now rising again.

V.A.

Nazareth House, Stoke Bishop

In 1920 the Poor Sisters of Nazareth bought a house called Cote Bank plus twenty-seven acres of land at Westbury-on-Trym from the Misses Pease, and in the following year the first Nazareth House opened when Mother Scholastica, eight sisters and fifty-four boys arrived from Cheltenham. On 29 September 1921 Bishop Burton said the first Mass in the new chapel. In 1925 they were joined by seventeen babies and three more sisters but soon Bristol City Corporation produced plans to build a road through the grounds and new premises were needed.

In 1929 Sneyd Park House in Stoke Bishop and twelve acres of land and the adjoining property of Little Sneyd House with a further nine acres were purchased. On 4 August 1929 the second Nazareth House was opened and Cote Bank was sold the following year.

By 1943 numbers had increased and one hundred and forty-six boys, five girls and forty babies were being cared for by twenty sisters. Some boys attended St. Bernard's school in Shirehampton and others the Pro-Cathedral School. Nazareth House continued for almost another thirty years, but numbers steadily declined in the late 1960s and in 1970 the property, now comprising further buildings and thirty-two acres, was sold to Southmead Development Company and the remaining nuns returned to Cheltenham where they now care for the elderly.

V.A.

Bristol: St. Gerard Majella, Knowle

In 1908 Bishop Burton invited the Redemptorists, who were then in charge of the parish in Kingswood, to develop a new parish in Knowle. For a brief period they agreed, and dedicated the mission to St. Gerard Majella (1726–1755), a Redemptorist lay brother who had been canonised only four years before. Eventually they found that they were unable to continue this responsibility, so the Bishop then asked the Benedictines of Douai, who were in charge of the parish at Chipping Sodbury, and they agreed. St. Gerard started in a shop, Tozers Dairy at 17 Jubilee Road, a stone's throw from the site of the new church, and this was also the residence of the first parish priest, Dom Joseph Horrigan. An altar was set up in the shop and the congregation frequently overflowed into the passage. The Benedictines bought the site for the new church in 1908 for the sum of £575, and appointed the architects Pugin and Pugin and the local building firm of Stephens, Bastow and Company. The church was erected in ten months in 1909, and Fr. Horrigan moved to what was then 2 Jubilee Road. This property remained the priests' house until the building of the present presbytery in the early 1950s. Fr. Horrigan maintained the Benedictine presence in Chipping Sodbury, travelling there each Sunday by train. The early headed notepaper of the parish referred to St. Gerard, Knowle and St. Lawrence, Chipping Sodbury.

At this time St. Gerard was on the edge of the built-up area of Bristol, and open fields separated it from Brislington village. Finances were a major concern in the early years, as the cost of building had incurred a huge debt, and offertory collections were small. Fr. Horrigan spent much time writing appeals for help. By 1912 the east window, the Stations of the Cross, the baptismal font and the shrine of St. Gerard had all been donated. In that year Fr. Horrigan started the tradition of the parish bazaar: the first lasted four days and took place in the Colston Hall. When he died in 1922 his successor, Fr. Murty, organised a memorial fund, which resulted in the present High Altar being installed in his memory in 1925. Fr. Murty also became a well-known figure as he walked round the parish with his huge shaggy dog. He made several improvements to the church, but his greatest contribution was the purchase of 'The Paddock', formerly part of the old Knowle racecourse, which is now the Broadwalk Shopping Centre. This was to be the site of the parish school, but in the meantime a fun fair and summer carnival became a feature of the life of South Bristol and brought in much needed funds. In 1935 the parish was handed over to the diocese.

The first parish priest, Fr. (later Canon) Patrick Barry presided over many major changes including the formation of the new parish of St. Dunstan, Keynsham, the building of the convent and school at Knowle West, and the building of the present church hall. Fr. (later Mgr. Canon) Joseph Sutton became parish priest in 1951, and during his tenure two more parishes were born: Christ the King, Knowle West in 1952 and St. Bernadette, Whitchurch in 1968. The consecration of the church finally took place on 29 April 1959 as part of the Golden Jubilee celebrations. Fr. Thomas Keane took over the parish in 1979 and served till his retirement and death in 1989, when Fr. Joseph Bredin, who had served in Brazil for many years, succeeded him.

V.A.

Arnos Court: Good Shepherd Convent 1851–1948

This convent was founded in July 1851 and only two months later received a visit from Cardinal Wiseman. The Good Shepherd Sisters had arrived in England from their Mother Homes in Angers, France in May 1841 and opened a convent and Home for Women in Hammersmith, London. The Bristol property at Arnos Court was purchased for the sisters by William Austin Gillow who, having visited the Hammersmith convent and seen the good work done for women who had been brought from a life on the streets, 'desired earnestly that a similar house be set up in Bristol for the same purpose'. Gillow was a member of an old Lancashire Catholic family who married Miss Agnes Markland of Pemberton Villa, Clifton Park, in 1851. Included in the gift was the land which is now the Cemetery of the Holy Souls.

At first a room in the house was used as a chapel, but in May 1858 the foundation of the present building was laid, and the completed building was dedicated by Bishop Clifford in March 1859. By that time the sisters had spent large sums in the erection of buildings, including a laundry. Bishop Clifford took a great interest in the chapel, to which he was a generous benefactor, his gifts including a chalice given to him by Pope Pius IX, and the four marble pillars, still to be seen in the present day restaurant, which divided the sanctuary from the sisters' choir. The first apostolic work established in Arnos Court was the traditional one of the sisters, a Voluntary Home for older teenagers and women who had personal and social problems. Their ages could range from seventeen to forty.

Later, in 1856, another apostolate was started. In view of the great need in England for a home for Catholic girl ex-prisoners, the ecclesiastical authorities asked the Provincial Superior of the Good Shepherd Sisters to consider undertaking the direction of a Reformatory School instead of the Voluntary Home in Bristol. At this time child offenders as young as nine years of age were being sent to prison to serve time in hard labour followed by a specified time in Reformatory Schools. Since there was no such provision for Catholic girls they were being sent to non-Catholic establishments.

After due consideration, and because the number of women seeking places in the Voluntary Home had decreased, it was agreed that this new apostolic work for girls be undertaken. The Certificate of Registration for Arnos Court as a Reformatory School for Catholic girls up to the age of sixteen was accorded by the Home Office on 22 April 1856. Thus was Arnos Court Reformatory School, known as St. Joseph's School, established and it was to continue uninterrupted under the direction of the Good Shepherd Sisters through the statutory changes of name, and changes of location (Eagle House, Bathford, and Ashwicke Hall, near Chippenham) from that day until November 1986.

The two separately run apostolates flourished for many years. During the wartime blitzes on Bristol in 1940 and 1941 the property suffered so severely that it was estimated that more than two-thirds had been destroyed. The Home Office insisted that the school be evacuated to a safer area. After much search Eagle House, Bathford was found and accepted by the Home Office as being suitable. On 3 March 1941 two sisters left Arnos Court with twenty of the girls for their new temporary home. Three days later they were joined by four more sisters, seven auxiliaries and the remaining sixty girls. By this time the name Reformatory School had given way to that of Approved School.

Eagle House is a lovely Georgian residence suitable for a family of eight or ten to live in some style. Now it was being called upon to accommodate six sisters, seven auxiliaries and eighty girls. However, it was seen as welcome after months of living and sleeping in underground shelters. Bishop Lee offered the first Mass there on 7 March and then consecrated the house to the Sacred Heart. There followed a very difficult period of adjustment during which a Home Office Inspector allowed the registered number, as a concession to the cramped accommodation, to be reduced from eighty to seventy-two.

After a very severe bombardment on the night of 10 September 1943 the sisters decided to sell Arnos Court and look for another property. It was a sad decision as the house had been established in the lifetime of the Foundress, St. Mary Euphrasia Pelletier. (see Batheaston).

Hill End House: Henbury 1948–1976

This property on the outskirts of Bristol received three sisters and a few girls in September 1946. When the necessary alterations had been completed the rest of the community and girls joined them on 28 October 1948. This date also marked the closure, after ninety-seven years, of the original Bristol foundation at Arnos Court. Later a second apostolate, for unmarried mothers was initiated in Henbury in the newly acquired Severn House. It became known as St. Raphael's Mother and Baby Home. This work continued until November 1976 when it was closed and the sisters withdrew.

Ashwicke Hall: Chippenham 1947–1982

At the end of the Second World War the Home Office, with plans for new child care legislation, decided that an entirely new location be found for

St. Joseph's Approved School. Ashwicke Hall had been occupied for some time by the Royal Air Force, who eventually moved out on 25 March 1946. Major alterations were carried out and the sisters and girls moved back in from Eagle House, Bathford on 10 December 1947. They were to remain for thirty-four years.

By the late 1970s the geographical isolation of Ashwicke Hall was proving to be a disadvantage in the changing approach to the rehabilitation of the girls, and an alternative was considered. This was the acceptance, for five years, of a formal invitation from Barnardo's to enter into a partnership with them in the re-establishment of their service to trouble teenagers at Duncroft School, Moor Lane, Staines, Middlesex. Barnardo's announced 'the move will witness the coming together of two Christian inspired organisations, each of which has been committed to the caring of troubled teenagers for over a century'.

So it was that on 3 January 1982 four sisters, a small number of lay staff, and twenty girls left Ashwicke Hall for good, drawing to a close 131 years of residence and service to the diocese of Clifton.

Sr. Rosaria Kenny

Bristol: St Patrick, Redfield

The Irish who poured into Bristol as a result of the potato famine wanted the church founded to accommodate them to be called after St. Patrick. In the event it was dedicated to St. Nicholas of Tolentino, the name in religion of their priest, but the bishop of the day promised that if ever a new parish were created from St. Nicholas then it would be given the name of St. Patrick.

Some seventy years later this pledge was honoured. In 1920 a shop, bakehouse and adjoining cottage were purchased in Redfield for £700. The shop and bakehouse were altered to serve as a chapel-of-ease to be known as St. Patrick's. In May 1921 this was sold and a new site purchased at Pile Marsh. The foundation stone of the new church was laid by Bishop Burton on 2 September 1922 and formally opened on St. Patrick's Day 1923. The architect was Sir Frank Wills and the builders Messrs. Sims and Son. Both had just completed work on what is now the nave of St. George, Warminster. The two buildings display strong similarities of style, particularly in the design of the roof supports. It was built at a cost of £3,783, and Fr. William Dillon was appointed parish priest. Three houses adjoining the church were purchased; one of which was to serve as a presbytery. By 1926 the parish was out of debt and in 1929 a field adjoining the church was acquired. On 9 July 1932 the foundation stone of a school was laid, and the building blessed by the bishop on the morning of 20 July 1933. The Lord Mayor of Bristol formally opened the school that evening. During his time at St. Patrick's Fr. (later Mgr. Canon) Dillon became a well-known figure, both locally and in the civic life of Bristol where, for many years, he served on the Education Committee. He died in 1955. In 1973, under Canon Owen Devaney, the church was consecrated and subsequently a new section was added to the building.

With the arrival in 1988 of Fr. Gregory Grant an ambitious re-development plan began. The £2 million project included: – a new church seating 350 parishioners, twenty-two retirement flats, a new convent, a new presbytery and the conversion of the old church into a parish centre. The principal features of the new church are, first, six wall paintings by Ramon Gaston depicting the life of the Blessed Virgin from the scriptures and Catholic tradition; second the sanctuary furniture: altar, lectern, two candelabra, crucifix and baptismal font. These are all by Arthur Fleishmann (1896–1990) an Hungarian who has pioneered Perspex as a sculpture medium. Eight stained glass windows relocated from the disused Pro-Cathedral, Clifton, complete the interior decoration of the church. Three of these windows had been inserted in 1903 to commemorate various bishops of the diocese, St. Hugh of Lincoln (Clifford), St. William of York (Brownlow) and St. Ambrose (Burton). Two more were added in 1912 in the presence of Cardinal Bourne, i.e. St. Patrick and St. George. Another three, all depicting saints associated with the diocese, were pierced in 1924 as a war memorial to those who perished in the Great War. St. Wulstan (who fought against the slave trade in Bristol), Blessed Richard Whiting (the last Abbot of Glastonbury) and St. Edith of Wilton. The final stage of the re-development is 'Riverside', a sixty-four bed purpose built Catholic nursing home in Crews Hole Road. It opened in May 1997 and was blessed by Bishop Alexander on 9 September.

J.A.H.

Bristol: St. Joseph, Fishponds

In 1907 the Redemptorist Fathers, established in the mission at Park Lane, Kingswood, founded a Mass centre in Fishponds for the local Catholics. A small chapel, 'St Philip's Oratory', was built in the garden of a house in North Devon Road, owned by Mrs. Heple. The rear entrance to the house via Guinea Lane provided the entrance to the chapel. Hence there was some confusion as to whether the chapel was in North Devon Road or

Guinea Lane. The Redemptorists served this little chapel until the Park Lane mission closed in 1911. They gave the bishop £960 towards the founding of a mission near St. Philip's Oratory in Fishponds. £600 of this was used to purchase a plot of land at the junction of Lodge Causeway and Forest Road as a site for the future mission. The corrugated iron building, which had been used in Park Lane as a temporary chapel, was dismantled and re-erected at Forest Road. There was no presbytery, so the parish priest, Fr. (later Archbishop) Michael McGrath, rented 'Myrtle Lodge', a house in Lodge Causeway. A presbytery was built but the 1914–1918 war prevented the building of a permanent church.

Bishop Burton laid the foundation stone of the present church on 18 November 1923. The architect was Sir Frank Wills and the builder the local firm of Clark. The cost of the building was nearly £10,000, no mean sum in the depression of the 1920s. On 18 March 1925 St. Joseph's church was opened and dedicated by Bishop Burton. Fr. Vassall-Phillips CSSR, who had earlier served at the mission in Park Lane, preached the sermon. To help the parish cope with the large debt, the Bishop allocated £2,300 of the money recently received from the sale of Prior Park; the parishioners and their priest, Fr. (later Canon) Timothy O'Riordan, had collected over £2,080; and Fr. Vassall-Phillips made a donation of £270. The outstanding debt of some £5,000 called for many years of fund-raising on the part of the parish, chiefly by the door-to-door weekly collection, and the annual carnivals held for many years in the Straits Field.

In 1923 the corrugated iron building was again dismantled and given to the newly founded mission at Chard in Somerset. In 1926 a group of the Sisters of St. John of God came from Wexford to found a convent in a house in Lodge Causeway. They also established an Independent Primary School in the parish hall with students paying one shilling a week. The convent was later moved to a house in Chester Park Road and closed in 1994. In 1929, when the convent of the Sisters of Perpetual Adoration at Taunton closed, the high altar from the convent chapel was presented to St. Joseph. The altar by John Bentley, who later designed Westminster Cathedral had been consecrated by Bishop Clifford on 13 November 1872 and at the time *The Tablet* described it as being 'principally of alabaster, relieved by various marbles, mosaics, gildings and paintings' (23 November 1872).

The primary school was absorbed into the state system in 1951, with some opposition from nearby parishes who feared losing some of the pupils from their school. The present building in Chatsworth Road was opened in 1991.

The parish is unique in that two of its former parish priests later

Bristol: Filton, former church of St. Teresa

became Archbishops: Michael McGrath (Cardiff 1940–1961) and Francis Grimshaw (Birmingham 1954–1965).

J.C. and J.A.H.

Bristol: St. Teresa of the Child Jesus, Filton

In 1926 a site for a new Catholic church in Gloucester Road North, outside the city boundary of Bristol, was purchased for £600. At that time all the area to the north of Bristol was in the pastoral care of the Friars Minor of St. Bonaventure, Bishopston. A presbytery and a temporary church were built in 1927 and the 'Little Flower', St. Teresa of Lisieux, who was canonised in 1925, was chosen as patron, so the new church was among the first who have claimed her name. The first parish priest was Fr. (later Canon) John Hayes, who when he was transferred to St. Nicholas, Lawford's Gate in 1925 was succeeded by Fr. (later Canon) Joseph Renehan until 1941 and then by Fr. (later Canon) James Rea until 1945. Canon Denis Lucey then served the parish until his death in 1971 and he was succeeded by a former curate, Fr. Timothy Barry.

In December 1940 the presbytery and church were twice heavily damaged by enemy action, and on the day following the second air raid a wedding was solemnised in the little church porch amid the debris. Services somehow managed to continue uninterrupted. After the war, although a bigger church was a pressing need, priority had to be given to the Southmead district. In

1955 it was expected that the opening of a new church would relieve the mother church, but after a few weeks the crowding at St. Teresa was as acute as before. The space left beside the presbytery for a permanent church was now far too small. Two expensive properties beside it had to be bought and cleared making the site just double the size with only adequate room for the development. The Roman basilica style was adopted, and the new church, designed by O'Brien, Morris and McCullough, was built by Henry Willcock and Company. The entrance is through an open colonnade which recalls the square forecourt of an ancient basilica, while inside one can set at a glance the rectangular shape divided into nave and aisles by ranges of columns. The effect is impressive. The sanctuary is well elevated and terminated by a great arch and apse within which the high altar stands.

Since it was opened in 1960 there have been many embellishments to the church including the addition of about eleven stained glass windows and the placing of a statue of the Risen Christ, made of plaster by two parishioners, behind the high altar. The statue is flanked by two other stained glass (cabinet) windows by Harry Clark, depicting Christ the King and Mary the Queen. The bell tower is now illuminated.

Other major developments in the life of the parish have been the opening of a primary school in 1963 and of a parish centre in 1975.

Based on an article by Canon Denis Lucey

Bristol: Our Lady of Lourdes and St. Bernadette, Kingswood

Catholicism came to Kingswood when a small community of priests of the Redemptorist Order established a temporary church in Park Lane, Kingswood to serve the Catholics in the area. From the outset the mission was beset by difficulties, with much hostility being shown to the priests by the local non-Catholics. The mission closed in 1901 and the Fishponds parish, which the Redemptorists had helped to establish with funds from the original Kingswood mission, served the area.

In 1935 a chance meeting, on the Irish ferry, between Bishop Lee and a member of the Oblates of Mary Immaculate, gave the Bishop an opportunity of explaining some of the difficulties which his diocese faced in providing Catholics living on the outskirts of a large city with the opportunity to practise their religion. Early in 1937, a small community of Oblates came to Kingswood and purchased a house in Hanham Road as a Mass centre. Later in that same year, a large house, Woodlands, the home of the Douglas family, manufacturers of the Douglas motorbike, was purchased by the Oblates as a more suitable site for the Mass centre, and it would also serve as a presbytery. On 28 November 1937 Mass was celebrated for the first time at Woodlands.

Bristol: Kingswood, former Church of Our Lady of Lourdes

In the following year a site for a church was purchased and building began. On 1 October 1938 Bishop Lee blessed and dedicated the new church. In 1939 a parish hall was built, but the outbreak of war stopped any further building. In the air raids of 1940–1941 the church buildings were damaged, but Mass was celebrated in the parish throughout the war years. The housing programme in the area in the post-war years increased the size of the congregation, and the parish primary school was opened in 1973. The Mass centre at Downside House, Winterbourne later became the responsibility of the parish. In 1989 the Oblates passed the parish over to the diocese.

Mass was also celebrated at Warmley, first of all in a public house, and later, as a result of a sharing agreement with the Methodists, in the Wesleyan Chapel which had been built in 1834. In 1980 the parish purchased the chapel but due to its age and structural deterioration the last Mass was celebrated in Warmley in August 1998. Some of the fittings, including the Stations of the Cross, have been donated to the new school chapel at Bradley Stoke to be opened in September 1999.

V.A.

Bristol: Sacred Heart, Westbury-on-Trym

The origins of Sacred Heart parish can be traced through a community of French nuns. The Visitation Order was founded at Annecy, in Savoy, in

Bristol: Westbury-on-Trym convent, pre-1939

1610, by St. Francis de Sales and St. Jane Frances de Chantal. It is enclosed
and contemplative. The order was introduced to England in 1804, by Mrs.
Tunstall, widow of Cuthbert Tunstall, of Wycliff Hall, Yorkshire, who
obtained for the English foundation three sisters expelled from their monastery at Rouen during the Revolution. They were hospitably received by
the Augustinian nuns at Spetisbury (later Newton Abbot) and they also
stayed for a short while at Wardour Castle, home of Lord and Lady Arundell, the latter being a relation of Mrs. Tunstall's. Finally they came to
Acton, near London, in 1804, and began to receive English postulants,
among whom was Mary Weld, daughter of Thomas Weld of Lulworth
Castle and sister of Cardinal Weld. She became the first English Superior.
In 1810 they moved to Shepton Mallet and then in 1831 purchased the
mansion of Westmead in Westbury from Mr. Irving, a Methodist minister.
The community decided to built a convent on the site with accommodation
for local Catholics to attend Mass. The choir, chapel and cloisters were
completed first, and the main buildings, commenced in 1859 were finished
by 1862. In 1868 the sisters opened a school in a converted stable and
coach house, the teachers being provided by the Sisters of St. Joseph of
Annecy. In 1896, when the Visitation nuns moved to Harrow-on-the-Hill,
London at the invitation of Cardinal Vaughan, the Sisters of Mercy took
over the convent and the school which became St. Ursula's. The boarding
school was closed in 1924 and the number of day girls increased. These
school buildings were largely destroyed during the war and rebuilt in
1948.

By the 1930s a new church was needed to relieve the overcrowding of the convent chapel so the Reverend Mother at the time gave the diocese a plot of land for a church and presbytery. The building was completed in 1939 and blessed by Bishop Lee on 13 September. The first parish priest, Fr. (later Mgr.) Cyril Hookway, introduced several fund raising schemes to clear the debt of £7,000.

The Holy Year of 1950 saw the consecration of the church on 20 June with three bishops and over fifty clergy attending. The ceremony had been preceded by a series of sermons given by eminent speakers including Mgr. Ronald Knox, the Abbot of Downside and Fr. Edwin Essex O.P. who had given the first mission in 1944.

By 1962 parish finances enabled the construction of a new hall. The architect was a parishioner, Gerard O'Brien of Ivor Day and O'Brien. The builders were Stansell and Co. Ltd of Taunton who had also built the church. The Newman Hall, as it was named, cost £28,000 and included a large mural of characters from Gilbert and Sullivan operas, painted by a famous local artist, Frank Shipsides. The mural was unveiled by Donald Adams of the D'Oyly Carte Opera Company. The hall later became the home of the Bristol Catholic Players, who continue their annual productions of Gilbert and Sullivan here. Dr. (now Mgr. Canon) Joseph Buckley, their founder, had become parish priest in 1957.

During the late 1960s the parish became the first in the country to have an elected parish council complete with Constitution. Two priests were ordained in the church: Fr. Michael Healy in 1971 and Fr. Richard Northey in 1974.

In 1985 considerable re-ordering and redecoration took place and new lighting and sound systems were installed. The Golden Jubilee celebrations included a parish pilgrimage to the Shrine of the Sacred Heart in Paray-le-Monial, the original home of the Visitation nuns which gave rise to the dedication of the church.

St. Ursula's school embarked on an extensive modernisation programme in 1972 when the convent was converted into additional classrooms. A window depicting the Visitation had earlier been moved first to the Lady Chapel in the Pro-Cathedral and then to the newly-built primary school of SS. Peter and Paul, Aberdeen Road, Cotham. In 1989 the Order of Mercy took the decision to withdraw from teaching to concentrate on social work. A trust was formed and bought the school to run it as an independent Catholic school from January 1991 when the remaining sisters moved to a smaller house in the parish to continue their pastoral work.

V.A.

Bristol: St. John Fisher, Frenchay

Until 1940 Catholics living in the Frenchay–Winterbourne area were part
of the parish of St. Joseph, Fishponds. In 1940, the parish priest at St.
Joseph, Dr. (later Archbishop) Grimshaw established a Mass centre at
Frenchay for the greater convenience of local Catholics. This was in a large
room above the riding stables near the village. In spite of the unsuitable
nature of the premises, reached by a steep staircase from the ground floor,
some fifty to sixty persons attended Mass each Sunday. The Mass centre
was still in use in 1949 when the then parish priest at St. Joseph, Fr. Donal
O'Connell, wrote to the bishop expressing his anxiety about the number of
Catholics who lived in the area and who found it difficult to attend Mass
because of the shortage of room. Although a plot of ground to build a
church was purchased in 1950 for £500, lack of funds prevented a start
being made on the building. However, the situation was less serious after
the hospital authorities gave permission for Mass to be said there each
Sunday. By 1957 200 Catholics were attending Mass at the hospital, many
of them members of staff. In 1957 a presbytery was built at 56 Begbrook
Park at a cost of £4,800, and, the following year, on land provided on
generous terms by the Burden Neurological Institute at Frenchay, a church
and hall were erected. In 1964 a Mass centre was established at Downside
House, Winterbourne. This was first served by Frenchay but later responsibility passed to the parish at Kingswood.

J.C.

Bristol: Christ the King, Filwood Park

When the new council house estate at Knowle West was being built in the
1930s most Catholics living there would attend Mass at St. Gerard Majella,
Knowle, some two or three miles away. In 1938 a Catholic primary school
was built in Hartcliffe Road and Mass was celebrated in the school hall by
one of the priests from St. Gerard. The first headmaster, Mr. Jack Anglin,
held the post until 1965. The school was originally called St. Gerard after
the mother church, because a site had been purchased and the money
raised for a school to be built in Broad Walk, Knowle. However it was
decided that the need was greater in Knowle West, much to the dismay of
the St. Gerard's parishioners.

A convent for the Irish Sisters of Charity, invited by Bishop Lee, was
also built nearby in Filwood Broadway, and the sisters taught in the school
and carried out welfare work in the area. In 1952 a new church was built
next to the school. Dedicated to Christ the King, it was blessed by Bishop

Rudderham in April and marked the establishment of the new parish. The name of the school was also changed at this time. A presbytery was built alongside the church. The first parish priest was Fr. (now Mgr. Canon) Joseph Buckley (1950–1957) whose interests in music and drama led to the founding in 1952 of the Filwood Catholic Players, later to become the Bristol Catholic Players, still renowned for their annual production of Gilbert and Sullivan Operas.

September 1953 saw the opening of the Men's Club, in its purpose-built premises, at a total cost of £5,600. By 1958 it was apparent that the church could not accommodate the increase in the number of parishioners, so it was enlarged at a cost of £39,000 by moving the side walls. In the early 1970s the parish passed briefly into the care of Vincentian Fathers James Rooney and Edward McGlinchy, who served the period between Canon Francis Rynn (1958–1960) and Fr. (now Mgr. Canon) Richard Twomey (1977–1981).

Social problems have always afflicted the area, and with the arrival of Fr. Richard McKay, first as curate and later as parish priest, several ecumenical projects were initiated which, in 1990, culminated in the signing of a joint covenant for all the churches in the area to work together for the benefit of the local community.

V.A.

Bristol: Our Lady of the Rosary, Lawrence Weston

The housing estate at Lawrence Weston was developed by the City Council to ease the housing shortage after the 1939–1945 war. The estate covers the area between Shirehampton and Henbury. The few Catholics who lived in the area before the war were in the parish of St. Bernard, Shirehampton, and it was from the parish of St. Bernard, Fr. (later Canon) Leahy, that the first moves were made to provide a church at Lawrence Weston. In 1951 a site was purchased at the junction of Tide Grove and Kingsweston Lane which cost £1,000. Bishop Rudderham laid the foundation stone of the new church on 16 July 1952, the feast of Our Lady of Mount Carmel. Current building regulations meant that the original building consisted only of the nave and side aisles, with accommodation for 300. The sanctuary, tower and side chapels were added in 1957–58. By that time Our Lady of the Rosary Primary School had been opened close to the church. A community of Missionary Sisters, the Servants of the Holy Ghost, had established a convent close to the school in which members of the community taught. By 1958 the church had been completed at a cost of £14,000.

In October 1959 the Diocesan Trustees purchased a 3.7-acre site, close to the church, on the opposite side of Long Cross, for the provision of a Catholic comprehensive school. This was possible because of the competitive price of land in the area. In 1961 work began on the building of the new school, dedicated to St. Bede. In spite of draining problems on the site, St. Bede's admitted its first pupils in September 1963, and church and civic dignitaries attended the official opening ceremony, in May 1964.

J.C.

Bristol: St. Vincent de Paul, Southmead

The first council estate at Southmead dates from between 1929 and 1939. Catholics who lived on the Filton side of the estate were able to attend Mass at St. Teresa, Filton and those who lived on the Westbury side were able to attend the church of the Sacred Heart at Westbury. The increase in building on the estate after 1945 made the provision of a church essential. Mass was said each Sunday at the local community centre and in 1953 a site for a permanent church was purchased in Glencoyne Square, close to the Westbury suburb. The site cost almost £900 and by 1955 the church of St. Vincent de Paul was completed. On Low Sunday 1955 the church was blessed and dedicated by Bishop Rudderham.

For several years there was no resident priest at St. Vincent and the church was served from St. Teresa, Filton. In 1963 Fr. Daniel Supple was appointed parish priest, and for the remaining twenty-nine years of his life served the Catholics of Southmead. There is an Angelus Bell which rings out each day at noon. Because St. Teresa's is nearer, chaplaincy work at Southmead Hospital continues to be the responsibility of the clergy at Filton.

J.A.H.

Bristol: St. Pius X, Withywood (formerly Hartcliffe)

Development on the south side of Bristol before and after the Second World War necessitated the provision of a place of worship for Catholics living in Bishopsworth, Hartcliffe and Withywood. Until 1956 priests from Holy Cross, Bedminster, said Mass in the Pavilion, Donald Road, Bedminster Down. In that year Fr. Gerard Carroll was put in charge of the new parish, dedicated to Pope Pius X who had been canonised two years before. A temporary church was opened in Hareclive Road with Mass being said for those in the west of the parish in The Elm Tree Inn, Bishopsworth. The priest at that time lived at 7 Dyers Close, Hartcliffe.

Bristol: St. Pius X, demolished 1987

Soon a school became necessary and St. Pius X Primary School was opened in 1961 on part of a site in Gatehouse Avenue, Withywood, earmarked also for a permanent church. Mass in the Elm Tree Inn was now discontinued in favour of the school hall. It was about this time that the Sartan Club was opened – the family name of Pius X was Sarto – and subsequently became the largest Catholic social club in the diocese.

St. David's Centre, Queen's Road, Bishopsworth was opened in September 1972. It had been built almost entirely by parishioners and superseded the school hall for celebration of Mass. Under Fr. Michael Fitzpatrick, 1987 witnessed the completion of parish development with the opening of a new church by Bishop Alexander on 9 December. The architect was John Webster. The wooden church in Hareclive Road was no longer deemed safe and was vacated, but St. David's Centre continues to serve as a parish hall. On 5 December 1993 Sunday Mass was televised from the church. During its first forty years the parish has witnessed three ordinations to the priesthood and one to the permanent diaconate.

J.A.H.

Bristol: St. Antony, Henbury

St. Antony, in Keinton Walk, Henbury, was provided in 1956 as a Mass centre for Catholics living on the new housing estate then being developed in the area between Westbury-on-Trym and the railway line along the city boundary. Mgr. Canon Hookway, at the church of the Sacred Heart in Brecon Road, had a temporary building erected on a plot of land at the junction of Satchfield Crescent and Keinton Walk. Fr. Francis O'Leary was responsible for the new mission. The Catholic convent of the Good Shepherd at Hallen, adjacent to Henbury, had its own resident chaplain who was able to help Fr. O'Leary at weekends. (The convent closed in 1980.)

In 1957 a council house was made available to Fr. O'Leary who thus became the first parish priest, and the house in Edington Grove became the first presbytery. He visited Severn Beach each Sunday to offer Mass in the bungalow belonging to one of the Catholic residents. In 1961 the Beach Cafe was purchased and converted into a chapel so that the increasing number of parishioners could attend Mass. Unfortunately the little chapel was destroyed by fire in 1974, and Sunday Mass is now celebrated in the local **Anglican Church of St. Nicholas**.

Fr. O'Leary was moved to Bath in 1963 and Fr. (now Canon) James O'Brien replaced him. During Fr. O'Brien's time the present presbytery was built adjoining the church. Fr. Gerald Rogers succeeded Fr. O'Brien and remained until 1978. During this period the parish hall was built and the permanent atrium (porch) was built to improve the entance to the church. Fr. Rogers was replaced by Fr. (now Canon) William O'Callaghan who remained at St. Antony until 1985. The Henbury housing estate, in common with other council estates developed in the immediate post-war years, has seen a decline in the number of residents, and this trend is reflected in the decrease in the number of parishioners at St. Antony.

J.C.

Bristol: St. Augustine, Downend

In the early years of the century Catholics living in the Downend area could attend Mass either at the Redemptorist mission in Park Lane, Kingswood, or St. Philip's Oratory, the Mass centre in North Devon Road, Fishponds also served by the Redemptorists. When the Kingswood mission closed the temporary church was moved from Park Lane to Forest Road, Fishponds, where St. Joseph's church was eventually built in 1923.

By 1945 the situation in the Downend area had become so serious that Bishop Lee was very anxious to find a suitable site for a temporary church. The most favourable one appeared to be the one in Stanbridge Road, but uncertainty over the route to be taken by the new roads planned for the area caused the Bishop to hesitate. A large house, 22 Salisbury Road, was purchased to provide a Mass centre in Downend and, possibly, a future presbytery. The cost of the house and the necessary alterations amounted to £3,800. It was in use by October 1947 but, sadly, Bishop Lee's death in 1948 caused any further work to be shelved.

In 1953 a temporary solution to the problem was found by hiring the British Legion hut in West Park Road each Sunday for use as a Mass centre, while funds were collected for the purchase of a site for a permanent church. In 1961 the present site in Boscombe Crescent was acquired for £16,000. Although the price seemed excessive at the time the site of 3.9 acres in extent had room for a church, a primary school, playing field and a presbytery.

A temporary presbytery was purchased at 62 Westbourne Road and in the summer of 1962, before building work began, the site was used for a Summer Fair which has been held every year since then. On 25 April 1965 Mgr. Thomas Hughes laid the foundation stone of the new church of St. Augustine. On 23 April 1965 a large crowd assembled to see the pre-fabricated steeple brought to the site by helicopter and lowered into position alongside the almost completed church. On 29 August 1965 Bishop Rudderham opened the new church.

Meanwhile a community of the Sisters of Our Lady of the Missions joined the parish in September 1973 and established their convent in Sutherland Avenue. On 6 December 1969 Mgr. Hughes came back to the parish to lay the foundation stone of the new primary school, the opening of which was celebrated with Mass on 14 September 1970. Under the leadership of Fr. Francis Daly, parish priest 1966–1993, a church, presbytery, and primary school had all been built, and a Mass centre established at **Pucklechurch H.M. Remand Prison**, served from St. Augustine.

J.C.

Bristol: Holy Family, Patchway

During his twenty-six years as parish priest of St. Teresa, Filton, Canon Denis Lucey was responsible for the building of three churches. One of these was at Patchway; part of a large development area on the north side of Bristol planned to accommodate many of the employees of the Bristol Aeroplane Company (now British Aerospace).

The site was bought in 1954 for £900, but it was not until 1962 that plans for a new church were set in motion. This delay meant that it was possible to take into account the liturgical changes envisaged by the Second Vatican Council. The sanctuary runs the full width of the church and is

separated from the nave by marble altar rails. The church, which cost
£34,000, seats 300. It is a simple traditional building, yet with a modern
look, faced in reconstructed stone with a plain tiled roof supported on a
pre-cast concrete frame. The primary school was opened in September
1968 and Holy Family became an independent parish in 1972.

The parish boundaries now encompass the recently developed estate
at Bradley Stoke which has been described as Europe's largest 'one-off'
development with a projected population of 26,000 (8,500 houses). To
cope, at least in part, with this massive increase, Fr. Gerald Rogers (now
retired) initiated the building of a new primary school, St.Mary, with a
parish community centre forming part of the school complex. It is planned
for the school to open in September 1999. The Sisters of Mercy moved into
the area in 1998.

J.A.H.

Bristol: St. Bernadette, Whitchurch

When the civil airport at Whitchurch opened in 1930, it was envisaged
that it would become an important crossroads in international travel and
indeed it did play a significant role in the Second World War. However,
because of the urban expansion of Bristol which eventually linked the city
with this outlying area, the City Council revoked its decision and opted to
close Whitchurch and to open Lulsgate.

Already in 1947 Bishop Lee had intentions for a Catholic secondary
school in south Bristol and his diary records that on 23 March he visited a
site at Knowle. When in 1954 St. Thomas More School was opened to serve
the north of the city, it was at first thought that its counterpart in the
south should be dedicated to St. John Fisher. However this name gave way
to St. Bernadette as the year of its opening (1958) coincided with the
centenary of the apparitions at Lourdes. The opening ceremony was performed by the American born Apostolic Delegate to Great Britain, Archbishop Gerard P. O'Hara, on 21 October 1958.

The first Mass centre in the district, served by the clergy of St. Gerard,
Knowle, had been at the Hengrove Youth Centre in Fortfield Road, but
when the school opened Sunday Mass was celebrated there. In 1968 St.
Bernadette was opened and blessed, serving the now independent parish of
Whitchurch, Hengrove and Stockwood. The distinctive design of the build-
ing, with its pointed silver metallic roof, still catches the eye of the passing
motorist. The architect was James Leask of the Nealon Tanner Partnership,
Bristol, and the shape is described as a double hyperbolic paraboloid. It is

a tent-like structure, reminding us of the temporary nature of our sojourn in this world. In 1982 a striking suspended crucifix of Christ in Glory by Frank Roper of Penarth was added to the sanctuary. It is made of a metallic alloy and, although large, weighs only twenty pounds.

A primary school serving the parishes of St. Bernadette and St. Gerard was opened in 1971. The church and the two schools are built on the same campus.

Stockwood, originally part of the estate belonging to Keynsham Abbey, and forfeited in 1534 at the Dissolution of the Monasteries, has since the 1930s been developed as a housing estate. At first Mass was said in a public house and then at Waycroft School in Selden Road. For many years there has been a sharing agreement, now formalised, with the Church of England, whereby Mass is said each Sunday and Holyday in the Church of Christ the Servant (opened in 1964). The sisters of La Retraite, well known for the girl's school which they used to run in Clifton, opened a convent in Hollway Road, Stockwood in 1982. Although the community left in the autumn of 1998, many people came for a final Mass in the chapel on 5 February 1999.

J.A.H.

Bristol: Polish Church of Our Lady of Ostrabrama

When at the end of the Second World War Poland was under the domination of the Soviet Union many Poles made their way to the West and to the USA. Those who arrived in Britain went initially to camps and then settled in nearby towns. Many came to Bristol and with their own priest celebrated Mass at 10 a.m. each Sunday in the Pro-Cathedral at Clifton. However, it was always their ambition to secure a building that they could call their own.

In July 1968 they purchased Arley Chapel in Cheltenham Road, Stokes Croft from the Congregationalists. The chapel, which is Italianate in style, cruciform in shape, and built completely in Bath stone, has a porched entrance which faces the street corner, and was originally opened in 1847. The architects were Foster and Wood who also designed the Trinity Almhouses in Old Market.

The building was re-ordered in 1968, with a grant from English Heritage, before its re-opening on 4 August by Bishop Wladyslaw Rubin, delegate of the Polish Primate, Cardinal Wyszynski, in the presence of Bishop Rudderham. The Lady Chapel houses a silver icon of Our Lady of Ostrabrama. A stained glass window, made in Poland, shows the priest martyr of the concentration camps, St. Maximilian Kolbe, who died at Auschwitz in 1941.

J.A.H.

University of Bristol

The Catholic chaplaincy in Bristol University is in an imposing Georgian building situated in Clifton next door to the students' Union in which the chaplain had previously occupied an office. The building had formerly been the vicarage of St. Paul's Anglican Church, and was acquired by the diocese in 1964, with the aid of a grant from the Van Neste Foundation. At that time the future Bishop Alexander was chaplain. The chapel, dedicated to St. Catherine of Siena and St. Thomas Aquinas, is the centre for many ecumenical activities. The present full-time chaplain is Miss Margaret Fraser and the building also has accommodation for twelve students.

University of Bath

Bath University Chaplaincy on Claverton Down, established in 1967, opened its new ecumenical chapel in 1972. Student accommodation is also available in the centre of Bath, but unlike Bristol, its chaplain, Fr. Thomas Gunning, is also parish priest at the nearby church of SS. Peter and Paul.

University of the West of England

In 1969 three Bristol colleges were merged to form the Polytechnic, and the Anglican, Methodist and Catholic chaplains worked together on plans for the new ecumenical day centre named the Octagon. This was built on Frenchay Campus and opened in 1972 by Bishop Alexander with 120 members of staff and many students of all denominations present. Fr. Rory Geoghan S.J., an artist employed by the Art College, was chaplain until his move to Leeds, and the current chaplain is Fr. Eugene Campbell, parish priest of nearby St. Vincent de Paul, Southmead. The Polytechnic was designated a University in 1992.

V.A.

Bristol: St. Brendan's Sixth Form College

Catholic secondary education in Bristol and Bath was re-organised in 1979 with provision for all sixteen to nineteen year-olds at St. Brendan's College.

Pupils in the eleven to sixteen age range were phased out and by 1983 St. Brendan's had become a fully fledged Catholic Sixth Form College with the ultimate expectation of providing a Christian education for a broad ability range of about 400–500 sixth formers. The first girls to be admitted to this hitherto all male institution was in 1979 when the La Sainte Union Independent School in Bath closed and a number of sixth formers transferred to St. Brendan's. Gradually over the years the proportion of girls to boys increased and they now slightly exceed the number of boys admitted to the College.

In September 1981 the Irish Christian Brothers, in order to comply with the terms of their constitution as being providers of exclusively male education, decided to withdraw from Bristol after a period of eighty-five years' dedicated service to Catholic education. From 1981 to the present the management and administration of the College has been in the hands of lay staff who have steered it through a very formative and successful period in its history.

By the late 1980s the College could boast of admitting students of a wide range of academic ability, from some seventy or more educational establishments, to a large variety of academic and vocational courses. In fact curriculum initiatives and development have featured in a major way in the progress of the College, while at the same time maintaining a strong emphasis on the Christian ethos.

Original hopes that the College would attain and maintain a figure of 400–500 students proved to be wide of the mark; in 1998 the numbers gaining entry exceeded 1000. This has necessitated building on a major scale, alteration and modification of existing buildings and the erection of temporary accommodation to absorb the growing demand.

M.McC.

For the earlier history of St. Brendan's see under
The Clifton Boys' Grammar Schools in Chapter 3.

Bristol: St. James Priory, Little Brothers of Nazareth

The most recently opened church in the diocese makes use of the oldest ecclesiastical buildings in Bristol, namely the nave of the Benedictine Priory founded in 1129 by Robert, Earl of Gloucester, under the jurisdiction of Tewkesbury Abbey. After the Reformation this housed the Anglican church of St. James until it was closed in 1983. It still retains the original Norman arches, built with stone brought over from Caen in Normandy at the time of the building of Bristol Castle, and houses a memorial to its founder, together with some original stained glass and several amusing bosses, the heads of prominent people of the time. In 1993 negotiations with the Anglican diocese of Bristol enabled the Little Brothers of Nazareth to acquire the buildings for a 'peppercorn rent'. Considerable restoration took place and the new St. James Priory was opened by Bishop Alexander on 8 September 1993.

In 1994 the community of the Little Brothers of Nazareth, three in number, moved into Church House, which adjoins the north aisle of the Priory, and may have its origins in the dormitory of the original twelfth century Priory, thus bringing the picture full circle, as the last three monks from the original community left 450 years earlier. The property is on a 100-yr lease from the Anglican diocese of Bristol.

In September 1995 Bishop Alexander and Bishop Doe, the Anglican Bishop of Swindon, came to St. James to lay the foundation stone of Walsingham House, a twenty-bed treatment centre for chemically dependent homeless men and women. This is one of the very few facilities in the United Kingdom dedicated to providing professional treatment for the homeless addict and was opened in June 1996.

The Little Brothers were able to buy the neighbouring almshouses in 1998. These will be renovated and converted into a hostel for the next stage of rehabilitation for former alcohol and drug abusers to open early in 1999. The Community itself is called to live a very simple religious life, at the heart of the city, with emphasis on Eucharistic Adoration alongside its work with the homeless, poor and marginalised.

V.A.

Brockworth, Gloucestershire: St. Patrick

Brockworth was formerly part of the parish of St. Peter, Gloucester. Mass was first said there in 1942, in the cinema of the workers' hostel of the Gloucester Aircraft Co. In 1954 the house Rathlea, now the presbytery, was bought by the diocese. From 1955 Mass was said in a dual purpose hall built with the help of volunteer Irish workers at the hostel. It became the parish church of St. Patrick when Brockworth was separated from Gloucester parish in 1960. The first parish priest was Fr. John McCarthy. The present church, by the Bristol architects Ivor Day and O'Brien, was opened in 1968 and extended in 1980, when a pipe organ was installed, and was dedicated in 1981.

In 1977 the Sisters of the Presentation of Our Lady acquired a house

Burnham-on-Sea: former La Retraite Convent, chapel

in Court Road, and members of the Order are involved in educational and pastoral care in Brockworth and nearby parishes.

J.A.F.

Brownshill, Gloucestershire: St. Mary of the Angels: See Stroud

Bruton, Somerset: See Shepton Mallet

Bulford Camp: Our Lady Queen of Peace: See Salisbury Plain

Burnham-on-Sea, Somerset: Our Lady and the English Martyrs

Until 1871 the Catholics of Highbridge and Burnham met each Sunday in a 'cottage chapel' where prayers were read by Joseph Burns and Joseph Austin Grimshaw, uncle of the future Archbishop Grimshaw. This cottage was owned by Mrs. Buckler whose husband was a Protestant.

The foundation of the parish owes much to the energy and dedication of the Abbe John Bouvier of the Bridgwater mission. He agreed to travel to Burnham once a month to say Mass for local Catholics. The first Mass was celebrated in August 1872 in Mrs. Buckler's cottage. Grimshaw gives a vivid account of the social background of these events in his unpublished paper, *In Nomine Dei*, in which he outlines the rise and progress of the Highbridge mission of Our Lady of Mount Carmel and St. Joseph 1871–1888.

The next milestone in the history of the parish came when Bishop Clifford gave permission to the Sisters of La Retraite to found a convent in his diocese. The sisters purchased a house from the Tucker family called The Rookery, moved in with a few boarders and eventually built a chapel. Their educational efforts were rewarded in the founding of a boarding school for one hundred pupils which proved very popular in the neighbourhood. Although the local press welcomed the La Retraite sisters when they first came, Grimshaw reports an outbreak of local hostility in the 1890s. A series of lectures was organised by the Protestant Alliance; devoted to prurient and sensational accounts by monks and nuns who had left religious orders. Grimshaw records that the local Anglican clergy refused to take part in any of these lectures and demonstrations and pointedly stood aloof from the whole affair. The restoration of community harmony was largely the work of Fr. Peter Treand. In 1900 the mission and convent were given their first parish priest and chaplain, Fr. (later Mgr. Canon) Hugh Lean (1857–1939).

In 1967 the parish church of Our Lady and the English Martyrs was opened, although many felt sad at the separation from the parish's long association with the convent chapel. The boarding and day school closed in 1984. One school now remains as the property of the La Retraite sisters, St. Joseph's primary school opened in 1891 under the first headmistress, Mother Mary Monica. The sisters are now, for the most part, engaged in various aspects of retreat work, parish activities and ecumenical commitments.

La Retraite sisters needing nursing and residential care moved from Clapham to the Burnham Nursing and Residential Care Home (run by Associated Nursing Services) in the autumn of 1996. The Home is in the former La Retraite convent and school.

K.McG.

Calne, Wiltshire: St. Edmund

After the Great War the growth in the numbers of Catholics living in Calne was due mainly to military and R.A.F. personnel from the nearby bases settling in the town and to the influx from the Midlands of workers in the Harris food factory. In the 1920s and early 1930s Catholics went on foot to the church at Chippenham. As the trains were not running on Sundays they were able to walk along the railway track, a short cut of about three and a half miles.

Mr. Edwarde, the superintendent engineer at Harris's, was the major influence in persuading the priest at Chippenham to come and say Mass in his home Rose d'Or, 4 Lickhill Road. He had built the house in 1926 in what was then a country lane following on from North Street. Mass was said in the front hall and parlour, the priest having been transported to the house by Mr. Edwarde in his pony and trap.

These were the arrangements that prevailed for most of the decade until it became obvious that the house could no longer cope with the increasing numbers. Mr. Edwarde then approached the Vicar and Parochial Church Council who made the hall at the back of St. Mary's Church available for Mass on Sundays and Holydays. This 'Red Cross Hall' continued to be used until the late 1940s when Gough's at 65 Oxford Road came on to the market. This was a large old property with spacious grounds including lawns, gardens and a tennis court. It also had a large garage adjacent to the house.

Bishop Lee needed little persuading to take advantage of the opportunity which presented itself. It was envisaged that the large garage could be used as a temporary church and the house as a presbytery. In due course an adequately sized church could be built in the extensive grounds. The purchase took place in 1947 and the garage was taken into use as a church. A resident priest was appointed the following year.

With the growth of **R.A.F. Lyneham** the number of Catholics settling in Calne was steadily increasing. At the same time the R.A.F. found that it was unable to supply a full-time Catholic chaplain to the Station. As a result Calne was selected as the nearest church to supply the needs of Catholics at the station. It was because of this that the R.A.F. felt able to make a contribution to the building fund of St. Edmund's church and, moreover, to make a financial allowance to the priest in his capacity as Officiating Chaplain.

In 1958 Fr. Guy Gibbins took over from Fr. Daniel O'Callaghan as parish priest. The new church was completed in 1964 but there is no record of its having been consecrated. During Fr. Gibbins' incumbency attendance at Mass was made easier by the use of a minibus which would pick up parishioners from the more distant parts of the parish such as Hilmarton, Compton Bassett and Yatesbury.

The furnishings of the church are of some interest. The baptistery was originally part of the entrance complex – since moved to the main body of the church – and the font is made of stone from the ruins of Stanley Abbey.

This Cistercian foundation stood about two miles from the present church and is within the parish boundary. St. Edmund Rich (*c*.1179–1240) was vicar of Calne prior to his appointment as Archbishop of Canterbury. He frequently went into retreat at Stanley and several tiles from the abbey ruins have been framed in the entrance porch.

In the early 1980s the altar was moved to the centre of the sanctuary where it was fitted with a new marble frontal embellished with a bronze winged chalice by a parishioner, Sean Crampton. The same sculptor designed and executed the Stations of the Cross.

A primary school was opened in September 1971. Fr. Gibbins, envisaging that it would be a convent school, invited the Sisters of Charity of Christian Instruction of Nevers into the parish where they took up residence at Chilvester Hill House. The plans, however, did not materialise. The sisters left in 1972 and were succeeded in 1974 by two sisters of St. Joseph who remained until 1979. The school became grant maintained in 1994.

Lyneham

By 1938 the R.A.F. had increased its presence in the area by opening stations at Lyneham, Compton Bassett and Yatesbury. During the 1950s and 1960s Lyneham had its own Catholic chaplain based on the camp. The wooden hut where Mass had been said was replaced in the late 1960s by a brick built chapel erected on the married quarters site and dedicated to **St. Joseph**. The chaplain has since been withdrawn so pastoral care of the camp now rests with the parish priest of St. Edmund, with the help of an assistant chaplain.

J.A.H.

Cannington, Somerset: See Bridgwater

Castle Cary, Somerset: St. Andrew C. of E.: Served from Wincanton

Chard, Somerset: English Martyrs

The foundation stone of the present church was laid by Canon (later Bishop) Lee on 24 September 1925. The completed church was opened and blessed on 22 June 1926 on the feast of St. Alban, the first English martyr. From that date Chard became a parish in its own right instead of being part of the Taunton parish of St. George. The building was designed by Sir Frank Wills, onetime Lord Mayor of Bristol, and is Victorian Gothic in style and built from local flintstone with freestone dressing. The present church grounds contain a church hall opened in 1933. Bishop Rudderham consecrated the church on 29 September 1966.

The churches in **Ilminster and Crewkerne** are daughter churches of Chard, **St. Joseph, Ilminster** was opened on 22 April 1953 and **St. Peter, Crewkerne** was built in 1937. Mass has been celebrated in and around Crewkerne since 1927, initially at Merryfield House and then at Riddle's factory in Merriot. The parish owed much in its early years to Fr. Edmond McSweeney who was parish priest from 1919 to 1929. His successor, Fr. William Mortland, initiated and planned the building of St. Peter at Crewkerne.

The district has historical associations with the English Martyrs: St. Alexander Bryant, Blessed John Hambley and Blessed James Fenn.

In 1919 Sister Thérèse of the La Retraite Sisters founded the Convent of St. Gildas. Gradually they built up a successful school which flourished until the changes demanded by national educational policy in the 1960s placed further provision beyond their means. The closure of the primary school in 1991 brought about the end of the convent and the departure of the sisters. Determined that the house and property should not be lost to the Church, the sisters agreed with Bishop Alexander that it should become a Retreat, Conference and Pastoral Centre. It is also used as a parish centre for local Catholics.

M.McC.

Cheddar, Somerset: Our Lady Queen of the Apostles

The earliest living testimony of Catholic life in Cheddar dates from 1922. There were only two Catholic families living in the village at the time and a journey to Wells was necessary to attend the nearest Catholic church. Between 1933 and 1938, when the Axbridge reservoir was being built, the presence of many Irish labourers on the site prompted the contractors to provide facilities for them to hear Mass. A priest from one of the surrounding parishes usually said this. When the war began in 1939 the Catholic population suddenly increased with the arrival of evacuees, together with the members of the forces who were stationed in the area. There was no church available in Cheddar so the local people had to improvise by having Mass said in any school, hall or hotel that happened to be available. Matters improved when the Pallotine Fathers purchased a small cottage in

Cheltenham: former St. Gregory's Church (from George Rowe's illustrated Cheltenham guide, 1845)

Tweentown, Cheddar. The first priest to occupy the cottage was Fr. Jeremiah Keogh. He started by converting a room upstairs into a tiny chapel for weekday Mass and relied upon temporary accommodation for Sundays.

In 1948 Fr. Gormley replaced Fr. Keogh and continued the struggle to keep the little chapel going. In the early 1950s local villages began to grow and more Catholic families arrived in the area. After a decade of financial difficulties the congregation set their sights on building a new church, which they eventually achieved under the direction of Fr. Daniel Hayes. During the 1960s the parish experienced a period of vigorous growth. In the 1970s attention had to be given to the construction of a parish hall for social events and to provide a place for the religious instruction of the children. In the course of time Fr. Hayes was succeeded by Fr. John Guidera.

Mass is also celebrated at **Sandford** in the Anglican Parish Church at All Saints and is served from Cheddar.

K.McG.

Cheltenham, Gloucestershire: St. Gregory

Towards the end of the eighteenth century Cheltenham was becoming established as a spa, and its visitors included members of the Irish aristocracy and French emigrés arriving in the wake of the Revolution. Their spiritual needs were first met from the mission in Gloucester, with extemporised arrangements depending on the accommodation immediately available. Emigré priests were also ministering at Cheltenham from the early years of the century until the death of the Abbé Cesar Robin in 1811. The Benedictine presence at Cheltenham, which was to last for nearly two centuries, began in 1805 when Fr. James Calderbank arrived from the mission at Bath, but he soon withdrew, and the Cheltenham mission did not become fully established until Fr. John Augustine Birdsall arrived in 1809. Fr. Birdsall was a forceful character whose altercations with Bishop Baines played a significant part in the history of the English Benedictine Congregation, of which he became President-General. He drew on his considerable private means to build a chapel on land purchased at St. James's Square. Opened in 1810, it was described at the time as 'a neat and commodious edifice, capable of holding 300 persons' and as 'neat and very chaste'; later, when funds were being sought for its replacement, it became 'an ugly square red-brick building of rather Methodistical appearance'. Before Fr. Birdsall ceased to be missioner in 1830 he extended it to accommodate a rapidly increasing community which by 1851 numbered a thousand. By then Catholic Cheltenham was a socially two-tier community; an appeal for funds in 1853 referred to two thirds of it being 'the poorest of the poor'.

Its growth was not always peaceful. Cheltenham was one of several missions in the newly formed diocese to experience violent expressions of the anti-Catholicism which, if of little moment compared with the Gordon riots in Bristol, nevertheless created great commotion at the time. This antipathy sprang from the appointment of the Evangelical zealot Francis Close to the parish church in 1826. It was something new to Cheltenham – in 1813 the local press had referred to the Catholics as 'a loyal, long-suffering class of our fellow subjects' – and it was slow to take effect: the controversies surrounding the Emancipation Act of 1829 led to no more than provocative placards and to a debate between Catholics and the Reformation Society which degenerated into acrimony. Feeling was inflamed by Close's annual anti-Popery sermons on November 5th, and boiled over during the nation-wide uproar which followed the restoration of the Hierarchy in 1850. Two 'Great Protestant Meetings' were held in Cheltenham, the latter causing the upsurge of a disorderly mob which did substantial damage in the town and mounted a destructive attack on the chapel. Its behaviour was not typical of Cheltenham: the local M.P. deplored the violence and the Unitarian congregation offered to help defray the damage. If the claim for compensation (of £30) suggests that the material damage proved to be less than cataclysmic, the effect on an otherwise tranquil community was long remembered.

Plans for a new church began with the arrival in 1852 of Fr. James Ambrose Cotham O.S.B., from service in Tasmania. The site was extended by the purchase of the house and grounds of 10 St. James's Square from the Benedictine trustees of the late Mrs. Sarah Neve, who had bought it in 1831 for the benefit of the Chipping Sodbury mission. At the time it was occupied by the Tennyson family, and *In Memoriam* was written there. An Early Decorated building which shows the skill of the architect C. F. Hansom in handling exteriors, it is, unusually, oriented roughly N–S, and was built almost piecemeal: nave, aisles and transepts alone were complete when it was opened, with Cardinal Wiseman preaching, in 1857. A free-standing tower and spire were finished in 1864 and the nave was not extended to meet them until 1876. (The spire was designed to outdo the parish church of St. Mary; the Anglicans counterattacked with the even taller St. Matthew, but they lost in the end – its spire proved unstable and only a truncated stump remains). By the time the nave was completed Fr. Cotham had retired from the mission, but he lived to see the completion of the church, which had been built largely on his initiative. He was succeeded as Missionary Rector in 1873 by Fr. Robert Aloysius Wilkinson, whose long incumbency continued until 1905, two years before his death. During his time, in 1883, St. Gregory's was designated a Benedictine priory. The Benedictines served Cheltenham until 1998, since when the parish has been a diocesan responsibility.

A rapidly expanding town with a Catholic population of well over 1200 at the turn of the century needed suburban Mass centres. At Prestbury as early as 1895 a nearly completed house was converted into a chapel accommodating fifty. It closed in 1902, and Mass was not again said at Prestbury until 1958, in the hall of the Women's Institute. The Holy Name Hall was opened there in 1964. As well as the future parishes of St. Thomas More and Sacred Hearts, a Mass centre (now served from Winchcombe) opened in the early 1940s at Bishop's Cleeve. At Hatherley, St. Margaret Clitherow Hall was built in 1978, though the Mass centre proved short-lived, closing in 1987.

Education has been centrally important to Cheltenham Catholicism, having a continuous history from pre-Emancipation times when in 1827 Fr. Birdsall opened a poor school above the then vestry. Known as St. Gregory's School, and described as 'for the instruction of the labouring poor in the parish of Cheltenham', it moved in 1855 to new premises in nearby St. Paul's Street. Fr. Scarisbrick (later Bishop of Port Louis, Mauritius, and titular Archbishop), then a curate to Fr. Cotham, invited a group from the Order of the Daughters of the Cross, which had been established at Liège in 1833, to come to take over the girls' education. Thus began a long association of the religious orders with Cheltenham education. They overcame substantial linguistic problems to remain until 1879, when they were replaced by the Sisters of Charity of St. Vincent de Paul, whose long stay ended in 1935. The Sisters of the Congregation of La Sainte Union des Sacrés Coeurs took their place. The school again moved in 1936, to its present position in Knapp Road.

In 1855 the Daughters of the Cross founded a fee-paying school at Montpellier Lodge. It closed nine years later. St. Gregory's High School for Girls (whose most famous pupil was the actress Lillah McCarthy) was at St. James's Square from 1891 to 1908, and the Ursulines maintained a Ladies' College at Fullwood Park from 1912 to 1931. More recently La Sainte Union opened the Charlton Park convent in 1939 and the Carmelites the independent Whitefriars in 1956. They came together in 1987 in the newly founded St. Edward's School, which now has a lay staff. The present arrangements for Catholic education in Cheltenham inevitably reflect national educational policies. St. Gregory's School, which was extended in 1990, now feeds into St. Benedict's Comprehensive School, which had been opened as a secondary school in 1962. In the recently established parish of St. Thomas More another primary school was opened in 1975.

J.A.F.

Cheltenham, Gloucestershire: Sacred Hearts

Mass was first celebrated in the Charlton Kings district of Cheltenham when in 1939 the sisters of La Sainte Union opened a boarding school and convent at Charlton Park. With the outbreak of war evacuees expanded the congregation and Mass was transferred to the school hall. The mission was then served by Benedictines from St. Gregory. In 1947 the parish of the Sacred Hearts of Jesus and Mary was created and land acquired for a church. The presbytery was completed in 1954 and the church opened in 1957.

Within the parish is Nazareth House, maintained for the care of the elderly by the Poor Sisters of Nazareth, who acquired the house Springfield in Charlton Kings in 1965. They had first come to Cheltenham eighty years before. New premises were begun in 1966 and opened two years later. The parish has also recently seen the return of the Carmelite Order to the diocese. In earlier days they cared for Whitefriars School but left when it became a constituent part of St. Edward's School (mentioned under St. Gregory above but actually in Sacred Hearts). Now the novitiate of the order is at St. Edward's.

J.A.F.

Cheltenham, Gloucestershire: St. Thomas More

Prior to 1960 the growing residential districts of St. Marks and Hester's Way to the NW of Cheltenham were served from St. Gregory: first in a scout hut and then in St. Marks community centre. In that year Fr. John Nolan arrived and the mission became an independent parish. Bishop Rudderham had told him that 'there is nothing except a plot of land and a growing and zealous congregation'; yet the parish hall was opened in 1962, the presbytery completed by 1964 and the first services held in the church in 1966. The architect, Anthony Thompson, gave an account of how this was done in the parish's anniversary brochure of 1981. Partly because of restrictions of space, partly in consequence of the liturgical requirements of the Second Vatican Council, the church is hexagonal. A remarkable feature is its 30ft. fibre glass spire which arrived complete on a lorry from Essex. Fr. Nolan did not long outlive his achievement. He died in 1969, and was succeeded by Fr. Thomas Lane, who served there for nearly thirty years.

J.A.F.

Chew Magna, Somerset: The Sacred Heart

On 15 May 1806 a mission was opened at East Harptree, five miles from Chew Magna. It had developed from the one at Shortwood and eventually, in 1883 when it was consecrated, superseded it. The dedication to St. Michael was retained. As a building the church was simple and functional. In addition a house, garden and schoolroom were purchased at a cost of £340. The payment was partly covered by the legacy left to Shortwood by the Beaumonts.

In 1937 Bishop Lee appointed Fr. Timothy Sheridan to take over the parish of St. Michael. The Second World War opened a new chapter in this church's history for in 1940 the Sisters of Our Lady of the Missions bought the Manor House, Chew Magna, where there is reputed to have been a priests' hiding hole, as a reception centre for their evacuee boarders from London and the South-East. The Bishop then arranged for the transfer of the parish priest from East Harptree to Chew Magna. At first the convent chapel served as a Mass centre for the local parishioners and when this proved too congested a temporary hall in the grounds was erected by Fr. John Flynn who was parish priest there until his transfer to Frome in 1952. The Church of the Sacred Heart was opened by Bishop Rudderham on 26 July 1964.

The Sisters of Our Lady of the Missions have remained in the Manor House, which is now a Retreat Centre, but the Senior School closed in 1985 and the Junior School has now passed to lay management.

East Harptree continued to be a Mass centre until, in 1994, an agreement was made to celebrate Mass and other ceremonies in the Anglican church of St. Mary, **West Harptree**.

J.A.H.

Chilcompton, Somerset: St. Aldhelm

Chilcompton village is very close to Downside Abbey and for many years local Catholics attended Mass at St. Benedict in Stratton-on-the-Fosse. Information about the Abbey always gave Chilcompton as the nearest railway station, although this has long since disappeared.

Writing on 19 September 1938, the Downside priest responsible for Chilcompton, Dom Gregory Murray, invited Bishop Lee to come and dedicate the new chapel of St. Aldhelm, who had been Abbot of Malmesbury and Bishop of Wessex. Although a small building, measuring some thirty feet by twenty-three feet it proved adequate for many years, until it was replaced in 1976 by a new church designed by Francis Pollen. Its interior is notable for a mural of St. Christopher by Maurice Percival.

Although the closure of the Somerset coalfield had a serious effect on the population in this area, the Mass attendance has remained stable at between seventy and eighty.

V.A.

Chippenham, Wiltshire: The Assumption of the Blessed Virgin

Chippenham owed the return of organised Catholicism to two converts: Mrs. Elizabeth Fellowes, the wife of a local solicitor, and Sir Richard Hungerford Pollen, of nearby Rodbourne House, who was also a generous benefactor of the Malmesbury mission. In the 1850s a school with about twenty pupils was established under Mrs. Fellowes's aegis, and in 1855 Archbishop Errington opened the chapel of the Assumption of the Blessed Virgin. Visit-

Chippenham:
former church
(*Acknowledgement
A. B. Coggles*)

ing priests served a congregation of forty, first from Frome, then from
Bristol.

When, as is told in the accounts of Malmesbury and Devizes, Captain
Dewell's intentions for the Malmesbury mission were frustrated, Fr.
Francis Larive came to serve Chippenham, thereby inaugurating the Fransalian apostolate in England. Chippenham was then serving Devizes, and
Larive, seeing greater opportunities there, left the care of Chippenham to
a fellow Fransalian, Fr. Bouvier. Meanwhile in 1858 Sir Hungerford Pollen
had obtained a rescript for the celebration of Mass in a cottage in the
grounds of Rodbourne House, and when in 1863 permission was given for
Reservation, Larive went there to live. Later he returned briefly to Chippenham, but when the church was opened at Devizes the focus of the mission became established there, and Chippenham was thereafter served by
diocesan priests. Dewell's influence at Chippenham continued with the
arrival of three Sisters of St. Joseph of Annecy from Devizes to occupy a

house that had been bought for them by Mrs. Fellowes. They stayed until 1884, running the school and caring for the infirm.

In 1890 there were about sixty Catholics living in the town. In 1902 a presbytery was purchased near the chapel but as the town continued to grow it became increasingly clear that a larger church was needed in the north of the county. A plot of land had already been secured in 1870 and so with the generous support of the parishioners a new church was eventually opened and blessed by Bishop Lee on 29 February 1936. Fr. (later Canon) Denis Ryan, who had been appointed in 1934, remained in Chippenham for fourteen years and then moved to Corpus Christi, Weston-super-Mare.

The Poor Servants of the Mother of God were invited by Bishop Lee to open a house in 1937, and in 1939 a convent and private school (St. Margaret's Independent School) were sited on Rowden Hill. In 1958 a primary school was established on the same site which continues to this day, but St. Margaret's closed in 1968. The sisters continue in education and parish ministry.

In 1944–45 Fr. Ryan was instrumental in establishing a new parish in Corsham (to the west of Chippenham). Today the congregation at Chippenham numbers some 700 people. Over twenty priests have served the mission and parish since the early days, the longest serving being Fr. James Kelliher. He was in charge at St. Mary for twenty-eight years and is now living in retirement in the parish.

Acknowledgements to a history of the parish by A. B. Coggles

Chipping Campden, Gloucestershire: St. Catharine of Alexandria

The Catholic mission at Chipping Campden, which was inaugurated in 1854, was founded by Charles Gordon Noel, Viscount Campden, who was converted from the Anglican church while at Cambridge. Services had been held from 1851 in a private chapel in Campden House, dedicated to Our Lady of the Annunciation. With the appointment of the former Anglican priest Fr. William Henry Anderton as chaplain Campden House became a well-known centre of Catholicism, and there Count de Montalembert wrote part of his *Monks of the West*. Campden continues to be a centre of attraction: recent parishioners include Graham Greene and the Old English scholar J. R. R. Tolkien, who is best known as a popular author and was also a contributor to the Jerusalem Bible.

The Catholic community grew rapidly and outgrew the private chapel.

A chapel built in the town served for twenty years. In 1889 the Noels provided the site, and most of the cost of the building, of the present church. It was opened in 1891, and in 1928 the family handed it over to the diocese. It was consecrated in 1954. Sometimes called the 'Catholic cathedral of the Cotswolds' it is arguably the finest Catholic church in the diocese, reflecting the strong concentration of artists and craftsmen around Chipping Campden about the end of the century. A Gothic revival building by William Lunn of Malvern, in local stone, some of it from the old Manor of Campden destroyed in the Civil War, it displays individuality in the saddleback roof on the tower, the asymmetry of its N and S aisles, and in its twenty-one windows, all different and making ingenious use of tracery. The chalice, ciborium, crucifix and processional cross all come from the Guild of Handicrafts by then established at Chipping Campden, and much of the glass is from the workshops of the local Catholic artist Paul Woodroffe (1857–1944). The priest's house (by Frederick Landseer Griggs, another local man) is important in its own right, with a relief by Eric Gill.

Education has played a large part in the history of Campden Catholicism. It began with the opening of a school in 1954. From its earliest days it has been in the charge of the Congregation of the Sisters of Charity of St. Paul, members of an Order first established in this country in 1847. They are now responsible for St. Catharine's Primary School.

The long incumbency of Fr. Henry Bilsborrow (1914–1939) did much to consolidate the standing of Catholicism in the local community, to the extent that in 1957 a thousand people attended the garden party of his successor, Fr. Daniel Hyland. In 1990 there came the tragic death of Fr. Andrew Burns, a Paraclete from Brownshill, while celebrating a requiem Mass. The present incumbent, Fr. John Brennan, is maintaining the strong aesthetic tradition. He has had restored a seventeenth century painting of the Flemish school, *The Adoration of the Shepherds*, which was in his previous parish at Weston-super-Mare, and now hangs in the chancel at Chipping Campden.

Moreton-in-Marsh is served from Chipping Campden. Mass had been said there, at Redesdale Hall, during the First World War. In the five years from 1951 Mass centres were established successively in the YMCA, Lilac Cottage in Church Street, and in St. George's Hall. Now Mass is said in the Congregational church at Moreton.

J.A.F.

Chipping Sodbury, Gloucestershire: St. Lawrence

The history of Chipping Sodbury begins with nearby Horton where a branch of the Paston family (the 15th century letter-writers) maintained a mission from the early eighteenth century until its last member died in 1794. Thereafter Horton was served in primitive accommodation by the Benedictine mission at Bath. In 1838 the focus of the mission moved to Chipping Sodbury when Sarah Neve, the Catholic wife of the vicar of Old Sodbury (also a benefactor of Cheltenham and patroness of the Benedictine mission to Australia), bought the Swan Inn, an Elizabethan house, for £1,300. The ostler's accommodation was converted into a sacristy and the stables and brewhouse into a chapel, dedicated to St. Lawrence. She also endowed the mission, which continued to be served by the Benedictines.

The subsequent history of the mission, unusually, is one of decline; the explosive growth of the Catholic population in the nineteenth century largely passed by Chipping Sodbury. Fr. Ralph Maurus Cooper was appointed in 1846 to what was seen as a comparatively easy mission. In 1858 he gave an account of what was still a typical far-flung rural mission of earlier days. There were sixty-eight Catholics, of whom twelve were at Chipping Sodbury and the remainder scattered as far as Thornbury, twelve miles away. Problems of distance meant that attendance at Chipping Sodbury then averaged little more than ten. After Fr. Cooper's death in 1869 the mission continued to be served by Benedictines, until 1890 from Ampleforth and Downside and thereafter, following changes in the constitution of the English Benedictine Congregation, from Douai. In 1891 the newcomer Fr. Ignatius Stuart found the mission 'in a shameful condition', with a Mass attendance of only seven. For a time at the end of the century it was served from Great Malvern and elsewhere, with only three or four at Mass. In 1908 the Benedictines wished to discontinue the existing arrangement, and the Chipping Sodbury endowment was transferred to Knowle, a suburb of Bristol, with Chipping Sodbury served from it.

In 1928 secular clergy were appointed to the parish, the first of whom, Fr. Bertrand Ellis, remained until 1948 to see the beginning of the post-war expansion. This was especially marked at nearby Yate, and Mass centres were opened in the parish hall there in 1965 and at Rodford junior school in 1970. When St. Paul's junior school was opened in Yate in 1974 both were superseded by a centre there, which, in turn, gave place to St. Paul's Church. These developments have taken place during the incumbency of Fr. Edmond Murphy, appointed in 1970 and now the longest-serving priest of Chipping Sodbury.

Yate, Gloucestershire: St. Paul

The rapid growth of Yate meant that by the late 1970s the Mass centre at St. Paul's school was no longer adequate, and a new church was planned adjoining the school. Designed by the architects Ivor Day O'Brien Stephens, it is a multipurpose building capable as a single hall of accommodating a congregation of 400, but adaptable as a smaller church and a parish hall. Its design is based on A-frame structures, with exposed structural steel with emphasis on sloping roofs (clad in blueblack slates) which have earned it the soubriquet of 'St. Paul-without-the-Walls'. The interior makes ingenious use of direct and indirect lighting with the altar the focal point of illumination. With the school the church makes an attractive enclave set back from the road. It was opened in 1981.

J.A.F.

Churchdown, Gloucestershire: Our Lady of Perpetual Succour

Catholic Churchdown has grown explosively since pre-war days when local Catholics in what was still essentially a rural community numbered fewer than a dozen. Now, as judged by Mass attendance (375 in 1997) it ranks as one of the larger parishes in the diocese.

Churchdown's rapid wartime expansion began with the influx of workers in the nearby aircraft component industry, and its Catholic element particularly by the evacuation from Birmingham of the staff and 200 pupils of a Catholic school. Mass was said in Churchdown on the first day of the war, offered by the parish priest of St. Peter, Gloucester, in the Assembly Room of the Chosen Hotel. Thereafter Churchdown was served variously from Gloucester, by the Benedictines of Prinknash, and by the Salesians of Blaisdon Hall. The Mass centre was moved first to the skittle alley of a local public house and, towards the end of the war, to the Sandycroft Social Club. Here a setback occurred when the main hall of the club was destroyed by fire, and with it the altar and other furnishings which had come from the chapel of Hartpury House. The club was able to continue to provide accommodation until the completion in 1954 of the conversion of brick barn buildings to a church where the first Mass was said in that year with a congregation of 192.

In 1992 the church, by then in a poor state of repair, was replaced by one of the most unconventional and effective compositions in the diocese. The line of its rectangular form is broken only by a gable symmetrically placed over its entrance (illustrated on the cover of the 1993 diocesan yearbook). Unusually the alignment of the sanctuary and the rectangular deployment of benches around it emphasise the narrow axis of the building rather than its length. Four coloured ornamental windows of conventional design contrast with, and in an otherwise unornamented interior compete with, a remarkable icon painted above the altar by Sr. Petra Clare, a well-known iconographer. Its unusual blue background was chosen to relieve the dark red brick of the walls. An account of the icon and its complex symbolism by Sr. Petra Clare appears in Journal 28 of the Gloucestershire Catholic History Society. The single story presbytery and St. Mary's primary school are nearby. While they make no claims to architectural distinction, they combine with the church to form a spatially attractive Catholic enclave.

In 1997 the death occurred of Miss Lillian Bell, who had been associated with the parish since the days of the Second World War. She was a devoted servant of the parish and deeply interested in its history. Through her initiative a brick was recovered from the Chosen Hotel when it was demolished, and incorporated into the structure of the new church – a tangible link with the formative days of Churchdown parish.

J.A.F.

Coleford, Gloucestershire: St. Margaret Mary; Cinderford, Gloucestershire: Our Lady of Victories

In recusant times Catholicism in the area of the Forest of Dean was marginal to its very strong presence in Monmouthshire and the Borders, and for a long time after the dioceses were founded it continued to look to Cardiff rather than Clifton. As late as 1924 Mrs. Radclyffe of St. Briavels, who then maintained a mission in her house which was served from there, wanted it to be part of the Cardiff archdiocese. Until recently the Forest was wild and remote. Much of what we know of it in the early days of the Clifton diocese comes from the recollections of Fr. Thomas Abbot, a nephew of Bishop Burgess, who was granted missionary facilities there in 1855. Throughout his long service of forty years he was much concerned that the Forest might be by-passed by Clifton. He described his flock as 'a few old native Catholics, and poor Irish labourers who come to the Forest coal pits when work is slack in Wales'. Soon after his appointment he supported a petition from fifty-one Catholics in the Coleford area which said that they had no place of worship nearer than Gloucester and no funds for a school for the thirty children there. A poor school was established there in 1852 and, supported by a predominantly Baptist local community, seems to have flourished briefly. Thirty-one attended in the following year, about half of them Catholic, but many inaccessible Catholic children were 'running about in the Forest'. Problems of accessibility and distance dogged Catholicism in the Forest until the next century. Fr. Abbot established a station for occasional Mass at the Indulgences at a farmhouse near Coleford, owned by Mr. George Morgan, a nephew of a rector of Oscott. According to Fr. Abbot, after Morgan obtained a papal rescript for a private oratory there he closed the door on the local Catholic population. The next owner seems to have been more generous and Mass was again celebrated there, in what was rather ungratefully termed a closet. The arrangement did not last. For a short time in the 1890s Coleford was served by the chaplain at Courtfield, and Canon Chard of Gloucester officiated in emergencies, sometimes going as far as Lydney. In 1896, two years after his retirement, Fr. Abbot introduced an Italian priest, Fr. Coletti, to Coleford. In his brief and unhappy stay he found few Catholics, no money and no centre, and, in contrast to the climate of thirty years before, encountered bigotry.

The twentieth century saw an improvement with some individual initiatives. Mass was celebrated at St. Briavels from 1911 to 1928, and in 1910 the convert Miss Gwenllian Myers, with the powerful support of Dom Bede Camm, obtained permission for Mass at Eastbach Court. Less fortunately, in 1930 two former members of an Anglican order established a school at Coleford and with it an oratory served from Monmouth. Their standing in the Catholic church and the integrity of the school's prospectus were gravely suspect and they soon went.

Permanent arrangements in the Forest began in 1930 with the appointment as parish priest at Coleford of Fr. Andrew Waters, and in 1933 the church of St. Margaret Mary, a modest building built by local labour, was opened. He also celebrated Mass in a room in the Swan Hotel in Cinderford. The privations of those early days are vividly, and idiosyncratically, recalled in a *History of how the Faith came back to the Forest of Dean*, a testament of unsophisticated piety by George Hare (1891–1967), who although totally impoverished worked indefatigably for the infant parishes. For a time the Salesians of Blaisdon Hall served Cinderford, and shortly before the outbreak of war the Oblates of Mary Immaculate took over. They continue to serve the Forest to the present day. The spacious neo-Gothic church of Our Lady of Victories was opened at Cinderford in 1939. In the same year the Sisters of Our Lady of Hope, a branch of the Holy Family Sisters of Bordeaux, took over Abbotswood House at Cinderford as an evacuation centre, and ran it as a nursing home until 1956. In 1960 the Franciscan Sisters of the Immaculate Conception arrived to occupy the former presbytery, where they opened a school which, with buildings much extended, is now St. Anthony's Convent, an independent junior school.

George Hare was probably right in saying that 'this is the largest mission [*sic*] in the United Kingdom, with its flock scattered all over the place'.

Cirencester: former chapel of the Immaculate Conception (1855) *Mr. J. K. Vose*

As soon as he arrived Fr. Waters had become chaplain to Beachley Camp, where Mass was said until the mid-1980s. A church was built there in 1962 by the Ministry of Public Building and Works. By then Coleford's responsibilities included Sedbury, where the Sacred Heart Chapel was opened in 1988, and Cinderford looked after Micheldean, Newnham-on-Severn and Lydney. Lydney became the largest Mass centre, with congregations of 100 attending Mass in the coffee bar of a hotel and confessions heard in a cloakroom. The much needed Church of St. Joseph was opened at Highfield Hill, Lydney, in 1977.

J.A.F.

Cirencester, Gloucestershire: St. Peter

Until the 1850s Cirencester was part of the Fairford mission. A survey of about 1847 named eight Cirencester Catholics who went there. When Fr. Glassbrook moved from Fairford in 1851 (see the account of Fairford below) he built a chapel, which became his own property, on what was then the outskirts of Cirencester. It still stands, now adapted to commercial uses. It was described severally as 'a neat little Gothic edifice' and (by a later Bishop of Clifton) as 'very miserable, hardly to be called anything but a pigsty'. It was opened with considerable ceremony in 1855, dedicated to the Immaculate Conception, defined in the previous year by Pius IX.

Fr. Glassbrook had a difficult time in Cirencester, and resigned in 1857. Bishop Clifford was concerned about the financial management of the mission and left it to him to dispose of the chapel. It was closed in 1858 and used for industrial purposes. For a time the mission, now served by the Dominicans of Woodchester, used temporary accommodation so poor that it deterred the congregation. Consequently in 1861 the chapel was rented back from Fr. Glassbrook: renting arrangements continued until the present church was built. In 1862 the Dominicans recorded a congregation of forty-four and a modestly successful financial year, but held out no hope of continuing. The prospect of their withdrawal prompted a pious and wealthy Chilean student at the Agricultural College to offer £20 p.a., a substantial part of the mission's income, to ensure that Mass was not lost to Cirencester. Thereafter the mission was served by a rapid succession of priests until the arrival in 1894 of Fr. James Aloysius Martin, in whose time the church of St. Peter was built.

Successive surveys showed an increase in the Catholic population of Cirencester to eighty-four in 1876 and over 100 ten years later; almost all of them poor and predominantly of Irish origin. The idea of another church was mooted as early as 1863, when a plot of land was bought with money given by the Chilean, and plans for a new and large church prepared. They were quite disproportionate to the resources of the parish and nothing came of them. The matter was reactivated some twenty years later and led to the purchase of a new site near the middle of the town. £500 towards it was given by Canon John Mitchell, who half a century before had done much for the Fairford mission, and now, in his eighties, was the parish priest of Taunton. In 1892 he said that had he known what difficulties there had been at Cirencester he would have helped earlier.

The church was built by the diocesan architect, Canon A.J.C. Scoles: nave, sanctuary, sacristy and western gallery in competent Early English. It was opened in 1896 by Bishop Brownlow at a service with the homily preached by the Prior of Woodchester. The Bishop said that he would be happy to consecrate the church; in fact it was consecrated by his successor four times removed in its centenary year of 1996.

The 20th century has seen a growth from 130 in 1896 to 390 Mass attendances in 1997. During the First World War it saw a short-lived influx of Belgian refugees, and in 1939–45 a Polish community was established in Cirencester. It is remembered in the dedication in 1997 of a window by the Nailsworth artist Graham Dowding, which is named after St. Maximilian Kolbe, a Polish priest who died at Auschwitz in 1941. Many of the changes of recent years coincided with the long pastorate (1953–1987) of Fr. John O'Donnell, who did much to foster the ecumenical spirit of the times. It is a spirit faithfully reflected in the centenary celebrations, which included a joint service with the neighbouring Methodist church, which was also founded 100 years previously. At one centenary service the homily was given by Fr. Graham Leonard, a former Anglican Bishop of London.

In 1939 the Sisters of the Poor Handmaids of Jesus Christ, a teaching order, established a convent in Chesterton House, a one-time country residence in Cirencester, and in September of that year opened a school with about 120 pupils aged between $3\frac{1}{2}$ and 17. A new wing was opened in 1954, and in 1960 the school was recognised by the Ministry of Education as efficient, but increasing costs finally led to its closure in 1973 with the transfer of the few remaining sisters to the provincial house at Hendon.

J.A.F.

Clevedon, Somerset: The Immaculate Conception

In 1880 religious orders were being expelled from France and a community of French Franciscans found refuge in the disused Dominican convent of St. Catherine, Park Place, Clifton, offered to them by Bishop Clifford. In 1882 the Friars moved to Portland House, Wellington Terrace, Clevedon to start a new mission, and their chapel was open to the public when the first Sunday Mass was celebrated on 14 July. The congregation numbered five, being the total number of Catholics known to be living in the town at that time.

Portland House soon became too small as more Friars arrived from France, so it was sold and the Royal Hotel purchased for £3,800 with money promised by friends in France. The first Mass was celebrated in the Royal Hotel, which had become the Franciscan Friary on 18 February 1883. In February 1884 *The Tablet* reported that 'fire destroyed the room over the cellar which was the Chapter room and private chapel, and that the community at that time comprised thirty-seven friars'. They had hardly settled into their new home when they decided to build a small church at nearby Portishead, which was served by a priest from Clevedon until 1906.

Increasing numbers attending Clevedon Friary created the strong feeling that a church should be erected in the ample grounds of the Royal Hotel. Overcoming initial difficulties from the local council the foundation stone was laid on 16 February 1887. The architect was Canon Scoles and the builder James Hillier Kitch. The cost was £3,000, subscribed mainly by the Tertiaries of Amiens in thanksgiving for the hospitality given to the French Franciscans. In 1902 members of the English Province replaced them, and in 1925 a generous legacy of £18,000 from Mr. Erasmus Smith, a parishioner, enabled the community to transform the interior of the old hotel to a suitable Friary.

A Mass centre was set up in a private house in **Yatton** but, very soon, the numbers became too big for this, and an arrangement was made with the Claverham British Legion in 1935 to hire their wooden hall on Sunday mornings and Holy days. In times of petrol rationing, a local car hire firm transported the priest to Mass, but for all other visits (catechism classes and similar) the friars had to cycle regular twenty-mile round trips. In the early 1960s the hut was sold to the parish and the **chapel-of-ease**, named **St. Dunstan and St. Anthony** after local and Franciscan saints respectively, was established.

Another rapidly developing area was **Nailsea** and in 1936 a regular Sunday Mass was celebrated in the Royal Oak Hotel. During the war Clevedon also provided a Sunday Mass and pastoral care at **R.A.F. Locking** in Weston-super-Mare. In 1974 negotiations with the Anglican diocese enabled Mass to be celebrated in the church of St. John at the other end of the parish and this continued for several years.

In 1937 the church was rewired and redecorated at a cost of £1,600, but the days of the old Royal Hotel were numbered, and it raised much resentment when plans were announced for its demolition in order to build a new Friary next to the church. The project went ahead, however, and the new building was opened in 1978 with some of the land being used for housing.

Clevedon has been home to several congregations of Sisters over the years: first the Franciscan Sisters (1887–1911), then the La Retraite sisters arrived in 1904, leaving in 1924 to take over St. Joseph's Academy for Young Ladies in Clifton. This became La Retraite High School for Girls, closed in 1982 when St. Brendan's Sixth Form College was established. In 1936 the Sisters of Mercy purchased the premises of the former Royal York Hotel in which they founded a boarding school. This later became St. Anthony's private infant and primary school which closed in 1993.

The Mass Centre at **Nailsea** became the parish of **St. Francis of Assisi** in 1982, but Clevedon continues to serve **SS Dunstan and Anthony** at **Yatton** and the **Chapel of Christ the King** at **R.A.F. Locking**, The R.A.F. station will be transferred to Cosford in 1999 and this ecumenical chapel will be closed early that year, but Fr. Maurice Ryan O.F.M., appointed chaplain in 1996, will continue to celebrate Mass in another chapel on the site and carry out all the other duties of chaplain.

V.A.

Corsham, Wiltshire: St. Patrick

The church was built in 1848 as Pickwick School on land given two years earlier by Lord Methuen and his tenants. The purpose was 'for the education of children and adults of the poorer classes of the labouring and manufacturing people in the district of Pickwick'. It was to be conducted in accordance with the principles and practice of the Established Church.

The architect was Henry Edmund Goodridge of Bath who exhibited the design at the Royal Academy in 1857. The school, as built, is illustrated in the stained glass windows to Sir Gabriel Goldney in Chippenham Parish Church. The building was designed in the Victorian Gothic style with gables and a bell tower and had therefore an ecclesiastical aspect from the outset. By 1928 the state of the building coupled with a fall in the population at the end of the Great War caused the trustees to sell the building at a price of £900. After a gap of some years the building became first a glove factory and then, when war again threatened, a gas mask factory.

Before the Second World War Corsham was a village of some 3,000 people with, it is believed, only one practising Catholic. The war, however, brought about a major change as the three armed services established units there. The Ministry of Works took over the vast disused, underground quarries, and spent over £40 million turning them into ammunition storage depots, factories, and radar and signal stations, with the result that the population increased to over 32,000. A large number of workers building the new depots were Irish and Bishop Lee requested McAlpines to provide a large temporary Mass centre at Neston which was served from Melksham.

Soon it became necessary to open a Mass centre in Corsham itself. Fr. (later Canon) Denis Ryan of Chippenham celebrated Mass in the British Legion, then in Priory Hall and then in a wooden hut in Fuller Avenue. Meanwhile the workers collected £1,000 for a permanent Mass centre.

In 1944 the disused gas mask factory in Bath Road at Pickwick was on the market for £800. It was in a deplorable state but had spacious grounds and great possibilities. Bishop Lee purchased the building which he blessed and opened on 17 April 1945. Not unnaturally it was dedicated to St. Patrick. One Mass was said each Sunday by visiting priests from Chippenham until 23 September 1957 when Fr. (now Canon) John Supple was appointed first resident parish priest and remained for the next nineteen years. Initially he stayed at Mrs. Eden's house in Pickwick and later at Miss Sheppard's of Meriton Avenue. He then lived for a while in a cottage attached to the church.

A debt of £1,000 was paid off and new stained glass windows, seats, pulpit, altar rails and carpet were acquired. The church was enlarged to take in the whole ground floor of the old school and a new presbytery was completed in 1959.

A parish school was opened early in 1964 on a site at Pound Hill, taking pupils from Melksham, Lacock and other villages.

J.A.H.

Cothay Manor, Somerset: See Wellington

Corston, Bath, Somerset: St. Teresa's Nursing Home: See Keynsham

Crewkerne, Somerset: St. Peter: Served from Chard

Cricklade, Wiltshire: St. Mary: Served from Fairford

Devizes, Wiltshire: Immaculate Conception

The chain of events that followed the early frustrations of Captain Dewell's attempt to establish the Malmesbury mission (see p. 142) meant that the focus of the Fransalian mission moved from Chippenham to Devizes. There Mrs. Ann Davis, a resident, rented a warehouse where Mass was first celebrated in 1861, with a congregation of seven. Dewell had intended that two Sisters of St. Joseph of Annecy should come from India to Malmesbury. When this proved impossible he arranged for them to go to Devizes, buying two houses, Windham Villas, there, and providing for their support. There they were to support the Fransalians and run a 'poor school'.

A temporary chapel was built in 1862 on land which was named St. Joseph's Place. It was superseded by the Church of the Immaculate Conception, built by J. A. Hansom, which was opened in 1865. Of the nave, chancel and aisles originally planned only the nave was then built. It was extended in 1909 and again in 1995. The school moved to the now vacant chapel building. From the fourteen pupils of the original 'poor school' it had expanded to ninety-three by 1893. The present St. Joseph's primary school has 200 pupils.

The Fransalians and the Sisters of St. Joseph have an unbroken record of service to Devizes to the present day. The direct influence of Annecy lasted for nearly a century: it was not until the appointment of Fr. Alexander Daley in 1947 that Devizes was not served by a Frenchman. Annecy's influence at Devizes is still real. The association of the Fransalians with England stemmed from their mission to India: today an Indian Fransalian, Fr. Bernard Caszo, is the parish priest of Devizes. He is one of the four Indian priests now attached to the English province.

The growth of Catholicism in the Devizes area has seen the opening of a second church in the town and a church at West Lavington (see below), and the expansion of Mass centres at Marlborough and Pewsey into the separate parish of Marlborough. There were Mass centres at West Stowell until 1964, at Ogbourne Maizey until 1971, and at Upavon until 1990. The Mass attendance at the three Devizes churches is now nearly 500.

Devizes: St. Francis de Sales

The church of St. Francis de Sales was opened in May 1960 – almost exactly a century after Fr. Francis Larive's arrival in England. It stands in the middle of an extensive housing estate in the eastern part of the town. It was designed by the local architects Rendell and West in traditional brickwork but with an interior in a contemporary style characterised by a bronze relief of the Last Supper forming a part of the altar. It is served from the church of the Immaculate Conception.

Lavington, Wiltshire: St. Joseph

The needs of the Catholic community around West Lavington and nearby villages were recognised before the Second World War when Joseph Sainsbury came to live there in retirement. At first accommodation was provided in a small cottage; its limitations led him to expand his own house for a Mass centre serving a congregation of about sixteen. The influx of soldiery in the war meant successive makeshift arrangements for a community which was still enlarged after the Army went. Finally the Methodist church in Littleton Pannell was bought and converted into St. Joseph's church, where the first Mass was celebrated in 1971.

J.A.F.

Dinton, Wiltshire: See Tisbury and Wardour

Downend: See Bristol: St. Augustine of Canterbury

Downside Abbey: Stratton-on-the-Fosse, Somerset

The Benedictine community of St. Gregory, now at Downside, originated in the seventeenth century when a group of English monks, and a school for English boys, was accommodated and endowed at Douai by Phillip de Caverel, Abbot of Arras. From its earliest days it included men of distinction: John Roberts and Ambrose Barlow, two of the Forty Martyrs canonised in 1970; Dom Leander Jones, a Hebraist who arrived in London in 1634 as papal agent; Michael Ellis, the first Vicar Apostolic of the Western District; and Charles Walmesley, a mathematician of distinction and FRS, who was successor of Ellis as Vicar Apostolic in 1764, was an old boy of Douai.

A community that had survived the sieges of Louis XIV and then of Marlborough was ravaged by the French Revolution. It was rescued by a former pupil of the school, Sir Edward Smythe, who accommodated it at his seat Acton Burnell in Shropshire until Downside, twelve miles south-west of Bath, was acquired in 1814. The original building survives in the heart of the school.

Building began with a chapel in 1823, but the early days of the community were not easy. Bishop Baines, coadjutor in the Western District, was conscious of the fact that the Western District, alone of the four districts, had no seminary for educating its future priests and this was proving a great drawback to progress in the district. The Bishop, a member of the Benedictine Order, met Dr. Marsh, a former President of the Order, in August 1823 and outlined to him his views on the desirability of establishing a seminary at Downside to serve the Western District. At the outset Dr. Marsh appeared to be enthusiastic about the proposal, but expressed his fears there would be some opposition from other members of the Order. This proved to be true. Although the Bishop explained that there would have to be a college and a seminary for the Western District, and it would most certainly be established in the neighbourhood of Bath, his proposal was rejected.

The controversy over the establishment of the seminary at Downside soured relations between the Bishop and the Order to such an extent that he was not invited to the four-yearly Chapter Meeting which was held at Downside in July 1826, although, as a member of the order, he was entitled to attend. When Bishop Baines succeeded Bishop Collingridge in 1829 he withdrew faculties from the monks on the grounds that the monastery had never been canonically established. However, in April 1830, a decree from Rome validated this and Bishop Baines restored faculties to the monks who applied for them. An early entrant to the community had been the future Archbishop Ullathorne. His reading list reflects the beginning of the tradition of scholarship at Downside, which in 1841 became affiliated to the fledgling University of London.

In 1878 the future Cardinal Aidan Gasquet, at the age of thirty-two, became Prior of a small community already confident enough to initiate the building of a church comparable with the great Benedictine abbeys of medieval England. Its foundation stone was laid in 1873. Through its diocesan Bishop Clifford, Downside took the lead in petitioning the Holy See for an investigation of the form of government of the English Benedictine Congregation, which many felt to be biased in favour of missionary work in the parishes to the detriment of the conventual life. In 1914, the centenary year of the arrival of the community in England, Gasquet, who had been Prior from 1878 to 1885, was raised to the Cardinalate. If his reputation as an accurate historian has not survived untarnished he remains a major figure in Downside's history as Librarian of the Holy Roman Church and as a member of the commission set up by Pope Leo XIII to investigate the validity of Anglican orders.

The long-standing tradition of scholarship at Downside saw in 1880 the inauguration of the influential *Downside Review*. In the 1890s a small monastic group was set up near the British Museum with the layman liturgical scholar Edmund Bishop, whose permanent memorial is his bequest which forms an important part of today's library of international standing. Dom Hugh Connolly, a Syriac scholar who became a member of the faculty of oriental studies at Cambridge; Abbot Leander Ramsay, the editor of St. Cyprian; Dom Ethelbert Horne, the archaeologist of Somerset; and Abbot Cuthbert Butler, historian of the First Vatican Council, were members of a community broad in its intellectual outlook: the patristic scholar Armitage Robinson, Dean of Wells, was a frequent visitor. Three abbots from the 1920s had been ordained in the Anglican Church. A later generation saw Dom David Knowles as an exclaustrated monk the first religious since the reformation to occupy a chair at Cambridge. A prolific author, his *Monastic Orders in England* (1940), which was followed by *The Religious Orders in England (1948–59)*, established him in the forefront of medieval historians. *The Spiritual Letters of John Chapman* (Abbot from 1929 to 1933) continues to hold its place among modern classics of the spiritual life.

Basil Christopher Butler (1902–1986) was Abbot from 1946 to 1966. A convert, he served the school and community successively as lay master, monk, headmaster and abbot. He attended the Second Vatican Council in his capacity as Abbot President of the English Benedictine Congregation. Appointed a *peritus* (expert) and a member of the Theological Commission, he is credited with having played a major part in drawing up the document on the Dogmatic Constitution of the Church (*Lumen Gentium*). On his appointment in 1966 as auxiliary bishop of Westminster he took up residence at St. Edmund's College, Ware. During the heated debate which followed the publication of *Humanae Vitae* (1968) reaffirming the Church's ban on artificial contraception, Butler acted behind the scenes as a moderating influence especially among those Catholics who had been disappointed by the papal ruling.

From the seven boys who arrived at Acton Burnell in 1814 Downside School had grown to about sixty boys by the mid-century, a school 'small and stagnant' in Dom David Knowles' judgement. Progress towards its present standing was marked by two early influences: the generous if unconventional support of Mgr. (the thirteenth), Lord Petre in the seventies, and the appointment as headmaster in 1902 of the future abbot, Dom Leander Ramsay, formerly in Anglican orders who moved it towards the then accepted model of an English public school.

A tragic event in its later history was the death of nine boys and the pilot when an aircraft crashed on the cricket field on 15 May 1943. Thirty-three others were seriously injured. A musical tradition encouraged by the organist and composer Dom Gregory Murray has made school and abbey familiar to a wide public. Murray's recitals on the Compton organ in the abbey became famous. Recently a recording of Gregorian chant and polyphonic motets by school and community had vied successfully for popular acclaim with music of very different genres.

St. Gregory's Priory, Downside was raised to the status of an abbey in 1900 and the church was made a minor basilica in 1935, the year in which it was consecrated by Cardinal Seredi, O.S.B. the last Prince Primate of Hungary. The Basilica of St. Gregory the Great, the largest monastic church in England, is an important example of revived Gothic architecture. Pevsner described it as 'the most splendid demonstration of the renaissance of Roman Catholicism in England'. The design of the abbey church is a successful blend of work by several architects: the transept by Dunn and Hansom in 1882; the choir by Garner in 1905 and the nave by Scott in 1925. Dunn and Hansom planned a spire and between 1881 and 1884 a base was built up to the belfry at 132 feet. In 1938 Scott transformed this into a fine tower 'in the best tradition of Somerset', 166 feet to the pinnacles.

In the abbey church itself are many features of note. The central altar is made of Doulting stone from Glastonbury Abbey, donated by the Trustees. The altar in the north transept served as the original high altar. It has ornate carvings on the reredos representing biblical events relating to the mystery of the Holy Eucharist, the Old Testament on the left and the New Testament on the right. Adjacent is a casket containing some of the remains of the martyr St. Oliver Plunkett (Archbishop of Armagh 1669–1681). The choir stalls are a replica of those in Chester Cathedral which date from the late fourteenth century. Behind the stalls, to the south, is the tomb of Cardinal Gasquet (1846–1929). The art deco design is by Sir Giles Gilbert Scott, and above is suspended the cardinal's red hat. In the groined vault of the nave there are fifty-four bosses, each bearing the coat of arms of a pre-dissolution English Benedictine abbey or priory. The west front of the abbey church has still to be completed.

The Abbeys of Ealing and Worth were founded from Downside which also serves the parishes of Bruton, Chilcompton, Holcombe, Midsomer Norton, Norton St. Philip, Paulton, Radstock, Shepton Mallet and Stratton-on-the-Fosse.

Downton, Wiltshire: Served from Salisbury St. Osmund

Dulverton, Somerset: St. Stanislaus

The present church of St. Stanislaus was established during the Second World War. This was due mainly to the initiative of Mrs. Aubrey Herbert of Pixton Park. The old laundry close to her house was converted into a spacious chapel and was first served by a visiting priest. This arrangement lasted until 1944 and the coming of Fr. (later Canon) O'Brien who resided in a cottage on the estate. In September 1945 Mrs. Herbert contacted Professor Albert Richardson, a distinguished architect, over the building of a new church at Dulverton, Professor Richardson later became President of the Royal Academy but as he was a close friend of Mrs. Herbert he gave his services gratis. After an extended search for a site a disused stable on the High Street came on the market. This building was skilfully adapted by Richardson and opened in 1955.

The church contains a number of furnishings from the Pixton chapel. These include the sanctuary lamp, an Eric Gill crucifix suspended in front of the altar and the Portugese reredos behind it. The Lady Chapel has a copy of the icon of Vladimir. The statue of St. Stanislaus is sixteenth century Hungarian and stands on a plinth on which is carved an inscription to a former parish priest, Fr. (later Canon) Ronald MacDonald. Two two circular windows were made at Buckfast Abbey. The window on the left contains a panel by the Irish stained-glass artist Evie Hone.

The dedication of the church to St. Stanislaus of Cracow, patron saint of Poland and martyr, is probably unique among dedications of parish churches in England. This association is due to Auberon Herbert, Mrs. Herbert's son, who fought alongside the Polish forces during the Second World War. In peacetime he devoted his energies to the resettlement of Polish servicemen who were unable to return to their native land. The parish is geographically one of the largest in the diocese and has one of the smallest congregations.

Fr. Philip Caraman S.J. (1911–1998), the distinguished historian of English and Welsh Catholicism, was parish priest at Dulverton from 1986 until his death in 1998. Fr. Caraman was editor of *The Month*, Vice-Postulator, Cause of English and Welsh Martyrs 1965–1968 and Professor of Church History, St. Edmund's Ware 1968–1970. He was a parish priest in Norway from 1976 to 1979. A selection from his many writings is given in the Bibliography.

K.McG.

Durrington, Wiltshire: Our Lady: Served from Amesbury

Dursley, Gloucestershire: St. Dominic

In the 1850s there were fifteen Catholics at Dursley, whose urgent spiritual needs were supplied from Woodchester, who had to walk the five miles to Nympsfield to the nearest Mass centre. This proved very difficult. Suggestions that a house, and later a Methodist chapel, might be converted for Catholic worship at Dursley came to nothing, and it was not until early in the First World War that Mass was first said there, reputedly in a converted barn in Broadwell Lane. After the War the local Catholic population fell sharply and in 1920 the Dominican Provincial closed the missions at Dursley and the nearby Wotton-under-Edge. Catholicism in Dursley revived with the arrival of workers at the engineering firm of Lister. In 1932 a petition for a Mass centre gained forty signatures, and in 1933 Mass was once more said at Dursley, served from Nympsfield, in a hall loaned for the purpose by the local YMCA. The primitive arrangements there earned the adverse comments of the convert novelist Evelyn Waugh, then resident at Piers Court, a house in the parish. Mrs. Robert Lister, the Catholic wife of the Protestant head of the engineering firm, was active in fund-raising, and in 1938 the diocesan trustees purchased a site on the Jubilee Road in Dursley. The foundation stone of the church of St. Dominic was laid in that year and it was opened in February 1939.

The Second World War saw a further influx of Catholics. Dominican nuns came to occupy Piers Court, and later Italians came from a nearby prisoner-of-war camp. The congregation became still more cosmopolitan after the war and was said to include seventeen different nationalities. In 1961 Mass was said according to the Byzantine rite at St. Dominic.

The first resident priest, Fr. Littleton Powys, was appointed in 1950. He had previously been in Anglican orders and Principal of St. Stephen's House, Oxford. When in 1955 the chapel of Our Lady of Czestochowa at Babdown Camp was closed St. Dominic was given its altar cloth. In 1957 the parish hall, built by volunteer labour, was completed, and a purpose-built school opened in 1959. After the arrival of Fr. Philip Smyth as parish priest in 1995 the presbytery and parish hall were refurbished, and the sanctuary re-ordered. The church was dedicated by Bishop Alexander in 1997, nearly sixty years after it opened.

J.A.F.

East Harptree, Somerset: See Chew Magna

Fairford, Gloucestershire: St. Thomas of Canterbury

The antecedents of Catholicism in Fairford are found at nearby Hatherop, where a branch of the well-known Webb family occupied Hatherop Castle, a centre of recusancy since Elizabeth's day. The last resident priest, Fr. Francis Leigh, died there in 1831. Thereafter Barbara, Lady de Mauley, a Webb descendant married to an Anglican, provided for Mass to be said there by visiting priests. One of them was deranged, and so antagonised her husband Lord de Mauley, who himself was already committed to substantial benefactions, that he indignantly repulsed Bishop Baines' approaches for further support. It was Fr. (later Canon) John Mitchell, the young parish priest of Chipping Norton, who retrieved the situation: the first of several important services he was to give Clifton diocese during a long life. He came to help Fairford at the request of his own Vicar Apostolic in 1841, after having declined an invitation from Bishop Baines. Once a month he travelled the eleven miles to Fairford, sometimes starting at 5 o'clock. Hatherop Castle being closed to him he was, in his own words, 'driven from one cottage to another amidst the insults of the people and the Parson', on occasion being reduced to sitting on empty bags under a tree to hear confessions. By force of character and example he won Lord de Mauley round, persuading him to continue his late wife's payment of £40 per annum which was a vital part of the income of an impoverished mission.

In 1843 he received into the Church Richard Iles, a local farmer, and his wife Dorothy. They founded an important local Catholic hierarchy which included Mgr. Richard and Fr. Daniel Iles. With their help he provided the funds for building the present church, which became his own property. It is said to be a replica of a Pugin building. It was opened in 1845, when the congregation numbered fifty to sixty. The Iles family and their relatives continued generous benefactors throughout the century.

Fr. Mitchell stayed at Fairford until 1846. For a time thereafter the church was served by the Passionists of Woodchester, but they proved irregular, and by 1849 Iles was finding the situation so unsatisfactory that he considered moving elsewhere. It was an impoverished mission. In 1848 Fr. Thomas Tierney Fergusson, an Oxford convert, stayed only briefly as he found the means of support inadequate, and returned to London; Fr. Reilly, probably from a different background, thought the same. In 1853 Fr. Edwin Anselm Glassbrook, a Benedictine serving under the Bishop as a diocesan priest, was appointed to Fairford. He continued there until 1857, but in the meanwhile moved the focus of the mission to Cirencester, where he considered the prospects of success to be greater. Thereafter the Fairford mission, which in its earlier days had provided the only church for about twenty miles around, became less centrally important. Swindon, with some thirty sadly neglected Catholic families, was thought to be a better prospect, and in 1857 Fr. James Clark, previously vice-rector of the English College at Valladolid, was appointed to take care of both from Swindon. In 1863 Fr. Peter Seddon came from Swindon to Fairford. In his time benefactions from the Iles and from Joseph Garcia, the Chilean student who did much for Cirencester, built the presbytery and also a school. This, however, met with little success. In 1876 only seven out of an attendance of twenty-five were Catholics. It closed in 1888. The parish remained small throughout the nineteenth century: the diocesan return of 1894 recorded fifty-six Catholics in Fairford, and the parish priest said then that fourteen had fallen away from the practice of their religion, though seven others were potential converts.

Fairford was served by an unusually rapid succession of resident priests, not all of whom proved satisfactory. With the exception of Mgr. Edgar English, who was at Fairford from 1895 to 1910 and died in post there, none stayed long. Before coming to the Clifton diocese he had been Rector of the English College in Rome. From 1922 to 1927 Fairford was again served from Swindon and the presbytery occupied by a tenant. It was not until the long incumbency of Fr. Edmund MacSweeney (1932–1963) that expansion (and wartime disruption) came to the parish. Nearly a thousand Irish were employed in the construction of Fairford airfield, and over a thousand Poles came to live in a hostel in Fairford Park. Both communities left their mark in the church: the Poles gave a portrait of Our Lady of Czestchowa and the Irish a window with a portrait of St. Patrick. The United States servicemen at Fairford airfield showed their appreciation of Fr. MacSweeney in a more direct way by giving him a holiday in America where he met Cardinal Spellman, the Archbishop of New York. Today the Mass attendance is about 250: the church of St. Mary, Cricklade and (at the time of writing) the former convent chapel at Lechlade are now served from Fairford.

Cricklade, Wiltshire: St. Mary

Cricklade was formerly part of the parish of St. Peter, Cirencester. Catholicism at Cricklade had modest beginnings. During the Second World War Mass was said, mainly for servicemen, in an old building in Gas Lane. Later a Nissen hut was used, and after it the Town Hall. From 1946 local needs were also met at the chapel of the preparatory department of Prior Park school, which was served by the Congregation of the Irish Christian Brothers (who stayed there until 1980). In the fifties an old chapel, now the Cricklade museum, was opened as a church, dedicated to St. Augustine. In 1984 a major development took place, of a kind so far very rare in the annals of Catholicism in this country, when the diocese acquired a hundred-year lease of the Anglican church of St. Mary in Cricklade, which had been declared redundant in 1981. Though much restored it remained, and in external appearance still remains, a fine example of a medieval parish church. Mass was said there in 1984 for the first time since the sixteenth century. At that time Cricklade became part of Fairford parish. Some sixty now attend Mass there. In 1998 the Friends of St. Mary's, Cricklade were inaugurated with the blessing of the Bishop of Clifton and of the Anglican Bishop of Bristol.

Lechlade, Gloucestershire: Convent chapel of the Annunciation

In 1939 the Congregation of St. Clotilde acquired Lechlade Manor for their boarding school, at that time at Eltham. The Congregation was founded in Paris in 1821, and is especially devoted to the education of girls. The dining room of the manor became the chapel, and Mass was first celebrated very shortly before the war. In 1960 the chapel of Our Lady of the Annunciation was built. Its exterior was designed to blend with the manor, but the interior was strikingly original, with wide-span arches supporting a vaulted ceiling, its most distinctive feature. The altar was a single slab of Cotswold stone. At that time there were then about eighty Catholics in the vicinity; because of Lechlade's location they came from four counties and three dioceses. A former Master of the Guild of Our Lady of Ransom, Mgr. Laurence Goulder, is buried there.

The Congregation's house at Lechlade, their only one in Britain, was closed in 1998, and shortly after it was announced that the school was to come to an end. The future of its chapel is in doubt.

J.A.F.

Fairford, Gloucestershire: St. James

After the Second World War the United States Air Force made intermit-
tent use of the airfield at Fairford. Since 1979 they have been there continuously. The parish of St. James is centred there. Until 1950 it was served
by U.S. chaplains. Then they were replaced by English priests; an arrangement which continued until 1998. Since then the parish has been served
from St. Thomas of Canterbury, Fairford.

J.A.F.

Filton: See Bristol: St. Teresa

Fishponds: See Bristol: St. Joseph

Frenchay: See Bristol: St. John Fisher

Frome, Somerset: St. Catharine

The parish comprises: Frome, the villages of Beckington, Rode, Mells,
Nunney, Wanstrow, Witham Friary (where St. Hugh of Lincoln had spent
six years as a Carthusian monk) and several nearby hamlets.

During penal times the Catholic centre of the present parish was at
Nunney Castle where, until the Civil War siege of 1645, there was the
attendance of a Catholic chaplain. A further development occurred in the
1790s when two émigré priests came to Frome to escape the French
Revolution. Another French priest, Henri Goudemetz, stayed at Chatley
House, five miles from Frome. He used to say Mass in the private chapel
of 'a fervent English Catholic' Mrs. Porter who was a sister of Lady Fermor.

In January 1850 two Catholics, Elisha Dowling of Titherington and his
wife, set up a new grocery store at Frome. They prospered and soon a
Downside priest was visiting the town and saying Mass in a room at their
house at the corner of Milk Street and Selwood Road. The visits of Dom
John Placid Hall (who had been ordained in 1844) were to arouse an outburst of virulent anti-Catholicism in the town. A local minister, the Rev.
T. Corbett, arranged a course of lectures in the schoolroom of Ebenezer
Chapel. Posters displayed in the town announced that he would 'expose
the Blasphemies, Arrogancies, Jesuitical Sophisms, and refute the Dogmas
advanced, or that may be advanced, by that limb of ANTICHRIST called a
priest, in his Lectures at his rooms in Naish's Street, Frome'. The first of
Corbett's lectures was on 1 January 1852. A series of open air meetings in
Naish Street was also planned for Sunday afternoons.

Frome: former church of St. Catharine

In 1853 Fr. (later Canon) Richard Ward, an Oxford graduate and a convert of Newman, became the first resident priest in Frome since the Reformation. An old chapel in Whittox Lane was bought from the Irving-ites and the nearby St. Catharine's Tower was taken as a presbytery. The church was dedicated to St. Bartholomew.

The Vicar of Frome from 1852 to 1886 was the celebrated W. J. E. Bennett. Under his influence the town became a focus of High Church ritualism. His teaching and actions – particularly his being prosecuted for alleged heresy for teaching the Real Presence and the sacrificial nature of the Mass – provoked frequent controversies in the press, and in these the local Catholics sometimes became embroiled. It was often alleged that his 'Roman tendencies' were the occasion of many people leaving the Church of England to become Catholics. Itinerant anti-Catholic preachers, includ-ing the notorious rabble-rouser known simply as 'Murphy', visited Frome during Bennett's incumbency. Ironically their principal target was the vicar rather than the local Catholic priest.

In the same way that the French Revolution brought priests into Frome in the 1790s, so an outburst of French anti-clericalism in the early 1900s resulted in the arrival of a religious order in the town. In 1902 the Sisters of Charity of St. Louis opened a school and convent in the Whittox area. The sisters left in 1998 but the school continues today with lay staff.

Canon James J. Lonergan was priest at Frome for twenty-four years. At the time of his death in 1927 the present site in Park Road had already been purchased for a new church. Services were held for some forty years in what is today the parish hall until the present church, designed by Martin Fisher of Bath, was opened in 1968. (Interestingly plans were drawn up in 1933 for a church to be built along the lines of the present Sacred Heart church in Westbury-on-Trym, but these came to nothing.)

J.A.H.

Mells, Somerset: St. Dominic

In 1913 Mass was said at The Chantry, home of Edward Tylee, but when this had to close, the present semi-public chapel of St. Dominic at Mells opened at the invitation of the Asquith family. (Katherine Horner, who married Raymond Asquith, son of the Prime Minister, became a Catholic in 1922 after her husband's death.) Sunday Mass is still said here for about thirty Catholics.

It was at Mells that Mgr. Ronald Knox (1888–1957) spent the last ten years of his life. Much of his time here was taken up with his translation into English of the Bible from the Latin (Vulgate) of St. Jerome. One of the treasures in Knox's study is a glass case containing the veil worn by Mary, Queen of Scots, when she was condemned to death.

Mgr. Knox lies buried in the parish churchyard. Nearby is the grave of Siegfried Sassoon, the First World War poet and later convert who used to attend Mass at St. George, Warminster.

J.A.H.

Glastonbury, Somerset: Our Lady

Some account of the late nineteenth century history of Our Lady's parish may be gleaned from an account of the Highbridge mission written in 1917. It tells of the Missionaries of the Sacred Heart establishing an 'Apostolic School' at Glastonbury in the 1880s and 'attending to the care of resident Catholics'. It was from Glastonbury that the Superior of this Order. Fr. Peter Treand, ministered to Highbridge and Burnham until 1900. The Highbridge account goes on to say that the Missionaries built a school for postulants to the Order and that the building was designed by

Glastonbury pilgrimage in 1897

Canon Alexander Scoles. However the school declined in numbers and the Missionaries departed shortly after the First World War.

Glastonbury has close links with neighbouring parishes in the diocese as since 1862 the church at Shepton Mallet has been dedicated to St. Michael, to commemorate an ancient chapel that once stood on Glastonbury Tor. Through their links with the Missionaries of the Sacred Heart, the Sisters of La Retraite, who had arrived from France in 1891 and been given temporary accommodation at Sevenoaks in Kent, learnt of the sale of a property in Burnham-on-Sea which they were able to acquire to set up their school.

In 1926 the Sisters of St. Louis came to Glastonbury and established a convent where Mass was said in the chapel for local Catholics. The Catholic population began to increase and in 1941 a new church, dedicated to Our Lady, was opened, four hundred years after the dissolution of the Abbey. In 1955 the historic shrine of Our Lady of Glastonbury was restored in the presence of Bishop Rudderham and an estimated 18,000 people. Ten years later the statue of Our Lady was solemnly crowned in the Abbey grounds by Archbishop Cardinale, the Apostolic Delegate. The large gathering included the Anglican Bishop of Bath and Wells. The statue was designed

by Philip Lindsay Clark from the representation of Our Lady on a fourteenth century metal seal of the abbey. Our Lady is shown crowned and
bearing the Holy Child on her left forearm, with a flowering bush representing the Glastonbury Thorn.

Glastonbury Abbey is now the focus of many pilgrimages both Anglican
and Catholic and the church of Our Lady faces the old abbey and is frequently visited by pilgrims on 'Pilgrimage Sunday' which is celebrated at
the end of June.

K.McG.

Gloucester: St. Peter ad Vincula

In 1787 Mary Webb of the recusant family at Hatherop Castle left £1000
for the establishment of a mission at Gloucester. After some early transit-
ory arrangements Fr. John Greenway, who moved to Gloucester in 1790,
bought a house and land on the site of the present St. Peter's and there
erected 'a very humble and unpretentious chapel at the back of a house in
a little hidden garden', though circumstances may in fact have been less
modest than this suggests: in 1843 the *Catholic Directory* was to advertise
'well furnished apartments at the Chapel House to be let on moderate
terms'. Sixteen were confirmed at Gloucester in 1794. In 1828 the Abbé
Josse was appointed to Gloucester and established a Catholic day school.
Notwithstanding some opposition to this he became a well-respected Gloucester figure. When he died in 1841 the number of Catholics had risen to
250 from only forty in 1813. Other incumbents of distinction were Fr.
Thomas McDonnell (1848) who gave doctrinal lectures in Gloucester and
was considered by Cardinal Wiseman to be the best catechist in England,
and Fr. Leonard Calderbank (1850), a former vice-principal of Prior Park,
who moved the school to more commodious premises. Wiseman visited him
there. About this time another element in Catholic education was introduced with the opening of a boarding school by the recently arrived Institute of the Blessed Virgin Mary.

In 1858 the Gloucester mission was still serving a predominantly
agrarian community of farm servants and labourers which then numbered about 400, but the increasing cosmopolitan element at Gloucester
docks meant an expanding Catholic community and in 1859 a new
church was begun, to which Miss Frances Canning of the Foxcote recusant family was a generous benefactor. It was opened in 1860 and
completed in 1868, largely through funds from Canon George Case, a
wealthy convert from Anglo-Catholicism best known for his estrangement

Gloucester:
St. Peter

from the Church over the matter of Papal Infallibility at the time of
the first Vatican Council. Its most striking and original feature is the
open bell stage in the steeple. Expansion continued through the rest of
the century. A new presbytery was built in 1878 and stained glass, by
Clayton and Bell, installed in 1886.

Education played a large part from the early days of the Gloucester
mission. A new wing to the school, by the diocesan architect Canon
Scoles, was built in 1893. One of the most important contributions of
Canon Joseph Chard, 'bicycling priest and sportsman', during his long
incumbency (1894–1934) was to establish the status of Catholic education in the city. He became a member of its school board and later of
its education committee. He saw Gloucester's Catholic population
increase to 800. A site for a new church was bought in the 1930s but
the plan came to nothing: it was not until after the war that new

Gloucester: Beckford, chapel

parishes were hived off at Matson, Hatherley, Brockworth and Tuffley, though Mass had already been said at the last-named three as early as 1942. Canon Chard was succeeded in 1934 by Canon Matthew Roche, who also served for nearly fifty years before he resigned in 1983, having been appointed Protonotary Apostolic four years previously. He also made a major contribution to Catholic education with three new schools being built in his time, and like his predecessor serving on the county education committee. His services to the city are recalled in the street-name Roche Walk. All three schools have since been extended, notably St. Peter's where a £750,000 block was opened in 1991. Since 1939 the Poor Servants of the Mother of God have taught there.

The rich history of Christian Gloucester has been reflected in recent events. In 1981 Cardinal Hume celebrated Mass at the 13th centenary of St. Peter's Abbey, the Cathedral being made available by the Dean and Chapter. In 1989 the 200th anniversary of the mission was marked by a Pentecostal celebratory Mass held at Blackfriars, one of the best preserved Dominican houses in England and, coincidentally, near the site of the original Gloucester mission in Berkeley Street.

Hartpury Court

The manor house of Hartpury Court, about two miles from Gloucester, was in Catholic hands for 200 years from the mid-seventeenth century. From 1794 to 1839 Hartpury sheltered a community of expatriate Belgian Dominican nuns who ran a school there until 1832. A chapel dedicated to St. Mary was built there in 1830 by the owner, Robert Canning of the Foxcote recusant family. In 1859 it became a station attached to the Gloucester mission, and Mass was celebrated there at the Indulgences. After a period of desuetude it was restored in 1936 by the then owner, Mrs. Gwynne Holford, and rededicated, again being served from Gloucester. During the Second World War a community of nuns of the Congregation of Our Lady of Sion was evacuated to Hartpury House. Mass was then said three times weekly in the chapel. It remained in use until it was closed on Mrs. Holford's death in 1947, when its interior fittings went to the chapel at Churchdown. The chapel building became part of Hartpury Court Farm and was used as a shed until 1998, when, in poor condition, it was bought by the Hartpury Historic Buildings Trust with the intention of restoring it, now a Grade II listed building, together with the adjacent group of historic buildings.

J.A.F.

Gloucester: Hartpury chapel in 1905 (in foreground of Anglican parish church)

Gloucester: Ukrainian church in its Anglican days

Gloucester: The Good Shepherd Ukrainian Church

The Ukrainian Uniate Church is part of the Catholic Church, with about 400 members in the city of Gloucester. The Church of the Good Shepherd in Derby Road, Gloucester, was opened in 1977 in premises formerly a mission church of the Anglican All Saints', Barton Lane. Its parish, one of the relatively few in the United Kingdom which possesses its own church building, covers Bristol, Cheltenham and South Wales. The early history was sadly marred by demonstrations at its consecration involving rival factions of the Uniate Church.

J.A.F.

Gloucester: See also Brockworth, Churchdown Matson and Tuffley

Grittenham, Wiltshire: Greatwood Farm

Mass was said at the home of the Mapson family by the priest from Malmesbury from at least 1939 until 1966.

J.A.H.

Hartcliffe: See Bristol: St. Pius X

Hartpury Court, Gloucestershire: See Gloucester St. Peter

Henbury: See Bristol: St. Anthony

Henbury: Hill End House (St. Raphaels): See ARNOS COURT under Bristol: St. Gerard Majella

Highworth, Swindon: Served from Swindon: St. Mary

Holcombe, Somerset: St. Cuthbert

In 1926 Major and Mrs. Nicholas Leadbitter presented Downside Abbey with a small coach house in the gardens of their residence, Flint House, for use as a chapel-of-ease. Mass had previously been said in the house. Prior to 1985 the chapel ranked as a public oratory, but later became the parish church of St. Cuthbert. Its intimate and devotional interior is enhanced by a screen and by a stained glass window in honour of St. Cuthbert designed by John Redvers which was installed in 1987.

In 1996 the average mass attendance was thirty-two making it the smallest parish the diocese. This is characteristic of the eight parishes in the vicinity of Downside Abbey which are served from it. The average attendance at the seven of them for which figures are published was under 100 in 1996, compared with 340 for the diocese at large.

J.A.H.

Ilminster, Somerset: St. Joseph: Served from Chard

Inchbrook, Gloucestershire: See Woodchester

Kemerton, Gloucestershire: St. Benet

Kemerton parish owes much to its associations with old Catholic families in its vicinity, among them the Handfords of Woollas Hall and the Wintours of Huddington Hall, once owned by Sir Robert Wintour of the Gunpowder Plot. Mass was said at Beckford, the seat of the Wakemans, until 1836, when the house passed out of their ownership, and thereafter at Overbury Court, then leased by the Eystons. After generous contributions from these and other local families the present church (Decorated, by Hadfield and Weightman of Sheffield) was built on land provided by the Tidmarsh family and opened in 1843. The Kemerton mission covered a large area within Gloucestershire and Worcestershire. At the diocesan visitation of 1858 there were forty Catholics recorded at Kemerton, fifty at Overbury, thirty at Tewkesbury, and thirty at Conderton. It was substantially reduced when Tewkesbury, the largest centre of population in it, became independent in 1870. Consequently Kemerton now has an unusually well-appointed church for a parish which, judged by Mass attendance, is one of the smallest in the diocese.

Catholicism returned to nearby Beckford Hall in 1883 when it was bought by the Ashton-Case family. The chapel there was served from Woodchester. In 1894 there were 191 Catholics in the Kemerton and Beckford congregations. Beckford Hall was to become the novitiate of the Salesian Order in 1936. They remained until 1985 when the Hall again passed into secular ownership. The Catholic church at Kemerton has benefited from local generosity from the time of its foundation to the present. Especially striking was the gift of vestments worked in the seventeenth century by Helen Wintour, which are works of art of national standing. A recent generous benefaction has allowed several projects of renewal and embellishment in celebration of the church's 150th anniversary. Local support also led to the establishment in 1850 of what was then 'St Benet's Poor School', notable as one of the first Catholic schools to receive a Government grant. Its original trust deeds were a roll-call of local Catholic gentry: Eyston, Handford, Tidmarsh, Surman, Porter. Falling numbers finally led to its closure in 1943.

Kemerton is remarkable for the two successive incumbencies of Frs. Aloysius Ridgway and Alphonsus Thomas, which spanned a century from 1844. The tradition continued; Fr. Christopher Cunningham, appointed in 1947, was succeded in 1973 by Fr. Ambrose Crowley, who served the parish until his death in his eighty-sixth year in 1997.

J.A.F.

Keynsham: St. Dunstan

The foundation stone of the church at Keynsham was laid by Bishop Lee on 16 March 1935 and the first Mass was said on 20 October of the same year. Before that time local Catholics had to travel to Bath or Knowle, so in spite of the small numbers of Catholics in the area the bishop decided that there should be a church in Keynsham.

The parish is indebted to the generosity of Edwin Marshall who left his money in trust: 'to have compassion on Catholics who are living at a distance from a place of worship'. The money was used to purchase a property at 20 Bristol Road for a price of £1,280. There was some discussion about the dedication of the new church, and the name finally chosen was that of St. Dunstan who had been Abbot of Glastonbury and later Archbishop of Canterbury. The first parish priest was Fr. (later Canon) Michael Reidy.

A notable feature of the church is the Stations of the Cross given by Mr. and Mrs. Batten in 1934 to Bishop Lee, and afterwards presented by him to Fr. Reidy to adorn the church which had recently been opened. The stations are in the form of panel pictures and date from around 1770. The central figures are by the Dutch artist Boon, while those of less importance are thought to have been painted by his pupils. The central window on the west end of the church is by Angus and is a memorial to Canon Michael Reidy who served the parish for thirty-eight years. Windows at the side are by John Yeoman.

The church is close by the site of Keynsham Abbey, a foundation of Augustinian canons, established in 1170 – the year of the martyrdom of St. Thomas of Canterbury. The Abbey was located below the present Anglican parish church, to the east and at right angles to the bypass.

The initial phase of quiet growth was disturbed by the war and the evacuation of children from London who were in the care of the Sisters of Charity of St. Vincent de Paul. Local Methodists lent rooms to be used as a school. The war years also brought to Corston the Poor Servants of the Mother of God who in 1940 established their novitiate at St. Teresa's on a temporary basis during the London bombing. From 1942 to 1952 it was a country annexe to St. Mary's Hospital in Bristol, and then a convalescent home until 1958, when it became a nursing home for the care of the elderly. The Sisters' long association between Corston and Keynsham still continues today.

In the post-war years efforts were made to built a parish school, but the falling birthrate and the empty places at St. Bernadette Comprehensive School, Whitchurch, and St. Mary's Primary School, Bath, made this impractical. Canon Reidy retired in 1973 and was succeeded by Fr. Daniel O'Callaghan who, in turn, was succeeded by Fr. Michael Larkin.

J.A.H.

Kingswood: See Bristol Our Lady of Lourdes and St. Bernadette

Knowle: See Bristol St. Gerard Majella

Knowle West: See Bristol Christ the King

Langport, Somerset: St. Joseph: Served from Somerton

Larkhill Camp, Wiltshire: See Churches on Salisbury Plain

Lavington, Wiltshire: St. Joseph: Served from Devizes

Lawrence Weston: See Bristol Our Lady of the Rosary

Lechlade, Gloucestershire: See Fairford

Locking, R.A.F.: Served from Clevedon

Lydney, Gloucestershire: St. Joseph: Served from Cinderford

Lynham, Wiltshire: R.A.F.: Served from Calne

Malmesbury, Wiltshire: St. Aldhelm

From its beginnings Catholic Malmesbury has been closely associated with the English mission of the Missionaries of St. Francis de Sales (the Fransalians), an order founded at Annecy in France in 1838. In 1858 Fr. Francis Larive, a young Frenchman serving on the Fransalian mission in India, met Charles Dewell, a captain of the 91st Regiment stationed there. Dewell, a member of a Malmesbury family of substance, was a recent convert, and was inspired by a wish to bring the Faith to his home town. He became convinced that Larive was eminently suited to a Malmesbury mission, and in 1861 resigned his commission and returned with Larive to England, subsequently becoming a Jesuit lay brother. He had also observed the work in India of the Sisters of St. Joseph of Annecy (an order which came to Annecy in 1835, and were independent of the Fransalians), and planned that three of the sisters should go to England to support the work at Malmesbury. He intended to convey his house Cross Hayes in Malmesbury to the diocese for the use of the mission.

Dewell and Larive arrived to find Cross Hayes encumbered by a lease so that possession was not possible before 1866. Larive therefore went to nearby Chippenham, and opened a mission to Devizes where the sisters, with financial support from Dewell, were accommodated when they arrived in 1864. Thereafter the affairs of the Sisters and the Fransalians at Devizes and Malmesbury are intimately interrelated, especially in financial matters where the supposed ambiguities in Dewell's settlement led to a prolonged altercation, vigorously maintained by Fr. Decompoix at Malmesbury, who, finding a worthy adversary in the Sisters, remained combative until well into the next century (he died at Malmesbury in 1917 aged 93). Bishop Burton endorsed the plentiful correspondence as 'Malmesbury muddle'.

One of the few Catholics near Malmesbury was Sir Richard Hungerford Pollen at nearby Rodbourne House, six miles away. His family was for many years the benefactor of the Malmesbury mission. In 1858 he obtained a rescript for the celebration of Mass and in 1864 Fr. Larive went to serve there, moving to Cross Hayes when it finally became vacant in 1866. The little shed where he first celebrated there still stands, full of garden tools, with the original coloured glass incongruously still in its windows. Next year twenty-two people from the vicinity attended the first public Mass in the parlour of Cross Hayes. Larive opened a night school, and next year, in the face of great local opposition, a day school; first with the support of 'a Catholic young lady living with her parents in Malmesbury'. From 1870 it was run by the Sisters of Mercy from Bristol. A temporary church built in the former stables of Cross Hayes was replaced in 1875 by the present building, itself becoming St. Joseph's School, which remained until 1933. In 1884 the Sisters of St. Joseph finally came to occupy Cross Hayes and take over the school, thus after twenty years fulfilling Dewell's wishes. In that year Larive returned to Annecy because of ill-health. He was to return to England, to Petersfield in Hampshire, where after again meeting strong local opposition he died in 1893. His had not been a happy life.

The church of St. Aldhelm, dedicated to the seventh-century abbot of Malmesbury, is a simple but effective building distinguished by an organ gallery at its west end and by a striking nineteenth-century altar now surviving the Second Vatican Council in the guise of a reredos. An early seventeenth-century painting of Our Lady of Guadeloupe is believed to have been brought to a farmhouse at nearby Bradenstoke by an eighteenth-century Catholic owner. It was given to Bishop Burton in 1921 by the then occupier. The statue of Our Lady of La Salette, who is shedding a tear for the sins of mankind, was brought back from La Salette by Larive when he made a pilgrimage there to supplicate for the success of the Malmesbury mission.

It was perhaps as a result of that pilgrimage that Larive became associated with the Congregation des Religieuses Réparatrices de Notre Dame, a community founded in 1866 around a supposed visionary Marie Renaud, whose claims were gravely doubted by the Archbishop of Rouen. In 1868 the community moved to Malmesbury where, as Bishop Clifford shared the Archbishop's doubts, it had been set up for a trial period of one year. It now styled itself 'the mother house [of the order] at Malmesbury'. They were soon followed by their director, the Abbé Dupont, about whom the

Archbishop had equal doubts, and there began a prolonged recrimination between Dupont and Larive. Clifford, with Ullathorne's support, ruled that the trial period should not be extended, and the community was dispersed. This strange and forgotten episode is vividly but incompletely recalled in the diocesan and the Fransalian archives.

From their beginning at Malmesbury the Fransalian presence has extended both within and without the diocese of Clifton. They have served Malmesbury continuously to the present day: now a parish much diminished from the area of the mission in its early days but with a Mass attendance of 263 in 1997, and now responsible for St. Joseph's primary school.

J.A.F.

Marlborough, Wiltshire: St. Thomas More

In an article in *The Downside Review* of 1902, Dom Gilbert Dolan described the missionary work of his order in the Wiltshire town of Marlborough in penal days. A local Catholic family, the Hydes, maintained a chaplain at their house for their own benefit and for that of any of their neighbours who wished to attend Mass. Thus the old Catholic faith was kept alive.

Among the members of the order who served at Marlborough and are mentioned by Fr. Dolan were Dom Robert Goolde (*c.* 1754), Dom Anselm Geary (c. 1774), and Dom Edward Hussey (*c.* 1758). Fr. Hussey was a member of the old Catholic family at Marnhull in Dorset, and returned to serve at his family estate in 1785. When Dom Williams Cowley, who served at Marlborough around 1790, was appointed President of the English Benedictines, the mission seems to have been left without a priest.

This state of affairs seems to have persisted for more than a century as it was not till 1911 that a Mass Centre was established in a house in the village of Ogbourne Maisey some two miles from Marlborough on the Swindon road. It was served by the Missionaries of St. Francis de Sales who had established a mission in Devizes in 1861. The Mass centre was used until 1937. In that year, one of the missionaries, Fr. Joseph Anthonioz, opened a small chapel in a bungalow in Elcot Lane in Marlborough. He lived at the bungalow and, under his guidance, the mission prospered to such an extent that by 1939 it had become necessary to hire a local hall for the numbers attending Mass each Sunday.

In 1948, in spite of the building regulations, Fr. Anthonioz purchased the site in George Lane, and Marlborough soon had its first Catholic church although it was in the form of a large Nissen hut. In 1953 a house for the priest was purchased close to the church. Fr. Joseph realised that it could only be a matter of time before his temporary church became too small for his congregation. He inaugurated a building fund but sadly died in 1954 before the building commenced. Fr. Ronald Besant took on the task and on 6 November 1985 Bishop Alexander consecrated the new church, dedicated to St. Thomas More, to serve the Catholics of Marlborough and the villages around the Kennet Valley.

Pewsey: Holy Family

The church of the Holy Family, Broadfields Estate, Pewsey was blessed by Bishop Rudderham on 13 May 1964. This replaced the small private chapel of Lady Phipps at West Stowell, three miles away which had served the Catholics of Pewsey Vale since 1934.

The new church was built on modern lines with a large copper roof which extended to within eight feet of ground level. The building, with seating for 110, is lighted by two large triangular windows in a multi-coloured glass. One surmounts the entrance lobby and the other is above the altar. The baptistery has a stained glass window depicting the Baptism of Our Lord. Beside the church there is a single storey, two bedroom caretaker's house with a spacious car park. The church is served from **Marlborough**.

The whole project was designed by Messrs. Rendell and West, Planning Consultants of Devizes, and the builders were Messrs. Gaiger Bros. also of Devizes, The total cost including the purchase of the land was £20,000.

J.C.

Matson, Gloucestershire: St. Augustine of Canterbury

The locality of Matson, formerly part of the parish of St. Peter, Gloucester, expanded rapidly after the War, and local arrangements for Mass were made from 1952. Accommodation, always primitive, was first found in the canteen of Laing the builder, and then in the following year in the local community centre. In 1959 this arrangement was found to be unconstitutional, and a move was made to the skittle alley of The Musket public house. Following a local appeal for funds launched in 1960 the foundation stone of the present church was laid in 1962. Materials and techniques meant that Mass could be said there later in the same year. The church cost £32,000, all found locally. It is a late example of a church built in the traditional style of the days before the Second Vatican Council, with a nave and side aisles and a deep sanctuary. The architect was Egbert Leah. Its most striking internal features are a lifesize *crux decusata* by Patrick Conoley and a five-light window by Whitefriars Studios. It functioned as a Mass centre served from St. Peter, Gloucester until 1974, when St. Augustine's was established as a parish. A parish hall was built in 1982, at a cost in pounds nearly double that of the church. In 1987 Mass in the new church was televised on a national network. The service elicited many expressions of appreciation from many parts and from members of many creeds.

J.A.F.

Melksham, Wiltshire: St. Anthony of Padua

The origins of this mission go back to 1857 when Charles Conolly of Midford Castle, near Bath, purchased Cottles, a large mansion at Atworth, near Melksham. (Today it houses **Stonar**, an independent girls' school founded in 1921, which moved to its present premises from Kent in 1939.) Conolly's wife was Louisa Lucy Margaret Catherine Brancaccio, in her own right Marquesa de St. Agata. She was the only child of the Prince of Ruffano. Chamberlain to Ferdinant, King of Naples. This probably explains why the chapel attached to the house was dedicated to St. Francis of Paola (1436–1507), a hermit who had lived in the same part of Italy.

Fr. (later Mgr. Canon) Charles Parfitt was chaplain at Cottles from 1858 to 1876, when he moved back with the family to Midford Castle. Bishop Clifford's vicar general, Mgr. John Bonomi, died at Cottles on 1 September 1872, aged fifty-six years.

From the time that the Conolly's departed, for a period of over sixty years until 1939, Catholics had to travel to Mass either at Trowbridge or Bath or, more likely, Devizes. In November 1937 the Diocesan Trustees purchased for £750 a property known as The Southernlands, The Avenue, Melksham. The house was to serve as the presbytery, and part of the garden was utilised for the building of a church. The foundation stone was laid by Bishop Lee in March 1938 and the church opened on 5 March 1939. This was a period of extraordinary activity just before the war when Bishop Lee opened a series of churches in north and mid Wiltshire, namely: Chippenham (1936) Westbury (1938) Warminster (1938) and Melksham (1939). At the opening ceremony of St. Anthony the guard of honour was provided by personnel from the R.A.F. base at Yatesbury – a compliment to Fr. (later Canon) Owen Devaney who for some weeks, while assistant priest at Trowbridge, had attended the station on Sundays to celebrate Mass for the recruits.

In his address the bishop gave more details of exactly how the church, which had cost £2,500, had come to be built. He spoke of Mr. and Mrs. Seymour, natives of Melksham, whose wish it had been that Catholics should have their own place of worship in the town. They left £1,500 of their life's savings to start a building fund. Then a lady from Somerset came to Melksham, secured the site and transferred it to the diocese. A contemporary newspaper account stated: 'the church is dedicated to St. Anthony of Padua and is built in a pleasant modern style, with a statue of the saint surmounting the tympanum above the main entrance. The architect is J. H. Willman of Taunton'.

A parish hall was opened and blessed in 1998.

J.A.H.

Mells, Somerset: The Manor House: Served from Frome

Mere, Wiltshire: St. Mary: Served from Wincanton

Midford Castle: See Bath, Combe Down

Midsomer Norton, Somerset: Holy Ghost

The mission at Stratton-on-the-Fosse remained the only one in the locality associated with Downside Abbey until well into the next century, when members of the community mounted a campaign to establish more, it is said as a result of a chance remark by an Anglican clergyman who wondered why Downside did not do more for Catholics in its vicinity. As a result the mission at Midsomer Norton (and that at Radstock) were established in 1913.

Midsomer Norton has one of the most remarkable churches of any denomination in the country. It is converted from a tithe barn once belonging to the Augustinian Canons of Merton, which passed to Christ Church, Oxford at the dissolution. It fell into neglect with the commutation of tithes and in 1886 passed into private hands. The story of its acquisition in 1906, with the title deeds pushed silently across the table by a seemingly hitherto unenthusiastic Abbot, is told in *The Downside Review* of 1913. By then it was sadly dilapidated and obscured by an accretion of ramshackle buildings. Its restoration was one of the earliest commissions of Giles Gilbert Scott. Many features have been retained, the finest being the timber roof with its arch and wind braces.

Its fittings and furniture are also remarkable as illustrations of many facets of Catholic history. The Jacobean panelling comes from the original

Minehead: convent chapel

house of the Downside community and the pulpit served for long as the prefects' desk in the school. The tabernacle came from the Bavarian church in London. The Stations of the Cross are eighteenth century Flemish work, and are probably among the earliest examples in England that incorporate visual representations of the Passion.

The growth of the Midsomer Norton mission owed much to Dom Robert Turnbull, who served it from Downside for twenty-six years from 1923. The Mass attendance had grown from about twenty in its early days to 190 in 1996. The present St. Benedict's primary school was opened in 1975.

J.A.F.

Milborne Port, Somerset: Served from Wincanton

Milton, Weston-super-Mare: See Weston-super-Mare, Our Lady of Lourdes

Minehead, Somerset: Sacred Heart

The origins of the Minehead Mission owe a great deal to the Franciscan Convent at Taunton. This convent was originally founded by nuns of the Third Order Regular of St. Francis who came to Taunton from Bruges, via

Winchester, in 1808. In 1888 Mass was only available in Minehead at infrequent intervals. The situation improved when Mr. and Mrs. Incledon invited Fr. Matthew Guerrin to say Mass in their home. A quick survey found that there were about thirty Catholics in Minehead who would attend Mass if it were available. Consequently, a small house with a large thatched barn was hired in Selbourne Place. This was opened as a chapel in 1891 by Bishop Clifford. The congregation soon increased and there followed an enthusiastic drive to build a new church. The funds for this project were collected by Fr. (later Canon) O'Shaughnessy who had been appointed priest-in-charge. Fr. O'Shaughnessy had come from St. George, Taunton, to which he was later to return.

The foundation stone of the new church was laid on 9 April 1896 by Bishop Brownlow. The architect was Canon Alexander Scoles who had already designed several churches in the diocese. The building, which consisted originally of a nave and sanctuary, was quickly completed, and opened on 15 September 1896. Two porches were situated at the rear, the one on the south side being the main entrance; while the one on the north side was a small Lady Chapel. Later this became the baptistery which had an octagonal Bath stone front with carvings on the bowl. The roof of the nave and sanctuary was sealed and boarded with pitch pine frames, creating bays. Fr. Richard Chichester was appointed parish priest on 9 September 1896. A statue of the Sacred Heart was presented to the church by Mrs. Marshall, the first convert at Minehead. The statue of Our Lady was given by Mrs. Incledon, already mentioned as a benefactor to the church. One of the windows in the nave is dedicated to her memory. On 10 September 1898 a new High Altar and reredos were unveiled during a special celebration of High Mass.

By 1900 there was a much larger congregation, especially in the holiday period, and it was decided to build a new aisle on the side of the nave. A church hall was built in 1927 and this was completely refurbished in 1996. In 1984 an extension was added to the church.

From the 1920s onwards Mass was occasionally said by a priest from Minehead at Broome Close, West Porlock, the home of Mr. and Mrs. R. V. Awdry. In 1932 land was purchased with the intention of building a chapel. The plot consisted of one and a half acres of land in what was known locally as 'the Coniger field'. This was purchased for £221 by Miss Alcock who was a maid in service at Bossington. In 1939 a Mass centre was opened in Porlock which continued until 1960 when the late Lord Lyttleton offered to build a chapel-of-ease on the plot of land originally bought for that purpose. Plans were submitted to the district council but were not approved. Mass continued to be celebrated in the village hall but in the late 1980s it was found increasingly difficult to sustain, and with the Bishop's permission, it was discontinued.

The Mass centre at **Watchet** came about with the celebration of Mass at the R.A.F. Station, Donniford in 1943. It has since had various venues, the latest being the primary school at Knight's Templar, Flowerdew Road. Mass at Butlin's Holiday Camp was discontinued in 1988.

Catholic education in Minehead owes a great deal to the Sisters of Charity of St. Louis. These French sisters came to England from Vannes, Brittany in 1898 as refugees from a hostile secular government. They were helped by the generosity of Baroness le Clement de Taintegnies who lived at Ashley Coombe. They also worked hard themselves. A laundry was built in the grounds adjoining the convent, and became a useful source of income. A home for orphan girls was established. The girls were brought up in the convent and when they reached fourteen years they worked in the laundry for their keep and pocket money. In the 1920s the sisters purchased Blair Lodge Hotel and converted it into St. Teresa's Day and Boarding School for girls and small boys. This establishment was separate from St. Louis Orphanage. In July 1967 St. Teresa's School was closed and sold to Somerset County Council. The sisters are now dispersed to the various other establishments belonging to the order.

In 1996 a special Mass was said at Leigh Barton to commemorate the 350th anniversary of the martyrdom of Blessed Philip Powell who stayed there and said Mass when he was not visiting other 'safe houses' in West Somerset. He visited his scattered parishioners in Washford, Williton, Glastonbury and Wells. Blessed Philip was executed at Tyburn on 16 June 1646.

K.McG.

More Hall, Gloucestershire: See Stroud

Moreton-in-Marsh, Gloucestershire: Served from Chipping Campden

Nailsea, Somerset: St. Francis of Assisi

Nailsea was formerly a quiet Somerset village on the main road from Bristol to Weston-super-Mare, even sharing its railway station with neighbouring Backwell. Priests from the Franciscan community at Clevedon had said Mass on Sundays in the village for many years. In 1950 they purchased a site for a church and in the following year erected a temporary building to be used as a Mass centre. The 'temporary building' was to serve this purpose for almost thirty years.

The population of the Nailsea–Backwell area increased very rapidly in the 1950s and 1960s and the first permanent school and chapel were opened in 1979. In September 1982 it became a parish in its own right. (Until then it had still been served from Clevedon).

A new church, dedicated to St. Francis of Assisi, was blessed and opened on 2 February 1986. The building is seen not just as a service to the Catholic community but to the community at large and this idea is reflected in its design. The sanctuary, for example, may be partitioned off, thus leaving the body of the building suitable for non-worship purposes.

One of the two stained glass windows in the sanctuary depicts the patron of the parish, the other window St. Alexander Briant. He was a Somerset man who was educated at the English College at Douai and, after his ordination, returned to minister in England. He was arrested in 1579 and, after two years imprisonment, in spite of being cruelly tortured, he refused to renounce his Faith. He was executed at Tyburn with St. Edmund Campion on 1 December 1581. The Stations of the Cross, while fourteen in number, unusually begin with the Last Supper and end with the Resurrection. They were designed by the children of St. Francis' School under the direction of the architect, John Webster. The Lady statue is the work of local sculptress Sue Bachelor of Nailsea.

Nailsea: The Novitiate of the Claretian Order at Backwell

In 1958, the fiftieth anniversary of the arrival of the order in England, the Claretians, or, to give the congregation its full title, the Sons of the Immaculate Heart of Mary, established its novitiate at Backwell Hill House, Backwell, about ten miles from Bristol on the Weston-super-Mare road. The congregation takes its name from its founder, St. Anthony Claret, who was canonised in May 1950 by Pope Pius XII. The future saint, an Apostolic Missionary, had served for many years as Archbishop of Santiago in Cuba, and had attended the First Vatican Council of 1870.

At first, the congregation held its services in one of the large rooms at Backwell Hill House, but by 1963 a new chapel had been built. On 21 August it was opened and blessed by Bishop Rudderham who afterwards clothed eight novices with the cassock of the Claretian congregation. The new chapel, with accommodation for 100 persons, is simple in the extreme. In conformity with the custom of the Claretians it was built in triangular form to express 'hands clasped in prayer'. The altar is of Portland stone and the tabernacle is of an artistic design carried out by Gunning and

Newent: Blaisdon Hall

Sons of Dublin. Mass was celebrated daily in the chapel which was open to Catholics living in the surrounding district. Sadly, the expected increase in the number of novices entering the congregation did not materialise and the novitiate was closed in 1968.

J.C.

Nailsworth, Gloucestershire: See Woodchester

Nazareth House: See Bristol: St. Bernard, Shirehampton

Newent, Gloucestershire: Our Lady of Lourdes

Organised Catholic worship in Newent is closely linked to the Salesians (the Society of Don Bosco), which in 1935 bought Blaisdon Hall, a nineteenth-century house near the village of Longhope. There they opened a school for disadvantaged boys. Many of the intake came from the Crusade of Rescue of Westminster diocese. Initially a school of agriculture, it became in 1950 a conventional school for boys with educational difficulties. From 1936 to 1950 Blaisdon Hall was also a theologate for Salesian students, many of whom were ordained by Bishops Lee and Rudderham. At first the school grew rapidly, but in recent years changes in national educational policies made it increasingly difficult to send pupils there, and it closed at the end of 1993. The Salesian community remained until the end of 1995, when the Hall was sold and the community dispersed. Blaisdon is now served from Newent, with Mass celebrated in the Anglican church of St. Michael.

The Salesians opened a Mass centre in a private house in Newent in 1935. Later, Mass was celebrated in the historic Market House. The church of Our Lady of Lourdes, opened in 1960, was financed through local endeavour and largely built by volunteer labour. It is an unpretentious but effective small building in the conventional style of nave and chancel. The Salesian presence is maintained in Newent in the person of the present (1998) parish priest, Fr. Aidan Murray.

J.A.F.

Norton St. Philip, Somerset: Our Lady

The first priest to celebrate Mass at Norton St. Philip was Fr. Ambrose Agius of Downside. In 1913 he had become responsible for the newly founded mission at Radstock, ten miles away. His vigorous ministry there was extended to Norton St. Philip, where in order to say Mass for an old lady and her crippled daughter living in a cottage at Norton, he regularly made the ten-mile journey from Radstock on his motor-cycle. Gradually a small and diverse concregation accumulated: an Irish family, a Swiss companion to a county family and a district nurse. In a small cottage they were a crowd, and the bed had to be pushed aside to make room, sometimes with the old lady in it.

In 1923 a small property was bought for £400 and a temporary church built, followed by the social amenities of a skittle alley and a parish hall. Thereafter Norton St. Philip continued to be served from Downside. In 1954 the appointed of Dom Edward Lee in 1954 was especially fortunate as he was a professionally qualified engineer who followed in Canon Scoles's steps as a clerical architect, and not only did he design the new church but did all the metalwork for its interior fittings. His mechanical abilities also helped indirectly as he gave the church the proceedings of the sale of a working model of the Flying Scotsman that he had made. The new church, opened in 1961, was dedicated to Our Lady. When Fr. Lee left the parish in 1978 he was succeeded by Dom Denis Agius, Dom Ambrose's nephew.

Based on Dom Denis Agius

Nympsfield: altar in the
Red Lion Inn (later
Chapel House)

Nympsfield, Gloucestershire: St. Joseph

As with neighbouring Woodchester, Catholicism in Nympsfield owes much
to the Leigh family. From the 1840s Mass was said there by the Orders
introduced to Woodchester by William Leigh – for a few years the Passionists and then, for over eighty years, the Dominicans. In 1847 it was
said in a small cottage, now known as Barberi Cottage, and from 1852 in
a room in the Red Lion, a former coaching inn, later named Chapel House
because Mass continued to be celebrated there until the opening of St.
Joseph's Church in 1923. Plans for a church were drawn up by Charles
Hansom (the architect of Woodchester Priory) in 1878, but lack of funds
delayed their implementation. The Dominicans did much for the local community, opening a night school and a reading room in the 1890s, but by
then the Catholic community had lost some of its initial vigour, and it was
reported to the diocesan visitation of 1894 that the many 'bread and
butter' converts made at the beginning of the mission had by then fallen
off entirely. From the turn of the century it was reinvigorated by the Misses
Blanche and Beatrice Leigh, granddaughters of William. St. Joseph's was
made possible by their bequest. The building, which realised much of Hansom's intentions, was designed by the Stroud architect E. P. Dromgole. In
it are incorporated a fifteenth-century font and a twelfth-century niche,
and it has a remarkable east window by Edward Payne of Box (1964). A
memorial cross at the crossroads near Chapel House incorporates a bullet-
ridden figure of Christ which was recovered from the Somme. The Nympsfield congregation included the family of the American ambassador Ken-

nedy, among them his son John, on their occasional visits to Berkeley Castle, and the novelist Evelyn Waugh and his family.

The Dominican presence, which lasted until 1932 when the church became the responsibility of the diocese, meant that several eminent priests were associated with Nympsfield, among them Fr. Thomas Burke who was to become famous as a preacher in the nineteenth century, Fr. Aelred Whittaker, a polymath who taught wood carving and music to the villagers, Fr. Vincent McNabb and Fr. Bede Jarrett (a cousin of the Leighs), who preached at the dedication of the church. The Dominican presence continued in diocesan times with Fr. Edwin Essex, who for sixteen years supplied the Marist convent and was buried in the village.

Catholic education in Nympsfield owed much to the Leighs. A school had been opened in Chapel House in the 1850s, but languished when ill-health meant that William Leigh could not maintain his interest, and by about 1870 it had been discontinued. In 1903 St. Joseph's school was opened, funded by the Misses Leigh. It expanded rapidly, not least because of secessions from the local Church of England school which was then having major problems of management. St. Joseph's affairs became something of a *cause célèbre* when the Parliamentary grant, which had been expected when it was founded, did not materialise, with questions in Parliament and, in 1912, a public enquiry. Nevertheless it continued to flourish. In 1938 Evelyn Waugh was one of its managers.

After the First World War the Misses Leigh, with the encouragement of Cardinal Bourne, also sponsored the establishment of an orphanage, and in 1929 a community of Marist sisters came to occupy a block of alms-houses, appropriately called the Barracks, living at first in primitive conditions. They also became closely involved in the school. In 1949 the local authority at last agreed to recognise it, but on condition that new buildings were constructed, to which both the Leigh Trust and the Marists made major contributions. It was not until 1962 that staff salaries were provided from public funds: by then Leigh money had continuously supported education in Nympsfield for sixty years. The Marists to this day make substantial contributions to capital expenditures on the school. Meanwhile the Marists had up to the 1960s continued to extend and reorganise the orphanage, so that it was officially described as 'one of the most progressive Homes in the country'. Changing national policies on the care of children led to its closure in about 1970. St. Joseph's Homestead is now a retreat centre, still cared for by the Marists.

J.A.F.

Painswick, Gloucestershire: Our Lady and St. Thérèse: Served from Stroud

Patchway: See Bristol: Holy Family

Paulton, Somerset: Our Lady Help of Christians

In the nineteenth century the most expeditious route from Bath to Paulton was by way of the coal canal which had been built to obtain access to the Somerset coalfield. In April 1814 this canal carried a boatload of Benedictine monks and boys on the last stage of their journey from exile at Douai in Flanders, via a temporary refuge at Acton Burnell in Shropshire, to their new home at Downside. It was at Paulton, the terminus of the coal canal, that the Downside community first set foot in a Somerset village. And it seems probable that the local inhabitants saw Downside boys in the dress which was not unlike that worn today by Christ's Hospital and the other Bluecoat schools, which were founded much about the same period as the original Downside community (1605).

For over 150 years the scattered Catholics of Paulton and the villages and hamlets around have been cared for by monks from Downside. In the early days this pastoral work was done on foot, the monks covering some fifteen to twenty miles to reach outlying families. The faithful would also have to walk similar distances to reach the nearest Mass.

St. Benedict, Stratton-on-the-Fosse, was established as a parish in 1855. The nearest parish at that time was St. John, Bath. This was also served by monks from Downside who built the church which was consecrated in 1863. Paulton lay in between on the distant boundary of the Stratton-on-the-Fosse parish. In 1913 Midsomer Norton became a pastoral entity and took responsibility for Paulton. It was not until 1957, however, that a Mass centre opened at Paulton, in the home of Mr. and Mrs. John Buckley at Geradene, Main Street. At the time Mr. Buckley was on the staff at Downside and played the organ at Midsomer Norton. Soon this accommodation, so generously provided, became too small. The premises at the Lamb Hotel were secured and here the needs of the faithful were provided for by the landlady Mrs. Evans and her husband, until Glenvue Bakery was acquired for the new church. The architect was Denis Poulton, the senior partner of Messrs. Poulton and Freeman, of Wyndham Place, London. Bishop Rudderham opened and blessed the new church on 24 September 1961.

An abridged account by Abbot Nicholas Holman O.S.B.

Peasedown St. John, Bath: St. Joseph

As with Norton St. Philip the beginnings of the mission at Peasedown were due to the indefatigable efforts of Dom Ambrose Agius of Downside and Radstock, who in 1920 began to say Mass there regularly in a cottage belonging to the O'Neills in 'The Bricks'. After a prolonged search he found a plot of land in 1926, which Downside bought, and a temporary wooden church was built.

Fr. Edmund Lee succeeded Fr. Agius in 1932 and built a hall behind the church. Fr. Lee was followed by a succession of priests from Downside ending with Fr. Julian Stonor. The Second World War brought a large increase of Catholics, evacuees from London, refugees from eastern Europe, and an influx of miners to the pits which were now working to full capacity. Three sizeable housing estates were built after the war, two of them on the opposite side of the village to the church.

In 1951 Peasedown became the responsibility of the diocese, and Fr. Littleton Powys, a former Anglican priest and principal of St. Stephen's House in Oxford, became the first resident priest-in-charge in November of that year. He lived in one room of a miner's cottage near the church, and at once set about building a presbytery. He died in post in February 1954 and was succeeded by Fr. (later Canon) Richard Norris who completed the presbytery. In 1958 the diocese acquired a stone building which had originally served as the village cinema, well located and near to the new housing estates. Gerard P. O'Brien, the architect, transformed the building into a place of worship which was blessed by Mgr. Canon Hackett, the rural dean, on 30 April 1959. In 1989 a new Mass centre was opened and the parish then again became the responsibility of Downside. In 1999 it was transferred to the pastoral care of SS. Peter and Paul, Bath.

V.A.

Pewsey, Wiltshire: Holy Family: Served from Marlborough

Porlock, Somerset: See Minehead

Portishead, Somerset: St. Joseph

In 1881 a community of Franciscans expelled from France were given a refuge by Bishop Clifford in the empty convent premises in Park Place, adjoining the Pro-Cathedral. In return the friars assisted in the work of the mission. One such work was to travel each Sunday to Sharpness to offer Mass there in the little chapel of Our Lady Star of the Sea which had been built at the expense of Mrs. Mary Gifford of Berkeley. Mrs. Gifford offered to build a house at Sharpness for the friars if they would serve the mission permanently, but they declined on the grounds that they were already planning to start a mission at Portishead. It was here, at West Hill, in two houses named Claremont and Belle Vue that the Portishead mission was founded in July 1883.

In his diary for 1883 Bishop Clifford describes how he travelled to Portishead by the 4 p.m. train on Sunday 2 December 1883 to open the friars' new chapel. The bishop wrote 'They have roofed in one of the gardens which makes a decent and roomy chapel ... it was crowded this evening at 5.30 p.m., chiefly by Protestants, there being only eight Catholics resident at Portishead and a few having come from Clevedon ... I supped and slept at the friars ... On Monday a.m. I said Mass at eight and gave confirmation to two.' Some idea of the rapid growth of the parish may be gained from the news that when the bishop visited St. Joseph's three years later, in 1886, he confirmed thirty converts.

The present church of St. Joseph was dedicated by Bishop Clifford on 19 March 1887. Shortly afterwards, in 1888, the friars withdrew to Clevedon, where they shared the Friary with another Franciscan community. However they continued to serve St. Joseph each Sunday until 1906. In that year, at the request of the friars, the diocese became responsible for St. Joseph. Bishop Burton's secretary, Fr. (later Bishop) William Lee, served the mission from the Bishop's residence at Leigh Woods. In 1907 a small community of two friars and a lay brother came to Portishead and, on 16 June 1907 Bishop Burton celebrated Mass in the church and formally welcomed the friars back to Portishead.

Over the years the mission steadily grew. In 1906 the Sisters of the Congregation of La Sante Union des Sacrés Coeurs founded their school at Rose Hill, close by St. Joseph. The house named Kenfield adjoining the church was purchased in 1936 and used as a Friary. In 1938 a Mass centre was established in the grounds of Ham Green Isolation Hospital. This was used by local Catholics until 1959 when a chapel, dedicated to St. Anthony of Padua, was opened in the nearby village of Pill.

The Franciscans eventually withdrew from St. Joseph in 1985, and the church and parish were taken in to the care of the diocese again. The first parish priest was Fr. (now Canon) William O'Callaghan. There is a plaque in the church which records the previous ministry of the friars.

J.C.

Pill: St. Anthony of Padua

The village of Pill, or, to give it its full name, Crockerne Pill, is situated close to the confluence of the two rivers, the Avon and the Severn, some seven miles from Bristol. Formerly the Catholic population of the village was small and were under the pastoral care of the Pro-Cathedral until the establishment of the Portishead mission in 1853.

In 1938 Fr. Roch, the Franciscan parish priest at Portishead arranged for Mass to be said each Sunday at the Ham Green Isolation Hospital on the outskirts of Pill, and local Catholics attended Mass there. But, in the post-war years house building programmes in the area meant an increase in the Catholic population and the facilities at Ham Green were inadequate.

In October 1956 a site for the building of a chapel to be used as a Mass centre, and eventually, a church was purchased in Springfield Road, just off the main Bristol Road. Meanwhile arrangements had been made to celebrate Mass each Sunday at the Pill Memorial Club, in the village. This continued for almost three years. Building work on the Mass centre began in March 1959, and on 10 November 1959 Bishop Rudderham blessed the new chapel, dedicated to St. Anthony of Padua. At the ceremony the total Catholic population of Pill, some seventy or eighty persons, were outnumbered by visitors, who filled the 200 places in the new chapel. Served from Portishead, it also provided Mass for the surrounding areas of Ham Green, Failand and Easton-in-Gordano until 1986. Falling numbers and increasing costs caused the Franciscans of Clevedon, who owned the property, to seek the Bishop's permission for deconsecration of the chapel so that it could be sold for housing.

J.C.

Postlip, Gloucestershire: St. James: See Winchcombe

Prestbury: Cheltenham Holy Name: Served from Cheltenham St. Gregory

Prinknash Abbey, Gloucestershire

The history of the Benedictine community at Prinknash began in 1896 when Benjamin Fearnley Carlyle, then still a medical student, founded an Anglican community conforming to the Benedictine rule. They made several moves in their early days and then, with the help of Lord Halifax and others, acquired the island of Caldey off the Pembrokeshire coast. Carlyle, who took the name Aelred, became Abbot in 1903, and in 1904 received

Prinknash Abbey: proposed Goodhart-Rendell design

Anglican priest's orders. The relations of the community with the Anglican church became uneasy and by 1913 the great majority of its members came to realise that their aims could only be fulfilled in the Catholic Church. The Holy See recognised Caldey as a canonically established Benedictine monastery of the Subiaco congregation and Carlyle was canonically blessed as Abbot of Caldey in 1914.

The Catholic community had a troubled start at Caldey, aggravated by the ending of the substantial support it was getting from Anglican sources. Relief came when the wealthy convert Thomas Dyer Edwardes left to them Prinknash Park, a spectacularly sited house near Gloucester which dates from the fourteenth century. The purchase of Caldey Island by the Cistercian Order made it practicable for them to accept, and by 1928 they were installed in what is now known as the Old House, St. Peter's Grange. In 1938 Prinknash Prior was promoted to abbatial status and the first Abbot, the Rt. Rev. Dom Wilfrid Upson, elected.

Plans were soon initiated for a new monastery destined to rival the magnificence of the great local Benedictine abbeys of the past. The architect was H. S. Goodhart-Rendel. In 1939 the foundation stone was laid by Cardinal Hinsley with great ceremony. No more than the crypt (which survives) had been built before the war put an end to construction. With the coming of peace the Abbey was completed to a less ambitious plan by F. G. Broadbent, the one-time partner of Goodhart-Rendel. Its cost was largely defrayed by the sale in 1969 of Bassano's *The Flight into Egypt*, which had been given in 1958 by Goodhart-Rendel, who was a confrater of the community. It fetched 260,000 guineas at Christie's; it had been insured for £2,500 during its journey to Prinknash. The present abbey, a sturdy four-square building clad in Guiting stone, harmonises well with its location in undulating country about a mile from St. Peter's Grange.

In popular estimation the community is perhaps best known by its ancillary activities, notably the Prinknash pottery (now no longer owned by the community) and the bird-park, but the *genius loci* is truly reflected in the community's journal *Pax*, which has been published since its earliest days, and in the pastoral role of St. Peter's Grange, now a centre for retreatants. Among the great leaders of the past are Carlyle himself, who after leaving Caldey through ill-health in 1921 returned in 1951, and Abbot Upson's successors, Dom Dyfrig Rushton and Dom Aldhelm Cameron-Brown. The rich variety in the lives of members of the community is illustrated by the lives of three members who recently died: Bro. Patrick Bergin (d. 1991), a lay brother and former blacksmith some of whose work is in the Abbey church; Fr. Bede Griffiths (d. 1993), who left Prinknash to become successively superior at Farnborough and creator of the Benedictine foundation in India; and Fr. Sylvester Houédard (d. 1992), poet and scholar who played an important part in the production of the Jerusalem Bible.

For a modern foundation Prinknash is remarkably rich in possessions. Some of the best work is relatively recent, including several items by George Hart, the silversmith of the Guild of Handicrafts at Chipping Campden, and vestments made in the Abbey workshops. Among its older possessions is a carved oak statue of the Virgin and Child which was given to the community by a descendant of St. Thomas More to be placed in a shrine for the conversion of England. The Abbey also owns the library of Mgr. Ronald Knox, who had a special affection for the community from the days when he, and Mgr. Vernon Johnson, were Anglican visitors to Anglican Caldey.

J.A.F.

Pucklechurch: See Bristol St. Augustine

Radstock, Somerset: St. Hugh

Radstock was one of the missions established in 1913 through the enthusiasm of members of the Downside community (the other one was Norton St. Philip). A temporary building of thin wooden beams and asbestos blocks was etected in 1913 and dedicated to St. Hugh, the patron saint of Dom Hugh Mackey, the first priest to serve it and one of the members of the 'pressure group'. Its altar rails and benches came from Prior Park. Fr. Mackey was succeeded in 1918 by Dom Ambrose Agius, who acquired a disused printing works, formerly a barn, and converted it into the present church, which opened in 1929. It was rebuilt after a serious fire in 1991. It has a statue of the patron on its façade.

The early days of the Radstock mission are vividly recalled in Fr. Agius' typescript autobiography at Downside. His battle with the prejudice and bigotry that he encountered in the earlier days is described in detail: he was a happy warrior who relished a tussle. From his Downside schooldays he had been a notable athlete, and he deliberately set out to use his sporting interests to gain the confidence of the village. He turned out for the football team and organised several other sports, including the Fosseway Ladies hockey players. When he left the mission in 1933 its foundations had been firmly laid. In 1955 Mass was celebrated on two weekdays (albeit with a small attendance) and on Sundays Mass attendance had grown from twenty-five in 1914 to about sixty.

J.C.

Ammerdown

In 1970 the Sisters of the Congregation of Notre Dame de Sion, founded in Paris in 1843, established a convent at Ammerdown, on the outskirts of Radstock. In 1973, with the encouragement of Lord Hylton, who lived nearby, the sisters opened a study centre and retreat house. It was originally intended for different Christian groups to meet and work together to improve understanding of each others traditions. However it soon became apparent that other faiths should become involved, and Rabbi Lionel Blue was one of the first non-Christian visitors. Hinduism and Buddhism are also included in the study courses but the centre is not just for religious groups. Over the years it has developed the residential accommodation and can now offer holidays for senior citizens and a separate house specially for young people as well as conference facilities for various lay organisations, together with a wide range of courses open to all.

Its mission statement describes it as 'a Christian house dedicated to peace, reconciliation and renewal which provides a programme of opportunities for study, mutual learning and the chance to hear and appropriate new ideas and insights'.

V.A.

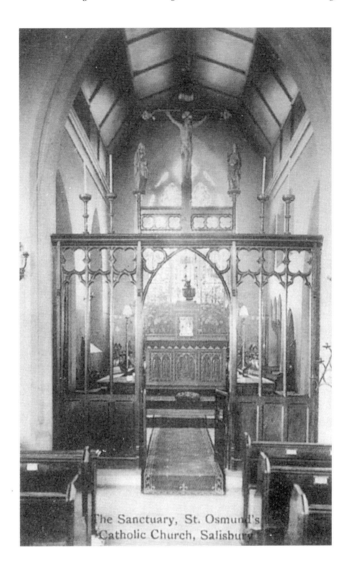

Salisbury: St. Osmund,
sanctuary

Redfield: See Bristol St. Patrick

Salisbury, Wiltshire: St. Osmund

The early history of Catholic Salisbury is linked with the history of two famous Catholic families. Gillow (iv, p. 106 seq.) records that there were several old missions in the vicinity of Salisbury, including that of the Webbs at Odstock, before the latter half of the eighteenth century. The Webb family were involved on the Royalist side in the Civil War between Charles I and Parliament. Sir John Webb had to flee the country after the failure of the Jacobite rising of 1745. At this period some of the Arundell family resided in the Close, and their domestic chapel was attended by the Catholics of the city. Their chaplains were Jesuits, among them Fr. Turner, who came in 1774. Shortly after his death in 1794, two French émigré priests, fleeing the Revolution, settled in Salisbury and ministered to the mission while maintaining themselves by teaching French.

A series of tragedies struck the Webb family during the later eighteenth century, and Odstock was sold to the Earl of Radnor who was a Protestant. The link with Wardour was provided by Thomas, brother of the eighth Earl Arundell, who settled in Salisbury in the mid-eighteenth century. Thomas kept a chaplain as part of his household, an arrangement that enabled local Catholics to attend Mass at his residence. Mgr. Marest later took charge at Wardour while Fr. Nicholas Begin remained, eventually 'to attain an excellent position in Salisbury, and was highly respected by the Anglican clergy'.

Meanwhile the Arundells had left the Close and Mass was said in a room of an old house in Brown Street, with the Arundells contributing £20 per year to the mission. In 1811 premises in St. Martin Street – formerly an inn known as the 'Worlds End' – were purchased for a chapel and priest's residence. This chapel continued to be used until the opening on '7 September 1848' of St. Osmund's church in Exeter Street. (Fr. Begin died in 1826 and was buried in the churchyard of St. Martin's on the south side of the church.)

The new church was designed by Pugin who had lived locally from 1835 to 1837 in a house which he himself had designed, St. Marie's Grange, Alderbury. At the Pugin Exhibition held at the Victoria and Albert Museum in July 1994, it was noted that the dwelling 'was a remarkably advanced house for its date for, although Gothic in form, it had no carved details, and was built largely of plain red brick with some contrasting stone trim and a slate roof. It was not a large house but, appropriately for a recent convert to Roman Catholicism, it did have a small chapel'.

The principal benefactor of the new church was John Lambert, a leading Catholic, who, in 1854, became Mayor of Salisbury and later, as a distinguished civil servant, advisor to a succession of prime ministers on such matters as health and electoral reform. He was knighted, sworn of the privy council and on his death in 1892, was buried in the small graveyard at St. Osmund. He was also the author of a number of studies on plainchant.

For the next hundred years St. Osmund was the only Catholic church in the area. A survey in 1865 by one of the missioners contains the names of 230 Catholics in Salisbury and the surrounding villages. That year of 1865 also saw the providential intervention of Lady Herbert of Lea, a recent convert to the Catholic faith. Lady Herbert sought to provide a school for the growing population of Catholic children. Gillow adds: 'In 1868, mainly through the munificence of Elizabeth, Lady Herbert of Lea, a poor school was erected on land purchased by her near the church'. The school was to last for sixty years and the building still remains as the Parish Rooms.

At the request of the Sisters of Charity she also founded an industrial school for young girls in need of care. This special school was housed in a property then known as St. Elizabeth's and now known as 131 Exeter Street. It closed in 1924 and the premises became available for the parish school.

Later embellishments of St. Osmund included the dedication in March 1893 of a window in memory of Sir John and Lady Lambert. Executed by Hardman and Co. of Birmingham it depicts St. John the Evangelist and St. Veronica. In 1895 *The Tablet* announced:

> The chapel of Our Lady in St. Osmund's church has been further
> beautified by the erection of a magnificent reredos and of a canopy over
> the statue of the Madonna. The screen in front consists of old oak work
> supposed to have belonged to a church in the neighbourhood some 300
> years ago. The canopy above is also carved in oak after the plan of the
> Rev. D. G. Hubert, priest of the mission, the work having been skillfully
> executed by Mr. W. M. Batt. The pinnacles and crockets are gilded, and
> the ground walk is blue, to correspond with the other portions of the altar,
> which is now rendered complete.
>
> *(30 November)*

The twentieth century witnessed further growth in the form of new residential areas and the pastoral commitments of the parish included the military establishments north of the city. A formative phase in the history of St. Osmund was the long pastorate of Canon Michael Hyland who was parish priest from 1932 to 1971. In 1938 the parish church of **St Gregory and the English Martyrs** was opened to provide for the expanding Catholic population, and Mass was being said at **Porton, Bemerton and Ludgershall**.

The Education Act of 1944 and the raising of the school leaving age created major difficulties for the parish. The school had suffered from overcrowding from the beginning of the century and the new legislation increased the pressures on cramped and limited accommodation. The opening of St. Joseph's in 1964 helped matters to a certain degree. St. Osmund's became a primary school under the guidance of the Sisters of Charity. However the sisters' numbers dwindled and the congregation withdrew from teaching in 1980. In 1982 the Sisters of Charity departed after 114 years in the parish. Also in that year Bishop Alexander, who had been an altar-boy and parishioner, returned to celebrate a Diocesan Mass in Salisbury Cathedral – an event attended by more than 2,000 people.

The sisters of La Retraite, who at one time had a school in Campbell Road, are now at 16 Bellevue Road.

There are now three parishes in Salisbury and the present St. Osmund's covers the centre and south of the city and extends for about ten miles to the south and west.

Downton: The Good Shepherd and Our Blessed Lady, Queen of Angels

In 1939 Lord Nelson of Trafalgar gave a bungalow and a piece of land to the diocese and in 1948 his successor sold a further acre of land to the diocese for £90. In 1950 a temporary church was built at a cost of £2,500.

In his will Lord Nelson (who died in 1947) gave to the diocese a legacy of £3,000 to be invested and the income applies

> 'towards the salary of the Roman Catholic priest who may serve the chapel in Trafalgar Park founded in 1147, or in the Oratory at Trafalgar House, or if at any time that is not possible in a chapel that may hereafter be erected and attached to the Chaplain's Presbytery at Barford, Downton'

On the sale of Trafalgar in 1948 Lord Nelson also gave to the bishop all the furniture, pictures, vestments, sacred vessels and ornaments in one of those chapels. Many of these are still in use in the church of the Good Shepherd, Downton, opened in 1950.

Salisbury, Wiltshire: Most Holy Redeemer

During the post war years Salisbury, in common with many other English towns and cities, experienced a growth in its Catholic population. Bishopdown estate to the east of the city had become in effect an appendage of St. Osmund's parish and so it seemed appropriate to make it independent, given that the clergy of the mother parish then had other commitments in **Alderbury, Bramshaw and Downton**.

For seven years Fr. Patrick Cronin had served as curate at St. Osmund and so was well aware of the pastoral needs of the area. Accordingly Bishop Rudderham appointed him parish priest of Holy Redeemer, although for about a year he had to live in a house on the estate until the presbytery was ready. Work began on the church site in 1960 but the building itself was not completed until 1964. It is of a typical modern design, predominantly in concrete and glass. The main altar is of striking dimensions measuring nine feet by three feet, and it was fortunate that at the last moment it was possible to re-locate it away from the wall so that the celebrant, in accordance with the new liturgical thinking, could say Mass facing the people.

At one time La Retraite Convent and school were at Campbell Road, within the confines of the parish. In 1953, long before Holy Redeemer had been established, the sisters had replaced the Institute of Christian Education at what was then known as Leehurst. La Retraite subsequently left Campbell Road and moved to their present convent in Belle Vue Road.

Fr. James Nolan served the parish for approximately seven years, and in 1996, when he moved to Tetbury, the pastoral care of Holy Redeemer reverted to the clergy at St. Osmund.

J.A.H.

Whaddon, Wiltshire: The Holy Family

This former Methodist chapel was opened as a Mass centre dedicated to the Holy Family on Whit Sunday 1991.

The church of England also hold their Sunday school in the building. A joint service is held in the village once a month.

J.A.H.

Alderbury, Wiltshire: The Hut

For three years until 1958 Mass was said in the home of Mrs. Thesiger at Hillside. In that year she gave the diocese a plot of land fronting the main Salisbury to Southampton road, and on this a church hut was erected. This became known locally as 'the Catholic hut at the Clarendon cross roads'. Mass was said here for thirty-two years before being transferred to **Whaddon**. During the intervening period of just over a year the priest from St. Osmund, Salisbury said Mass in St. Mary's parish church, Alderbury.

Bramshaw: Our Lady of Walsingham, Warrens

Although under the Local Government Boundaries Acts (1895, 1896) Bramshaw was transferred from Wiltshire to Hampshire, it nevertheless continued to be in the diocese of Clifton. The Papal Bull which established the diocese in 1850 had decreed that, irrespective of any subsequent change, the county boundaries 'as existing at that time' were to continue as the diocesan boundaries as well.

On 1 November 1934 Bishop Lee opened a chapel which (Sir) Oliver Crosthwaite-Eyre, later to be elected as M.P. for the New Forest, had built for public worship on his estate (Warrens) at Bramshaw. This was the year in which Cardinal Bourne had re-established the medieval shrine of Our Lady of Walsingham at the Slipper Chapel, and so it was fitting that the new chapel should have the same dedication.

During the next twenty-five years Mass was said regularly by the clergy from St. Osmund. Congregations were small, mostly family and retainers, although during the summer months groups of girl guides and others camping in the New Forest would swell the numbers considerably. In the course of time, however, the chapel was seen to be no longer pastorally viable and so a decision was made to close it. The final Mass was celebrated by Bishop Alexander on 27 October 1979.

Standlynch, Wiltshire: Trafalgar House

Trafalgar House is the name given to the mansion of Standlynch which, with the estate, was bought by the trustees in 1814 and bestowed on the first Earl Nelson, brother of the Admiral who had been killed in action. The Nelson family maintained an oratory at Trafalgar and a little pre-Reformation perpendicular church at Standlynch. The latter had been damaged in the Civil War, re-built for Anglican worship and then re-dedicated as a Catholic chapel on 20 June 1914 by members of the family who, some time before, had become Catholics. The full dedication is worth recording: Mary, Queen of Angels, St. Michael and all the Angels. The estate was sold after the Second World War and the family gave the furnishings to the church then being built at **Downton** on land which they had donated for the purpose.

J.A.H.

Salisbury, Wiltshire: St. Gregory and the English Martyrs

Just before the Second World War it became clear that a second church was needed in Salisbury. The diocese purchased some land in St. Gregory's Avenue, in the western suburbs of the city, for £500 and erected a church in a modernised romanesque style with a concrete roof. It was dedicated to St. Gregory and the English Martyrs and was opened by Bishop Lee on

22 June 1938. From then until 1951, when it became an independent parish, it was served by the clergy from St. Osmund.

In September 1950 the adjoining semi-detatched house, 44 St Gregory's Avenue, was purchased for £2,250 and a priest took up residence. In 1958 a church hall was built for just over £5,700. It has had a chequered history, was destroyed by fire and rebuilt. For many years it served as an annexe of St. Osmund Infants School. Later 42 St Gregory's Avenue was bought and linked up as a presbytery extension, but in 1980 most of it was again separated off and rented out to tenants.

From the late 1950s there was a weekly Mass at **Fugglestone Camp, Wilton**. In 1969 a two-storey Georgian building, formerly Wilton Methodist Chapel, was purchased for £5,000 and renovated. **St. Edith's Chapel** became a chapel-of-ease and Mass in Wilton was celebrated there. (St. Edith was a tenth century nun who died in the convent at Wilton while still in her twenties). In 1973 a small group of Holy Family sisters made part of the building a temporary convent and then, in 1975, moved to 44 West Street, Wilton.

When they left in 1983 the house was bought by John and Lee Proctor both as a family home and as the 'Maranatha House of Prayer' which was to be the focal point of the Alabare Prayer Community which they initiated. Inspired through prayer, since 1992 this community has opened three homes in Salisbury for the homeless, another for adults with learning difficulties, and initiated several other schemes to help the disadvantaged. Although the community is not strictly part of the parish, several parishioners have been involved in its work which is supported by the parish charity project. In 1989 the community's leader, John Proctor, was ordained permanent deacon.

When the Methodists left St. Edith's they had arranged to share the Wilton United Reformed Chapel, but when this building began to deteriorate, the joint congregations asked if they might share St. Edith's. As the result of a sharing agreement reached in 1984 the three congregations now worship in one building.

Fr. Richard Northey

THE CHURCHES ON SALISBURY PLAIN

The churches of **Bulford, Our Lady Queen of Peace and Larkhill, St. Barbara** (the Patron Saint of Artillerymen) are in the diocese of Clifton but served by Army Chaplains, and both are fairly modern additions to their respective camps. The Bishop-in-Ordinary to H. M. Forces, the Rt. Rev. Gerard Tickle, laid the foundation stone at Larkhill on 12 January 1967 and two years later, also on 12 January, dedicated Bulford church to Our Lady Queen of Peace. The new building had replaced a much older wooden structure which had been erected to the memory of Fr. W. Finn, the chaplain to the 29th. Division who died on D Beach at Gallipoli in April 1915. A modern 5-panel reredos on the wall behind the altar was painted by George Warner Allen, a convert to Catholicism, who for many years worked on the camouflage of aircraft. A large bell stands beside the church bearing the inscription: 'I have been named Eugenia Gertrude Cecilia by Mrs. Gertrude Radcliffe of Burgate, Fordingbridge, with the assistance of Eugene Cadic Esq. of Ormonde House, Cardiff and blessed by the Abbot of Notre Dame de Grâce in 1905', but its connection with Bulford is a mystery.

Tidworth: St. Patrick (now Diocese of Portsmouth)

The history of the oldest church on the Plain, consecrated in 1912, dedicated to St. Patrick but known as 'Tommy Atkins' Church', began during the early years of this century at Mooltan Barracks, where the Catholics were given permission to use the dining hall for celebration of Mass. The Royal Munster Fusiliers stationed there were Catholic almost to a man. The chaplain at that time, Mgr. Count Bickerstaffe-Drew, probably better known as the novelist John Ayscough, realised that a permanent church building was needed. Each Catholic soldier was asked to contribute 1d. per week and N.C.O.'s 6d. and these contributions were recognised in two of the stained glass windows dedicated to the 2nd. Battalion Royal Munster Fusiliers and 3rd. Battalion Worcestershire Regiment who are referred to as Founders and Benefactors.

In 1997 three glass windows commemorating three specific periods of the military history of the twentieth century were commissioned:

• *The Parish Window* commemorates post Second World War conflicts;

• *The Chaplains Window* – 42 Catholic chaplains who died during both world wars and Fr. Gerry Weston C.F. who died in the bombing of the Parachute Mess in Aldershot in 1972; and

- *The Brigade Window* commemorates units which have served in Bosnia under the United Nations. Throughout the decades various Regimental units have gifted the church with glass, benches and other furnishings to commemorate their comrades.

V.A.

See also Amesbury, Ludgershall, Tisbury and Wardour and Warminster.

Sandford, Somerset: Served from Cheddar

Sedbury, Gloucestershire: Sacred Heart Chapel: Served from Coleford

Severn Beach, St. Nicholas (C of E): Served from Bristol St. Antony

Sharpness, Gloucestershire: See Thornbury

Shepton Mallet, Somerset: St. Michael

This parish is one of the oldest in the diocese. Shepton Mallet had an organised community at the end of the eighteenth century. In 1765 Fr. John Brewer, a Jesuit, who served until his death in 1797, started a mission which included Wells and Ston Easton. The original chapel at Shepton Mallet was a room in the house of the Hippisley family in Market Place. (Before the arrival of Fr. Brewer the Hippisleys had walked either to Bristol or to Bath; in due course, however, they were able to persuade Fr. Alban Molyneux to come from Bonham every six weeks to officiate at Shepton). Fr. Brewer lodged with this staunch Catholic family, paying them twenty pounds *per annum*.

His successor was Fr. James Hussey who used his private income to buy a plot of land, part of Summerleaze Park. The chapel opened for public worship on 29 April 1804 and could seat a congregation of 200. Fr. Hussey died in 1810 and was succeeded by Dr. William Coombes, a man noted for his learning and courtesy, who served the mission for thirty-nine years. Born at Meadgate in the parish of Camerton in 1767 he had been expelled with others from the English College at Douai as a result of the French Revolution.

Ironically the Revolution brought another benefit to the town. The Sis-

Shepton Mallet: former church of St. Michael

ters of the Visitation, founded at Annecy in 1610, had also been driven from France and two of them eventually found their way to Draycott where in 1810 they opened a convent which they called 'Sales House' after their founder, the Bishop of Geneva, St. Francis de Sales (1567–1622). The buildings, which included a mansion, dye houses and mill, had been purchased for the sisters at a cost of ten thousand pounds by Mrs. Tunstall of Wycliffe, Yorkshire. The community opened a 'free school' which served both Catholic and Protestant children in the town. Because of repeated flooding from the river Sheppey in 1831 they left and established a new foundation (also 'Sales House') at Westury-on-Trym.

In 1851 the Jesuits handed over the mission to the newly formed diocese of Clifton. Twenty years later, in 1875, Wells became a separate mission.

In 1908 Mother Patricia and seven Sisters of the Saviour and the Blessed Virgin arrived and set up a convent in Paul Street, opening a boarding and day school for girls. The school was successful and in 1934 a new building was opened to accommodate the expanding numbers. Fr. Hussey's church – originally dedicated to St. Nicholas – served the Catholics of Shepton Mallet until 1965. Since 1862 the church had been dedicated to St. Michael. The present church of St. Michael, dedicated in 1965, was built on a site which formed the corner of Langhorne Park (latterly the Convent) and was given by the Order. Their generosity was matched by an anonymous gesture of £30,000, half of which was a gift and half an interest free loan.

The chapel of St. Nicholas is still preserved as a Grade 2 listed building. After a short spell as a temporary furniture store it is now the factory site of ICI Polymers Ltd. The high pointed windows on the west side are a remainder of its 163 years service as a Catholic chapel.

Bruton, Somerset

During the war Red Lynch Mansion, just outside Bruton, served as a Mass centre for surrounding Army units, and when they left in 1946 the nine local Catholics who had been attending Mass there were left without this facility. One of them, Mr. Thorn, approached the Prior at nearby Wincanton, and it was agreed that Mass would be celebrated first at the local school, then in a village hall. Later an arrangement was made with the Anglican Church of St. Mary which still continues today. Mr. Thorn's two daughters Lilian and Beatrice acted as sacristans, keeping the altar linen in their home for the next fifty years. The celebrant travelled from Wincanton until the Carmelites left there in 1995 and the area is now served from Shepton Mallet.

J.A.H.

Shortwood

Mass was said in what is now known as Shortwood House for almost one hundred years. Only the three Gothic windows upstairs on the west side indicate that it once contained a chapel capable of holding up to forty people. Access was by an outside stairway. The bay window at the front of the house and the section at the rear were added at a different date. Today, with a new landscaped garden, the house looks out from its elevated position above the Common towards Mendip.

The founding father was the Rev. Hunt. Born at Ston Easton in 1762, he was ordained priest at Douai in 1790 and, after a period of imprisonment, when the college was seized by the French authorities, returned to England in 1795. At **Ston Easton** he said Mass in the Beaumont chapel (later to become a farm building) beside the road to Clapton, and ministered to Catholics in the area from 1795–1838 (with a short break 1799–1802, when in Monmouthshire).

By 1806 he had built the house and chapel at Shortwood: 'previous to this I had no fixed abode'. Shortwood House was built on a piece of land

Shepton Mallet: Shortwood, former chapel (upper floor)

given by the Rev. John Brookes, formerly rector of Hinton Blewett. Brookes, who had married a Catholic, Ann James, whose mother was a Beaumont from Wells, had become a Catholic in 1804, when he resigned his living.

Oliver in his *Collections* tells the story of why Hunt wanted to establish a church in the area. Early in the eighteenth century William James was farming in the Hinton Blewett area. Among his labourers was an Irish drover whom he had brought over from the market at Salisbury. Instead of attending the services in the parish church, he used to make his way to one of the outbuildings on the farm where he worked, to make his own devotions, with his beads and a book of prayers. Impressed by his servant's example, William James asked for an explanation of this 'queer religion', as a result of which he was himself received into the Church before his death in 1720.

One of his sons, also William, married Miss Beaumont of Wells. They had three sons, all of whom became priests. Her father, Joseph, thus being deprived of a male heir, bequeathed his estate at Ston Easton to John Hunt, who had married Elizabeth James, on condition that he took the name Beaumont. This John Hunt/Beaumont, living at Ston Easton, was the father of Shortwood's first priest.

Although Fr. Hunt served Shortwood for some forty years, the remaining forty-five years of the missions' existence saw the incumbency of no fewer than thirteen priests, the most notable of whom was the celebrated contoversialist, Fr. T. M. McDonnell, who stayed from 1852 to 1860.

Shepton Mallet:
Ston Easton,
Beaumont Chapel

The Rev. John Skinner notes in his *Journal* for 1825 a growth in the number of Catholic chapels at Camerton, Shepton Mallet, Downside and Shortwood. Certainly the returns for 1840 show a congregation of 115. A little later there is a tradition that when the Coley reservoirs were being constructed about 1850 Mass was said at the old Button Factory, which can still be seen at Sherborne, for the Irish navvies who would be kneeling in the mud outside.

In 1883 a new Catholic church at **East Harptree** was opened and consecrated. This superseded the chapel at Shortwood, although, until about 1900, Fr. George Johnson continued to reside in the house belonging to the old mission. What is interesting is the pedigree of missions in this area:

STON EASTON
↓
SHORTWOOD
↓
EAST HARPTREE
↓
CHEW MAGNA

with Shepton Mallet also claiming a spiritual descent. Apart from Chew Magna (dedicated to the Sacred Heart) the dedication throughout has been to St. Michael – the same as that of the chapel on the top of Glastonbury Tor.

With the exception of the final paragraph, the above is an abridged version of an article by Robin Atthill in South West Catholic History, 2, 1984, by kind permission of the editor.

Shirehampton: See Bristol St. Bernard

**Somerton, Somerset: St. Dunstan and Langport, Somerset:
St. Joseph**

In 1886 the Missionaries of the Sacred Heart came to Glastonbury and in
1898 there began the construction of the railway line between Castle Cary
and Taunton. These two events in their different ways are part of the
origins of this parish. The former provided priests to say Mass in Somerton
and the latter brought in large numbers of Irish Catholics to form the basis
of a parish community. Since 1886 Somerton was served from Glastonbury,
though it has not been possible to find out exactly where Mass was said.

In 1903 the Sisters of Christian Instruction of St. Gildas fled from the
anti-Catholic legislation in France. They came to England and moved into
Hill House, Langport. They brought with them three lay brothers who cul-
tivated the garden for food. To earn some money the sisters took in wash-
ing, needlework and gave French lessons. In 1914 they opened a private
school for about a dozen girls. Over the years the numbers increased, partly
due to the railway which brought pupils in from Somerton. In 1953 the
convent school numbered 183 children of which only forty-seven were Catholics.

In 1927 a plot of land was given for the erection of a wooden church
on the north side of Langport Road. The church was named after St. Dunstan who was born in the nearby village of Baltonsborough. The stone
church of St. Dunstan was built in 1965 and successive priests lived in the
accommodation provided by the sisters at St. Joseph's presbytery. In 1972
the boarding school was closed but the Junior School continued until 1991
when it too closed. In August 1991 the Sisters of St. Gildas left Langport
and the diocese took over the convent as a Conference and Retreat Centre.

K.McG.

Southdown: See Bath Our Lady and St. Alphege

South Petherton, Somerset: St. Michael: Served from Yeovil

Stockwood: See Bristol St. Bernadette

Stonehouse, Gloucestershire: St. Joseph

There was an early attempt to establish a Catholic congregation at
Stonehouse in 1894, when the Dominicans of Stroud rented a room and

celebrated Mass once a fortnight, but the arrangement was short-lived. Prior to the First World War the regular congregation at Stonehouse numbered no more than about twelve. An unusually vivid account of the times has been left by the daughter of the late Mrs. Cicily Mary Cullis, who played a large part in the raising of funds for the construction of the present church. The arrangements were typical of the extemporisations which preceded many recent parishes. The first Mass centre was a converted outbuilding at Oldbury House near Eastington, the home of the Catholic Lady Makins. Thereafter, until 1933, Mass was said in the Subscription Rooms at Stonehouse. The billiard room, and later the stage, served as confessional and sacristy, and Mass was celebrated in a 'rather dingy hall with pictures of local worthies and Queen Victoria's coronation on the walls'. The Mass centre was served from Stroud, by the Dominicans until they left the parish in 1947, and thereafter by diocesan priests.

The inadequacy of the accommodation was aggravated by the wartime influx of Catholic evacuees. The efforts of local fundraising made it possible to acquire a site for a new church in 1947, and in the following year when Mrs Cullis's daughter had an audience with Pope Pius XII he sent his blessing for the project. Its foundation stone was laid in 1965. Designed by Anthony Thompson, its most striking feature is the segmental arrangement of seating which in conformity with post-Conciliar principles allows the congregation an unimpeded view of the altar. Stonehouse continued to be served from Stroud after the new church was built until 1973, when it became a separate parish. In that year the parish was entrusted to the Fransalians, who remained there until 1989, when it became the responsibility of the diocese.

J.A.F.

Stow-on-the-Wold, Gloucestershire: Our Lady and St. Kenelm

Before the First World War the few Catholics at Stow went to Chipping Campden and Chipping Norton, and in 1914 monthly masses were celebrated at chapels at Carterton and Witney in Oxfordshire. Mass at Stow began with the influx of Belgian refugees in the war. Mass centres were opened at Stow (and also at Moreton-in-Marsh): in private houses, a hall in Well Lane, then in St. Edward's Hall. They were served from Chipping Campden. After the number of refugees had dwindled away Mass was discontinued in 1917.

Catholicism in Stow was shortly afterwards revivified by the efforts of a remarkable man, George de Serionne. A Frenchman of aristocratic lineage, he matriculated as a non-collegiate student at Oxford after attending the Sorbonne, and devoted himself to Catholic apostolic work in Oxfordshire and adjacent parts of Gloucestershire. The first Mass was said in 1918 with a congregation of sixteen. In 1921 he bought a disused Church of England school then being used as a builder's yard, which was adapted to become the present church. He was helped there by a retired Mill Hill Father, Fr. van den Biessen, who was long remembered in Stow and described by de Serionne as 'a little odd, but a great man'. Otherwise single-handed, he maintained the mission, together with his extensive commitments in Oxfordshire, from a room in the Unicorn at Stow. The supply of priests was a constant preoccupation, which he seems to have met by exerting considerable influence – he is said to have prevailed upon Dominicans and Franciscans from Oxford, Jesuits from Heythrop, Servites from Begbroke, Passionists from Broadway, Fathers of Charity from Rugby, and Benedictines on holiday from Ampleforth. In 1939 George de Serionne was badly hurt by a fall from his motor-bicycle, on which he regularly toured his country, and was ultimately compelled to abandon his Cotswold mission. The church of St. Kenelm, previously his personal property, became a responsibility of the diocese in 1941, served from Chipping Campden. The first resident priest, Fr. John O'Donnell, later of Cirencester, was appointed in the next year. Meanwhile in 1941 de Serionne had moved to Ampleforth, where he died in 1960. He was buried at Chipping Campden.

Bourton-on-the-Water, Gloucestershire: Our Lady Help of Christians

Prior to the Second World War the few Catholics in Bourton attended Stow or Chipping Campden, though a small catechetic group was set up in the house of George and Mary Barnes, who did much towards establishing Catholicism there. The need for a Mass centre became more urgent when Service personnel came to Little Rissington airfield, and after a time when Mass was said in private houses the Church of England hall was used. Fund-raising events were initiated by Fr. O'Donnell, the parish priest of Stow, and continued after the war, so that in 1957 a site in Station Road was acquired and work began in 1960 on the present church. Though traditional in design it uses modern materials which lend themselves to quick construction, so that it was possible to celebrate Mass in it in October of that year. It continues to be served from Stow.

J.A.F.

Stratton-on-the-Fosse, Somerset: St. Benedict

A village Catholic community became established around the Benedictines of Downside shortly after their arrival in 1814. The baptismal register, which dates back to 1818, includes the name of Dom Bede Polding, the first Archbishop of Sydney (1842). A church and school were completed in 1857 to the design of Charles Hansom. It was extended and altered, with the removal of its spire, in 1913. Its furnishings included a highly decorated rood screen designed by Dom Ephraim Seddon of Downside and executed by a local craftsman, and a reredos with sixteen statues of figures associated with the locality and the West Country. The screen was dismantled when the interior was changed after the Second Vatican Council and a free standing altar was introduced.

Dom Bede Vaughan, who became second Archbishop of Sydney in 1877, was in charge of the mission from 1859 to 1861. One of his successors, the archaeologist Dom Ethelbert Horne, was a dominant and greatly respected figure for half a century from 1891. He is said to have baptised most of the community, irrespective of creed, and to have blessed their weddings.

Dom Bede Polding was already teaching in the village, in a cottage in the earliest days, in 1825. Ten years later there were 100 pupils. In 1837 they formed a Coronation procession through the village, surely one of the earliest Catholic parades since the Reformation. Hansom's school was enlarged in 1874. In 1897 the Servite nuns came to teach there and stayed for over fifty years.

The Guild of St. Gregory, a village sodality that was also a sick benefit club, was still in a healthy financial state when it was wound up in 1949 after 108 years' existence.

The theologian, Baron Von Hügel (1852–1925), is buried in the churchyard.

J.A.F.

Street, Somerset: See Glastonbury

Stroud, Gloucestershire: Immaculate Conception

The parish of Stroud is remarkable for the rich variety of Catholic institutions within its boundaries, and for the churches served from it. Organised Catholicism came to Stroud when in 1855 Emily Sandys (1800–1878), the convert widow of an Anglican clergyman, opened a school in a house in London Road, and in the following year the Stroud mission began there, served by the Dominicans of Woodchester. It immediately proved inadequate for a rapidly increasing Catholic population, which by 1857 numbered 220, with an unusually large proportion of converts who resisted a sustained attack from the Protestant Alliance. In 1855 the foundation stone of a church, designed by C. A. Buckler, was laid at Beeches Green. Dedicated to the recently defined Immaculate Conception, it was opened ceremonially in 1857, Cardinal Wiseman preaching. Initially the nave and aisles were built, with chancel and sanctuary to follow; they never did, because of the encroachment of St. Rose's Convent on the site, and the existing building was remodelled to give adequate accommodation for the sanctuary and to include a side chapel, dedicated to the Sacred Heart. It was opened in 1882, and consecrated a century later. In 1893 Cardinal Vaughan, a native of Gloucestershire, visited the church to bless the newly erected statue of St. Peter. He commented that the congregation of Stroud was one of the first in England thus to honour the Prince of the Apostles.

Until 1944 priests were appointed to Stroud by the Dominican Province, and thereafter appointments have been by the Bishop of Clifton. From 1978 to 1996 the incumbent was Canon Thomas Curtis Hayward, a member of a local family of Quedgeley. The churches of Painswick and Bisley, and the chapel of the convent at More Hall, are served from Stroud, as was Stonehouse until it became an independent parish in 1966.

St. Rose's Convent, Stroud

Emily Sandys established a group of lay Dominican tertiaries in association with the Stroud mission. In 1857 they were joined by Elizabeth Matthews (1815–1905), who had been received into the Church in 1852 and was then living *en famille* with the Catholic Bucknall family in Stroud. Largely due to her influence the group came to seek the regular religious life, and in 1857 the Dominican Provincial, Fr. Dominic Aylward, and Fr. James Bernard Morewood were received in private audience by Pope Pius IX and given permission to establish a convent of Sisters of Penance of the Third Order of St. Dominic, under the patronage of St. Rose of Lima. Elizabeth Matthews was clothed as Mother Mary Teresa, and became the first Prioress, an office she held for over thirty-five years.

In 1862 Emily Sandys bought land near the church of Our Lady, Stroud, for the convent buildings, and provided funds towards its construction, but it found no other major benefactor and was built from the 'pennies of the poor': progress was slow. The convent dates from 1867 and its chapel from 1888–1895: the community was fortunate in having the services of Benjamin Bucknall, an influential figure among Victorian architects. The interior of the chapel was not completed until 1950, when it was consecrated. A

Stroud: former St. Rose's convent, chapel

famous visitor to its organ was Sir Edward Elgar, whose sister was a member of the community. The periodical 'The Rosary', described as 'the only authorised source of information connected with the Rosary Confraternity in England', was published from Stroud. The order grew dramatically: so many vocations were attracted that by the end of the century three branch houses had been opened. By 1927 there were four. St. Rose's now belongs to the Congregation of Stone, in Staffordshire.

The Third Order has the special role of teaching and of visiting the sick. It is a role that has been fully enacted at St. Rose's from Emily Sandys' time to the present day. The last century and a half has seen mission schools, domestic service classes, a crèche for poor working mothers, an orphanage, and schools for the wealthier. Perhaps its greatest achievement is the school for physically handicapped girls, which from straitened beginnings in 1912 has now become famous. It is now centred on the house Stratford Lawns near the convent.

Stroud: Painswick, Our Lady and St. Thérèse (before the bombing)

Bisley: St. Mary of the Angels

Until the First World War the small and scattered Catholic population in
Bisley and its surrounding villages depended on the Dominican mission at
Stroud, four miles away. The local terrain made attendance difficult for
them, and in 1916 Edward Raymond Barker, a local resident related to the
Pusey family, received permission for Mass to be said in his private oratory.
He undertook that collections should go to the Stroud mission so that it
was not disadvantaged. More permanent arrangements came in 1930 when
Charles Meek, another Bisley resident (and a relative of Archbishop
Ullathorne) gave the funds for building a church at Bisley as an act of
thanksgiving for his conversion. It was built on lands belonging to the Ray-
mond Barker estate, designed in the local vernacular by Wilfrid Mangan.
It was opened in 1931, dedicated to St. Mary of the Angels. It is served
from Stroud.

Painswick: Our Lady and St. Thérèse

The unusually colourful history of Catholicism in Painswick owes much to
two redoubtable women. Frances Isabel Seddon, the wealthy convert wife
of an Anglican vicar who was for a time at Painswick, established an oratory
in her house Gwynfra, now the Painswick Hotel. She did much for the

Belgian refugees in the First World War. After leaving Painswick in 1917 she often visited More Hall until her death in her 94th year in 1951.

A more lasting influence began when Alice Howard, a kinswoman of the Howards of Norfolk, went in 1921 to live with a relative in Painswick. She converted the attic of a cottage into an oratory where Mass was occasionally said, and established a teashop whose profits went to a fund for a church. She acquired a dilapidated building in 1931 and with volunteer amateur labour (including her brother's) created a church where the first Mass was said in 1934, with a small congregation mostly Miss Howard's friends. Stroud lacked the resources to serve Painswick, and Alice Howard sought out her own 'chaplains' – among them, from 1934 until his death in 1936, *aet* 76, Mgr. Barnes, the former chaplain to both Oxford and Cambridge Universities, and later her cousin Canon Alfonso de Zulueta, whose varied career ended as Rector of the Holy Redeemer and St. Thomas More at Chelsea. In 1941 it fell to him, at 2 a.m., to rescue the Blessed Sacrament from the badly damaged chapel after a chance stick of bombs fell on Painswick. Alice Howard died in 1942, having established Catholicism in Painswick 'on a prayer and a shoestring'. Shoestring arrangements continued after the bombing until 1954, when restoration of the church began, largely through a donation from Alice's sister Jessie Howard. An otherwise plain exterior is decorated with an attractive cupola; inside, though obviously a converted room devised on a small budget, it is arguably one of the most effective Catholic church interiors in the diocese. Thus the generally accepted view in retrospection: at the time it attracted great controversy, with many, including the Bishop, strongly antipathetic. It was reopened in 1956.

Painswick has been served from Stroud since 1944. The fiftieth anniversary of the church's opening in 1934 was celebrated by the installation of a Madonna carved by Dom Basil Robinson, the son of Heath Robinson the cartoonist.

Brownshill: St. Mary of the Angels

The small village of Brownshill in the parish of Stroud is a centre of Catholic activity unique in the diocese. It originated in the early 1920s when Miss Katie Hudson and Miss Bertha Kessler came to the Cotswolds from London. There they already been concerned with the treatment of mental disorder, which they were to make their lives' work. Although not yet Catholics they had become convinced of the importance of faith to the healing of the mind, guided by Dr. W. E. Orchard, then an eminent nonconformist minister. In 1927 they bought the house Templewood at Brownshill, and in succeeding years acquired several other properties in the vicinity. There they established the Templewood Home of Rest, where women religious patients afflicted with nervous disorders joined with staff in what gradually developed into a regular way of spiritual life coupled with medical treatment. Miss Kessler and Miss Hudson became Catholics and in 1951 a Dominican Tertiary Chapter was erected with Miss Hudson (Mother Catherine) Prioress. In 1976 the structure which had long since developed was formalised by the foundation of the Little Company of Hope. They occupied St. Raphael's, a property formerly owned by the Kessler family, until the death of the last member, Sr. Philomena Murray, in 1998.

In 1938 Fr. Philip Darley O.P., who had been appointed to Stroud in 1930, became chaplain to the community. He had received Miss Hudson and Miss Kessler into the Church four years previously, and until his death in 1951 directed and fostered its spiritual life. At that time it was growing quickly, and now included a group of men based on Vine Farm, where outdoor work provided occupational therapy. He was assisted by Dr. Orchard, now a Catholic priest, who had come to live in the locality. Fr. Darley's last testament, recorded by Miss Kessler (Mother Margaret) a few days before his death, gives a moving account of his ministry.

Changes in social patterns meant fewer patients from the 1970s and most of the properties were sold. Religious communities were given first option so the Congregation of Mary Mother of the Church and St. Michael's House of Prayer (which has recently moved to Dursley), became established at Brownshill. Male patients were already also fewer when the fame of the work reached Fr. Gerald Fitzgerald, who in 1947 had founded in America the Congregation of the Servants of the Paraclete, a numerically small order dedicated to the care of priests and religious in need of psychiatric aid. This led in 1959 to their acquiring the house Firwood (previously owned by an Anglican bishop) where a group of the order continued its work. Miss Kessler and Miss Hudson, who died in 1963 within three weeks of each other, were thus able to see assured the continuation of their vocation. In the late 1960s the Paracletes moved to the premises of the former Anglican House of Mercy, which now became known as Our Lady of Victories. Described in an article in 1995 in *The Tablet* as a place of psychological and spiritual healing, it aims to set the most advanced methods of addiction therapy on a Catholic spiritual foundation. There are seven staff, all professionally trained. It accommodates twenty patients, who spend at least seventeen weeks in residence proceeding to aftercare.

There are also two tangible memorials of the work of the foundresses of Templewood and of Fr. Darley. The chapel of St. Mary of the Angels, superbly situated above the Toadsmoor valley, was opened in 1937, with

Stroud: More Hall before extension

the homily given by Fr. Darley. It is a late work of the prolific ecclesiastical architect W. D. Caroe, and is generally recognised as one of his best. Its dominating feature is the Norman arch separating the nave from the apsidal chancel. It is now served from Our Lady of Victories. Immediately adjacent are the ruins of Templewood, destroyed by a crashing aircraft in 1946. Fr. Darley, already infirm, escaped the conflagration via a drainpipe: an epitome of the indomitable spirit that illuminates Brownshill after seventy years of care for the distressed.

More Hall

More Hall, a late Tudor building in the Stroud valley, was acquired in 1901 by Frances Isabel Seddon (1857–1951), a member of the Dyson Perrins family of Worcester, and wife of an Anglican clergyman, who played a part in the early days of Catholicism in Painswick. She restored it from a ruinous condition, and for some years it housed the St. Mark's Home for Boys, which had been established in London by the Reverend James Addersley, an associate of Benjamin Fearnley Carlisle. From about 1907 it was occupied by the Anglo-Catholic priest Charles Henry Sharpe, to whom Mrs. Seddon gave it in 1912. Over the next four years Fr. Sharpe established a religious community there which he saw as a focal point for the remnant of the Caldey community which had not moved to the Catholic church.

Swindon: Holy Rood, prior to extension

Mgr. Ronald Knox in his Anglican days made a retreat there. During this time a chapel was added to the original building. Sharpe's attempt ended in failure and in 1917 he became a Catholic layman, still calling himself Fr. Sharpe. He lived until 1932, in his last years cared for by the Sisters of the Temple at Clifton. He left More Hall to them, and they continued their work there of caring for invalids and convalescents until 1968, when their place was taken by the Sisters of Grace and Compassion, who adopted the Benedictine rule in 1978. Until recently the chapel was served from Stroud.

J.A.F.

Swindon, Wiltshire: Holy Rood

Swindon has an extensive pre-Reformation history, but after the Reformation three centuries were to pass before the Mass returned to Hatherop Castle, home of Lady de Mauley. At her death in 1844 the Mass continued to be celebrated, in the cottage of a Catholic gamekeeper, by Fr. John Mitchell, who rode over from Chipping Norton. Fr. Mitchell encouraged Lord de Mauley to build a chapel in memory of his wife, together with a presbytery and a school, at Horcutt, near Fairford. This chapel was equipped with furnishings from Hatherop Castle and opened in 1845. A year later the priests from Woodchester took charge of the Horcutt mission, and, two years later, we find a chain of events that brings us back to

Swindon. In that year of 1848 there were six Catholic families living in Swindon. The names of the fathers have come down to us. They were: Thomas Deasy, Patrick Burns, Owen Murphy, Patrick Miles, Patrick Norris and James Atkinson. As there was no church or priest nearer than Fairford, these six men resolved to walk there every Sunday – a distance of fourteen miles – to hear Mass. After a brief period they persuaded the priest to come to Swindon once a month to say Mass for their families, and any other Catholics in the vicinity. So it was that Mass returned to Swindon after three centuries. This Mass was celebrated at the Greyhound Inn (which still exists in Westcott Place). Some time later Mass was said in a chapel built on a plot of land given by a parishioner, Mrs. Arkell.

From 1851 to 1856 the new Swindon mission continued to be served from Fairford. In 1857 the first resident priest, Fr. James Clark, was appointed. He was to remain for fifteen years. Swindon was now entering a phase of industrial expansion and population growth. A school chapel was opened in 1859 to provide for an expanding population of children. However, money was scarce, and as late as 1881 a debt of £450 still lay on the mission. The Catholic population now exceeded 300 parishioners and the congregation needed larger premises. St. John's Free Christian Church (now a furniture shop in Regent Circus) was acquired in 1881 and opened as a Catholic place of worship by Bishop Clifford on 8 February 1882. Here the Swindon parishioners were to worship for over twenty years until the building became inadequate for their purposes. The priest at this time was Fr. Herman Eikerling who was ordained in 1876 and died in 1915.

Fr. James Lonergan – later to minister at Frome – was in charge from 1891 until 1902. During his time the parish hall was built in Groundwell Road. The cypher of both bishop (W.R.B.) and priest (J.J.L.) may still be seen over the entrance. This hall served as a temporary place of worship during the building of the present church and presbytery, the foundation stone of which was laid by Bishop Burton on 3 May 1904. The architect chosen was E. Doran Webb of Salisbury.

In 1922 the Poor Servants of the Mother of God opened a convent at 34 Groundwell Road and the sisters worked in Holy Rood Junior School which was opened the same year. They also provided teachers for St. Joseph's Comprehensive School which opened in 1956 and still continue to serve the parish in education and pastoral ministry.

In this period began the long pastorate of Canon John Noonan which was to last for nearly thirty years. He embellished the building by adding marble altar rails and securing a magnificent stone pulpit from Cardiff Cathedral. The altars in the church (since enlarged) came from St. Catherine's Convent, Clifton, which adjoined the Pro-Cathedral. Until St. Mary's opened in 1953, Holy Rood ministered to the entire Catholic population of the town.

The growth of population, caused mainly by the overflow from London, created an acute problem in the provision of school places. In 1960 Holy Rood Primary School had over 1,000 children on the roll, and the school was spread over five sites. St. Joseph's Secondary Modern (now Comprehensive) was opened in Queen's Drive in 1957. Canon Michael Fitzpatrick was succeeded in 1963 by Canon (later Mgr.) Joseph Leahy and under his leadership new schools were opened in Upham Road, (primary) and Nythe Road (secondary). The money to build these was obtained, largely, by the transfer of grant from those areas in London where many of the children would have been educated had their families remained there.

In the late 1960s the limited capacity of the church had to be addressed, as well as the liturgical requirements of the Second Vatican Council. The church was turned on its axis with a new altar facing its northern side and the old high altar serving as the Blessed Sacrament chapel. In recent years new parishes were created from Holy Rood. These were: The Holy Family (1962) at Marlowe Avenue, Park North; Wootton Bassett, Sacred Heart (1967); and Wroughton, St. Joseph (1969). At one time Swindon was reputed to be the fastest-growing town in Europe. As time passed the railways gave way to other heavy industry which in turn gave way to electronics and the micro-chip. Mgr. Canon Richard Twomey, who had previously served fifteen years as assistant priest, returned as parish priest in 1988.

J.A.H.

Swindon, Wiltshire: Holy Family

Work on the estates of Walcot, Park North and Park South began in 1956 and many Catholics, principally from London moved in. The children attended Holy Rood Primary School and a bus was provided to take people to Mass. From 1960 Mass was celebrated in St. Joseph's Secondary Modern School in Queen's Drive. So great were the numbers, however, that in 1962 a decision was made to build a school, convent and church on a site in Marlowe Avenue in what was to become the centre of the parish. In August of that year Fr. (now Canon) William Roche was appointed first parish priest, taking up temporary residence in Woodside Avenue. During the period of building, baptisms, weddings and funerals were conducted at Holy Rood. New junior and infant schools were opened in January 1964, the remaining classrooms being completed by September of that year.

By the end of 1963 houses began to be built on the Nythe estate. One of these, in Ashley Avenue, was purchased to be used as a presbytery and just after Christmas, Fr. Roche took up residence. There were now three Masses on a Sunday, indeed the continued growth of the Catholic population made it necessary to have yet another Mass and so, in June 1966, the hall at St. Joseph's Upper School in Nythe Road became a Mass centre. So urgent had the need now become that a second priest was appointed to Holy Family even before the parish church had been built.

Some statistics for the period convey an idea of the challenges then facing the priest and his people. For example, the first Confirmation ceremony held in Holy Family Junior School hall on 7 April 1965, Bishop Rudderham administered the sacrament to 228 children. In 1967 two ceremonies were held, in May and June. Only the candidates and their sponsors could be accommodated – the parents were outside looking in. Bishop Rudderham gave directions that plans for a new church should be drawn up forthwith, and Canon Leahy laid the foundation stone on 6 October 1968. Responsibility for work on the furnishings and laying out of the grounds was assumed by members of the parish. The Bishop opened and blessed the new church of the Holy Family on 7 October 1969. In time Eldene became another growth area within the parish and from 3 February 1974 Mass was said there at the community centre.

Canon Roche's ministry in Swindon, lasting a quarter of a century, was recognised by the Borough Council when it named 'Roche Close' on the Liden Estate after him.

The foundation of the convent owed much to the friendship between Canon Michael Fitzpatrick, (parish priest at Holy Rood 1954 – 1962) and his counterpart at Bicester, Fr. Thomas Foynes. One day on the golf course the canon confided his wish to obtain the help of sisters in the rapidly expanding estates of Swindon. Fr. Foynes responded by persuading three Presentation sisters from his local convent to take up the challenge. They lived temporarily at Barcelona House, Wroughton, until May 1964 when they moved to their new convent in Marlowe Avenue. It was here that, for the first time, Mass was said in the Holy Family parish. Sr. Mercedes became headteacher of the new Holy Family School which had been opened the previous January.

Holy Family Church, Swindon, abridged

Swindon, Wiltshire: St. Mary

During and after the Second World War – and before the even greater expansion of the late 1950s and early 1960s – Swindon had been growing far beyond the pastoral resources of the town's only parish of Holy Rood. In 1954 a church dedicated to St. Mary had been opened at Pinehurst with Fr. Joseph Sheehan in charge. Initially he lived in a council house on the estate until the presbytery adjoining the church could be completed.

The railway line was to serve as the boundary between the two parishes. Even so, the area covered by St. Mary was considerable and included the districts of Rodbourne, Penhill, Gorse Hill and the village of Highworth. In the course of time mass centres were to be established at **Penhill** (first in the Community Centre and then in the Anglican church hall), and at Inigo Gardens, **Highworth** (the home of Dr. and Mrs. Dermot Gilmour).

For many years there had been only one primary school (Holy Rood) based on five sites and serving the whole of Swindon. Pupils from St. Mary's attended the school at Stratton St. Margaret. Clearly such a situation could not be allowed to continue. What was significant, however, was that the numbers involved justified the building, not of one, but two primary schools in the parish. The first of these was at Bessemer Road (opened in 1961) to be followed in 1969 by St. Catherine's at Stratton St. Margaret.

Fr. Sheehan served the parish for thirty-eight years until his retirement in 1991. He had been made an honorary canon in 1986 and died on 6 February 1992.

J.A.H.

Swindon, Wiltshire: Polish Catholic Centre

One of the most numerous of the Polish communities in the diocese is at Swindon. On their arrival in this country many Poles had been sent to camps at Trowbridge and Cirencester, but in the course of time the increasing growth and prosperity of nearby Swindon had drawn them to take up residence there.

Always closely-knit and industrious the community went from strength to strength, particularly during the time that Fr. (later Mgr.) Stanislaus Borek was their chaplain. In the 1960s it was estimated that there were 1000 Poles living in Swindon. His leadership was single-minded and firm and when he died in 1971 he left behind a flourishing community of Catholics.

From 1957 Mass and other liturgical celebrations for this community took place in Holy Rood church. In 1965 a Polish Community Centre was officially opened in Whitbourne Avenue. This was added to in 1977 when a chapel, dedicated to the Sacred Heart and served by two priests, was built adjoining the centre.

At the Saturday School children are instructed in the Polish language, history and geography. Traditional singing and dancing are taught as extra-curricular activities to pupils who, for the most part, are Polish by descent. The Polish bishop visits the centre to administer confirmation and on other special occasions.

J.A.H.

Swindon, Wiltshire: St. Peter

The close of the 1970s saw the West Swindon expansion underway. The history of the parish opens when in late September 1979 Fr. David Ryan came from Holy Rood to say Mass in the shared church at Toothill. In November of the same year Fr. (now Canon) Liam O'Driscoll was appointed to the new parish of St. Peter. In the following January he moved to 1 Liskeard Way to establish a presbytery and chapel. The chapel was set up in one of the two garages adjacent to the entrance hall and plans were made to provide a new church for a fast growing congregation.

In December 1985 the new church of St. Peter was in use for the first time for Midnight Mass at Christmas. The parish continued to develop under the guidance of Fr. O'Driscoll until May 1990 when he left for Trow-bridge. He was succeeded by Fr. Thomas Kelly who came from Marlbor-ough. One feature of the church is the statue of St. Peter which for many years graced the west end of the nave of Clifton Pro-Cathedral. The statue, blessed by Bishop Brownlow on 29 June 1894, had been purchased by Bishop Clifford out of the funds of a legacy bequeathed to him by Miss Agnes Matchinson. When the building was closed in 1973 the statue was eventually brought to its present position. It is an exact replica of the bronze twelfth century statue in St. Peter's, Rome, the right foot of which has been worn smooth by the kisses of countless pilgrims. In recent years the parish centre has been expanded and the layout of the church re-arranged. In 1985 the Missionary Sisters of the Holy Rosary moved to their present convent opposite the church.

J.A.H.

Taunton, Somerset: St. George

By 1770 there were an estimated ten 'papists' in Taunton. They were mainly of Irish and Italian origin, had no pastoral support and little oppor-tunity for worship. Their isolation was relieved in the early 1800s by the arrival of Fr. George Baldwin (or Baudwin), Taunton's first priest since the

Taunton: Franciscan Convent, chapel

Reformation. He was greatly helped in his mission by 'Dame Shattock' and
her daughter, Maria. Three generations of this convert family were to span
the many changes in the history of Catholic Taunton. Around the same
time there occurred another event that was to be a shaping influence on
the early history of the parish. Mother Gertrude Weld and her Franciscan
nuns arrived in Taunton from Winchester. Thirteen years earlier they had
escaped from Revolutionary France. Their arrival in England was facilit-
ated by the influence of King George III. They were to teach and minister
in Taunton for almost a century and a half. Indeed in the 1850s they were
to receive unwarranted notoriety in what became known as the Talbot Case
(see Chapter Six).

In 1818 Fr. Baldwin was succeeded by Fr. Samuel Fisher who immediately began working towards the building of a permanent church. A site at
the top of The Crescent was chosen; the foundation stone was laid on 13
April 1821; and in the same year twelve people were baptised by Bishop
Collingridge, the Vicar Apostolic. The church was opened in 1822 and
dedicated to St. George. In that year there was an estimated one hundred
Catholics in the town. Fr. Fisher was succeeded by Dom Richard Towers,
a scholar and controversialist, who had to deal with an upsurge of anti-
Catholic feeling in the town at the time of the passing of the Catholic

Emancipation Act 1829. Despite local hostility the congregation grew in the following decades and by the time of the establishment of the diocese in 1850 the Mass attendance had reached 300. Many of these must have been children as the Franciscan school became stretched to capacity. Three years after the foundation of the diocese Canon John Mitchell, who had played a central part in the early days of the Fairford mission and was to be a generous benefactor of Cirencester, arrived with plans for a church that would stand 'tall and proud' on the hilltop at Mountfield. The land for the church was purchased by the Franciscan nuns and the foundation stone was laid in 1858 by Bishop Clifford. The architect employed on the project was Benjamin Bucknall and the builder was John Spiller of Taunton. Dr. William Vaughan, Bishop of Plymouth, performed the opening ceremony on 24 April 1860. Canon Mitchell was a skilled apologist for the Faith and became a well-known and well-loved figure in Taunton. He was mourned by all sections of the community when he died in 1899.

In 1867 the Order of Perpetual Adoration of the Blessed Sacrament moved from Cannington to Taunton, and on 13 November 1872 the new altar in the convent chapel was consecrated by Bishop Clifford. A contemporary account stated:

> the building now erected, consisting of refectory, parlours, sacristies,
> sanctuary, mens' choir, and an outer chapel for external adorers, was designed
> by Mr. Bentley of John Street, Adelphi, and build under his superintendence;
> the whole of the outside is faced with stone taken from the ruined tower of
> the old Catholic churches of the town of Taunton, which adds greatly to the
> interest of the picturesque addition of the convent. The altar and sanctuary of
> the new chapel are of very handsome detail, all referring to the one idea of
> perpetual adoration. The altar is principally of alabaster, relieved by various
> marbles, mosaics, gilding and paintings (not yet finished). The tabernacle and
> throne are extremely beautiful and very delicately worked out.

The Tablet, 23 November, 1872

The convent, which was situated in Park Street in buildings now used by the Borough Council, closed in 1928 and the altar was taken to St. Joseph's, Fishponds, Bristol, the following year.

St. Francis School, which had served the community since 1810, was flourishing and overcrowded by the 1860s. In 1870 St. George's School was opened, replacing the small Catholic school in The Crescent universally referred to as 'The Poor School'. The development of Catholic education in Taunton was greatly helped by the energy and vision of Mother Francis Agnes Jerningham. As well as providing elementary education for the poor, she opened a 'middle school' in 1865.

Eleven years after the opening of the new church the original chapel of St. George in the Crescent was sold for £550 and used first as a warehouse and then as a Masonic Hall.

The year 1880 brought religious persecution in France with friars from Amiens crossing the channel and arriving in Taunton as refugees. They stayed for a while until Bishop Clifford invited them to Clifton. They eventually settled at Clevedon where they still administer a parish.

Canon Daniel Iles took the place of Canon Mitchell and served until 1911. He was followed by Canon James O'Shaughnessy. The church was consecrated on St. George's Day 1912. Canon O'Shaughnessy was succeeded by Canon (later Mgr.) Richard Iles who was the nephew of a previous incumbent. During his time as parish priest the Catholic population increased in the outlying towns. **The Church of the English Martyrs, Chard**, was the first daughter church of the parish of St. George. There were soon chapels in **Wellington, Crewkerne, Ilminster and Wiveliscombe**. In 1953 the Franciscan sisters departed after 150 years association with the town. Their work was carried on by the Sisters of St. Joseph of Annecy.

On 4 October 1997 the body of Joseph William Hendren, O.S.F. first Bishop of Clifton and then first Bishop of Nottingham, was re-interred in the precincts of St. George's church. Bishop Alexander conducted the ceremony in the presence of members of the bishop's family and representatives of the Franciscan Order and of the diocese of Nottingham. Since his death in 1866 his body had lain in the grounds of what had been the Franciscan convent (now King's College).

The great east window above the high altar is a fine example of nineteenth century stained glass, representing from left to right St. Dunstan, Joseph of Arimathea, The Blessed Virgin Mary, St. George, St. Walburga and St. Boniface. An important recent acquisition is the fifteen wood sculptures of the Stations of the Cross by Tom Praetor, a parishioner of St. James. They are dedicated to the memory of Mgr. Canon Iles.

St. Teresa of Lisieux

In 1955 the Mayor of Taunton signed a twinning contract with Lisieux, with the encouragement and support of many Catholics in Taunton. In the same year St. George's parishioners began a series of collections to build a second church dedicated appropriately to St. Teresa. A site on the Lyngford housing estate was agreed upon and in 1958 the foundation stone was laid by Bishop Rudderham. The new church was opened on 8 October 1959 and was described by Lt-Col J. A. Garton, Master of the Somerset Guild of

Craftsmen, as a church of 'distinctive design, with dignity and spacious interior beauty'. The architect was E. C. Francis, the builders Messrs. Stansell and Son Ltd of Taunton and the cost was £18,000. The crucifix in the apse, above the altar was carved by a local artist Escourt Clack. The Stations of the Cross are made of fabric and are believed to have originated from Buckfast Abbey. St. Teresa's became a parish in its own right for several years, until 1981 when the Sisters of Mill Hill took over the house acting as parish sisters. It is now served from St. George.

V.A. and J.A.H.

Taunton, Somerset: St. Teresa of Lisieux: Served from Taunton St. George

Tetbury, Gloucestershire: St. Michael

Early records of Catholicism in Tetbury are fragmentary: it is known that at the instance of the Belgian resident Baron de Brienen Mass was said in 1881 at the home of Mr. Hugginson, a confectioner of the town, and that from 1881 to 1883 Fr. Francis Larive came from Malmesbury to celebrate there. The congregation then numbered twenty or thirty. Thereafter the records are silent until the First World War when, as with many other Cotswold communities, an influx of Belgian refugees greatly enlarged the Catholic presence there. Mass was then said at nearby Chavenage House from Malmesbury. The Tetbury community did not secure a permanent place of worship until 1931 when Fr. Alphonsus Grorod, the parish priest of Malmesbury, bought York House in Silver Street. It was served alternately from Malmesbury and Devizes. With the outbreak of war large numbers of evacuees came to Tetbury and larger accommodation proved necessary: for a few months in Oak House, the home of a parishioner, then in the ballroom of the White Hart, whose landlord was a Catholic, and finally in 1941 in a former Baptist Chapel which was bought at auction. The Fransalians continued to serve Tetbury until 1995.

J.A.F.

Tewkesbury, Gloucestershire: St. Joseph

A plea for subscriptions for a chapel in Tewkesbury appeared in successive issues of the *Laity's Directory* in the 1830s. It was then said that Tewkesbury Catholics had to go eight or nine miles 'to attend prayer', and that gentlemen in the neighbourhood had expressed their willingness to assist. Subscriptions were to be sent to Bishop Baines. There appears to have been no sequel, and subsequently Tewkesbury became the most populous area served by the Kemerton mission. It became independent when the heirs of Thomas Porter, a wealthy Catholic resident in the area to the north-west of the town known as the Mythe, established a trust by which a church was built and a mission maintained. The church, a simple brick building in Early English with four decorated stone windows, made use of some courses of a dilapidated existing building. It was consecrated in 1870. In 1882 the congregation was said to number between thirty and forty. The first priest-in-charge, Fr. Thomas Fenn, served there for thirty-five years; his latter days were clouded by controversy over the matter of Masses for the intention of the benefactors. His successor, Fr. Arthur Jackson, left his estate to the diocese; it was used to improve the church and presbytery.

The church's location proved inconvenient from early times, and in 1977 its building was closed. Through the initiative of Fr. Michael Larkin a former telephone exchange was acquired and converted into a new St. Joseph's which was opened in the same year. In 1990, thanks to the generosity of Peter Vose, the then owner of the old church, the stained glass Annunciation window given by Amelie Pearce-Serocold in memory of her husband was moved to the new church. Mr. Walter Pearce-Serocold and Mr. Tony Packe, Amelie's great-nephews, attended the service of dedication.

J.A.F.

Thornbury, Gloucestershire: Christ the King

Long before the Church came to Thornbury, organised Catholicism had come to the Vale of Berkeley through the enthusiasm of Mrs. Mary Gifford of Berkeley, who in the 1880s gave £200 for the erection of a small chapel to serve the local community at Sharpness, on the bank of the Severn estuary about eight miles away. It was opened in 1883, dedicated to Our Lady Star of the Sea. It was served by the Franciscans from Clifton, but the expected large congregation never materialised, and the Franciscans soon withdrew to serve the mission at Portishead. Stopgap arrangements were made until the mission came to an end in 1888 and the building sold. Later it became the Anglican church of St. Andrew. A few Anglican churches have recently become Catholic, but a move in the opposite direction is rare indeed.

The next attempt to make spiritual and liturgical provision for Cath-

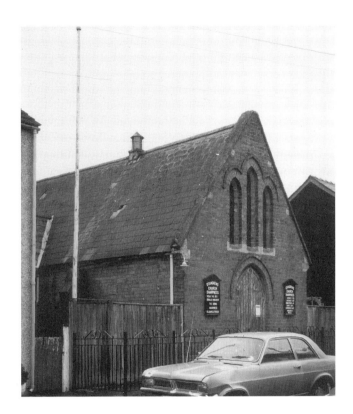

Thornbury: Sharpness, Anglican church of St. Andrew, formerly Our Lady Star of the Sea

olics in the Berkeley Vale area came in 1941 when the Provincial of the Salvatorian Order wrote to Bishop Lee offering priests to the diocese for the purpose of opening a new mission in an area where a parish did not already exist. Bishop Lee readily accepted the offer and assigned the Salvatorians to the Thornbury area, where the parish currently covers one hundred square miles.

The first Salvatorian to arrive in Thornbury was Fr. Kevin Kenny who was given £10 to get the parish established. Initially he took up residence in the Ship Inn, Oldbury where Mass was celebrated on weekdays and at the Anglican Church Institute in St. Mary Street, Thornbury on Sundays. With the help of generous benefactors a house was soon purchased in St. Mary Street where a room was converted into a small chapel for daily Mass while the Sunday arrangement continued as before. By the early 1950s sufficient money was raised to build a larger chapel at the back of the St. Mary Street house when it was estimated that the total number of Catholics in the area had reached close to 400.

The building of the Berkeley and Oldbury Power Stations within the confines of the parish led to a substantial increase in the number of practis-

ing Catholics by the late 1950s and early 1960s, and the chapel in St. Mary
Street was no longer adequate to meet the needs of the congregation. In
1961, therefore, after a variety of fund-raising activities, the site of the
present church, presbytery and parish hall was purchased. In the following
year the foundation stone of the new church was laid and in 1964 it was
opened by Bishop Rudderham. The Salvatorian Fathers have continued to
serve the parish to the present, as well as establishing a separate parish at
Wotton-under-Edge, and they have also established a Sunday Mass Centre
in the ancient **Chapel of St John at Berkeley Castle**. Christ the King has
seen the ordinations of two local men, Giorgio Malecki in 1976 and Alex
McAllister in 1984, both for the Salvatorian Order.

The liturgical changes introduced by the Second Vatican Council led to
the modernisation of the church in the early 1980s and the bringing of
the sanctuary closer to the congregation. Most of the building work was
undertaken voluntarily by local Catholics.

M.McC.

Tisbury and Wardour, Wiltshire: Sacred Heart

The parish of the Sacred Heart, Tisbury, is one of the largest in the south
of England. Situated in the south-west corner of Wiltshire, it is some sixteen miles long and ten miles wide, shaped like a diamong, covering seventeen C. of E. parishes. It stretches from six miles west of Salisbury to the
very edge of Shaftesbury. It contains not only its parish church in Tisbury
but also the chapel of **All Saints** in New Wardour Castle. Its connections
with the latter and with the Arundell family mean that it contains more
history than most other parishes.

For the 250 years between the Reformation and Catholic Emancipation
in 1829, Wardour was one of the major refuges of Catholicism in this
country. Through much of this period and beyond, the Arundells maintained Jesuit chaplains based at Wardour. Old Wardour Castle was, of
course, besieged and badly damaged during the Civil War. During the
1770s the seventh Earl of Arundell built New Wardour Castle and, within
it, the baroque chapel of All Saints which was one of the first two Catholic
places of worship constructed since the Reformation. Despite the law at
the time, this was permitted by George III providing the chapel was invis-
ible from the outside. It was constructed in 1776 and, for the next 120
years, served the whole Catholic population of the area. The boundaries of
the parish have remained basically unaltered since the diocesan structure
was set up when the Hierarchy was restored in England in 1850.

During the second half of the nineteenth century, Tisbury, by now on the railway network, expanded and developed some local industry. The main church, some four miles away at Wardour, became steadily more inconvenient for the growing population and, through the 1880s, various plans were developed to build a church in Tisbury itself. Also during that time, two other Mass centres, served from Wardour, one at Anstey, and the other at Barkers Hill near Donhead, were opened in properties owned by the Arundell family. These were to remain in use until around 1960. In Tisbury a sum of £1,000 was raised and a site purchased, but, in 1897, there was a change of plan. The land was sold and, instead, Ann Lucy, Lady Arundell, gave a site at the bottom of the High Street, with her husband donating the stone.

The foundation stone was laid on 13 October by Bishop Brownlow. As sufficient money for the whole building had not yet been collected, it was decided to complete just the nave, the sacristy and a 'heating chamber', but as funds came in during 1897 and 1898, notably a donation of £550 from Horace Chapman, the church was able to be completed as originally planned. It is interesting to note that Mr. Chapman had been the Rector of Donhead St. Andrew, one of the villages in the parish, and had been converted to Catholicism some years earlier. The church was dedicated by Bishop Brownlow on 3 November 1898. At that stage there was still a debt of £330 which was finally cleared in 1903; the detailed lists of subscriptions and expenses have survived.

Also in 1898 the chapel of All Saints in New Wardour Castle was transferred by the twelfth Lord Arundell to a trust, under episcopal control, which has meant that later changes in the ownership of the Castle have not, to any major extent, affected its availability for worship – though they have left the responsibility for some of the joint maintenance a somewhat vexed subject.

For the next thirty-five years the church in Tisbury continued to be served by the Jesuits from Wardour and was still, in effect, a chapel-of-ease. During the 1920s the Jesuits purchased a car which must have made the journeys to and from Tisbury and the other Mass centres in the parish somewhat easier. Until the car was bought, whichever priest was actually serving Tisbury used to stay over on Saturday night.

The 1920s and early 1930s also saw a period of dissension within the parish with the Dowager Lady Arundell trying to get the Tisbury church recognised as the parish church, with the chapel in Wardour Castle turned into a private family chapel. She also hoped that the priests would move to a proposed presbytery in Tisbury, even buying a suitable building there herself in 1924. In what appears to have been a compromise agreed to by

Bishop Lee in 1933 soon after his appointment, the Jesuits, who had been at Wardour almost continuously for over 200 years, left and the parish became the responsibility of the diocese. Then in February 1934 an agreement was signed between Anne Lucy, Lady Arundell, and Bishop Lee by which the church of the Sacred Heart at Tisbury did become the parish church for the district of Tisbury and Wardour, but all the existing rights of the public to use Wardour Castle chapel were retained as were all the Arundell family trust payments – of which there were at least four. In addition Lady Arundell virtually gave the property on one side of the church, which she had bought in 1924, as a presbytery, and a property on the other side of the church to be let to provide funds for the parish.

Reading the words of this agreement one would be led to believe that the parish was intended to remain as an entity with the church at Tisbury as the parish church and the chapel at Wardour, even though it was larger, now becoming the subsidiary. In fact, in circumstances which are not clear today, the parish had, within a few months, been effectively split into two and, for the next thirty-two it remained in these separate halves. On 12 September 1934 Bishop Lee, assisted by the Bishop of Plymouth and nineteen other clergy, consecrated the church in Tisbury. Just over a month later, the Dowager Lady Arundell, who had been so deeply involved with the parish in so many ways since her marriage in 1862, died. Also in 1934 the diocese paid for major building work both at Tisbury where, for example, a passage-way was built between the church and the presbytery, and at Wardour where the presbytery needed much in the way of repairs. Even after this there was still no electric light in the Wardour presbytery as, in the 1950s, the then parish priest, Fr. Paine, S.J., when inviting the Bishop to stay, warned him that he would find only paraffin oil lamps.

The history of the parish continued to be intertwined with that of the Arundell family. The last Lord Arundell, who had been captured early in the war, was repatriated to England in 1944 because of ill health and died within a few weeks of his return. With him the title became extinct and New Wardour Castle came on to the market to help pay off death duties. It was bought in 1946 by the Provincial of the Jesuits in England with the intention that it should be used for their novitiate. At that time it was agreed that the parish of Wardour would again be a Jesuit responsibility and they moved back into the presbytery there. For the next twenty years they served Wardour while the diocese continued to provide the priests for Tisbury. The Jesuits did in fact help Tisbury by saying Mass at a chapel-of-ease at Dinton, at the east end of the parish, which had been opened in 1921 and was only recently closed.

In 1966, the then Provincial of the Jesuits, having managed by this time

Tisbury: wayside crucifix on the A350 between Warminster and Shaftesbury commemmorating Neil Shaw-Stewart, killed in action in 1916. His parents became Catholics after the war and erected this cross to his memory

to sell New Wardour Castle to Cranborne Chase School, agreed with Bishop Rudderham that as Wardour parish was not viable for the Jesuits on its own, the two parishes should again become one and would be served by three Jesuits who would now live at Tisbury. The presbytery there needed some repairs and it was not till the middle of 1967 that the Jesuits family left Wardour presbytery for the last time. They have, of course, continued to serve the chapel, and at least half of the congregation of the parish goes to Mass there each Sunday. Although there were originally three Jesuits when they moved to Tisbury, this number was reduced by old age and retirement and for some of the 1980s only a single priest was available for the whole parish. More recently, the Jesuits have been able to provide two, admittedly elderly, priests to carry the responsibility for this large area and for the two churches it contains, plus all the accumulated history of four centuries.

Richard Long-Fox

Dinton, Wiltshire: Chapel of Our Lady of Pity

Even today Dinton is little more than a hamlet and yet during the reign of Queen Elizabeth I it provided the Church with two priests. Edward Mayhew, born in 1569, arrived in Rheims in 1583 and later (1590) went to Rome where he was ordained by Bishop Owen Lewis in 1594. His brother, Henry, also went to Rheims in 1583 but then proceeded to Vallodolid where he was ordained. In 1611 he was imprisoned in Newgate whence he was banished in 1613.

The chapel, under one of the old English dedications to the Mother of God, was established in the 1920s by George and Mary Englehart after they came to occupy Little Clarendon, an historic, listed house. Priests from the Tisbury and Wardour parish began to celebrate public Masses there in the 1930s, and they continued to do so for over half a century, until the chapel was closed in 1993.

Mr. and Mrs. Englehart are buried in the garden immediately west of the chapel. Their daughter, Katherine, died at Prinknash in 1963 and appears to have left no will. The senior Engleharts had generously given Little Clarendon, including the chapel, to the National Trust, as copies of their wills in the Probate Registry at York show. Mrs. Margaret Streader, who was the Trust's tenant at Little Clarendon in the 1950s and 1960s, cared for the chapel, and told her son, John Spalding, that there was an understanding that the house would always be let to Catholics who would care for the chapel as a place of worship.

K.McG.

Trowbridge, Wiltshire: St. John the Baptist

Catholicism in Trowbridge appears to have died out completely after the Reformation. By the middle of the nineteenth century there were few, if any, Catholics among the townsfolk who numbered about a thousand persons. However, the town had a garrison of soldiers who would have come from various parts of the country. There was at that time a high proportion of Catholics in the army so we may reasonably assume that there were Catholics serving in the garrison. This assumption is strengthened by a story told in the 1860s of a priest who was called out from Bath to give

Trowbridge: St. John
the Baptist, *c.* 1880

the Last Rites to a sick soldier. When this priest returned to Bath he reported that there was an urgent need to establish a Catholic church in the town. Unfortunately there was no money to buy land, let along build a church, and the purchase of land for Catholic churches could be difficult, even when the money was available. It seems that the army came to the rescue and arranged to provide Sunday Mass for the servicemen. The upper rooms of the Hope and Anchor in Frome Road opposite the barracks were booked and here Mass was said for the first time at Christmas 1873. This initiative was due to the influence of Bishop Clifford's brother who was a serving officer in the regiment. There was also a connection with Wardour in the person of Fr. Everard Arundell who persuaded his brother, Lord Arundell, to buy a plot of land in Wingfield Road to build a church. Accordingly the foundation stone was laid on 11 November 1875 by the Bishop's secretary, Mgr. Arthur Russell, who was the son of a rector of Lavington. Among those present were Fr. Francis Bartley of Frome and Fr. Arundell himself who was described by the local press as 'the priest of the mission'. The press coverage displayed an amused curiosity about the event, especially the ritual which was, apparently, strange to the people of the town. The church of St. John the Baptist was opened on 27 June 1876 and, for a time, was served from Bath. The newly-built church derived immense benefit from the generosity of Mrs. Helen Brymer, a convert. Mrs. Brymer was a sister-in-law of the Archdeacon of Wells.

The Tablet of 18 January 1896 stated: 'A convent has been opened in Wingfield Road by the Congregation of the Sacred Hearts and Perpetual Adoration direct from Paris. The premises, lately used as the "West Wiltshire College" have been secured on lease. The schools will be opened shortly.'

One of the original members of the parish was a young girl named Emily Francisco, the daughter of an Italian immigrant who had settled in Trowbridge. In the course of time she married a man named Alfred Carpenter. Their son, John entered the Jesuit novitiate at Milltown, Dublin, and became the first Trowbridge-born priest since the Reformation. Yet, for many years, there seems to have been no permanent appointment. The records mention the names of Fr. Edward Williams, Fr. George Bailey, Fr. Daniel Iles and Fr. John Archdeacon. These priests were resident for varying periods during the last decades of the nineteenth century. The indications are that the number of Catholics fluctuated, probably owing to the movement of the garrison. The first permanent parish priest was Dom George Herbert who came in 1902. A strong formative influence on the parish was the appointment in 1925 of Fr. (later Canon) John Hudson under whose vision and energy the parish grew and prospered. The accounts tells of this 'larger than life' character who became the source of many humorous anecdotes. He retired to Ireland in 1968 and was replaced by Fr. (later Canon) Moriarty.

In 1927 the Sisters of St. John of God came to the parish at the invitation of Bishop Burton. The driving force behind the education effort was Mother M. Cecilia. Her influence was to be great, and she was to stay in Trowbridge for thirty-seven years. Her spirit of self-sacrifice and her hard work kept the little school, St. John's in existence despite obstacles and hardships. She started with eleven pupils: four Catholic and seven non-Catholic. The school was in an old tin hut next to the church on the site of the present Junior School. In 1934 the school hut was dismantled and a new private school was opened in January 1936 by Bishop Lee. According to the 1944 Education Act St. John, an all-age school, had to become strictly for juniors with special provision for over 11. Consequently, in 1950 forty senior pupils were transferred to temporary classrooms in the convent. Bishop Lee had persuaded the Mother General to purchase Dulce Domum, a diocesan property in Wingfield Road, to use as a school. Although the school was successful national education policy was leading to plans for a new parochial secondary school, and the Convent School finally closed in 1966. By 1967 a new block was needed for St. John's School, and this was built on the playing fields along Wingfield Road. On 5 January 1967 St. Augustine's Secondary Modern School was opened with 140 pupils.

The war had had a strong impact on all the diocesan parishes and Trowbridge was no exception. There were numerous camps in the area for British servicemen: the congregation at St. John and St. Bernadette, Westbury would change weekly as soldiers came and went. In 1940, after Dunkirk, many French soldiers came to Trowbridge. For some time American troops were stationed nearby, and reminiscences of the time tell of the church overflowing with servicemen spilling out into the sacristy. The first Polish settlers arrived in Keevil Camp near Trowbridge in 1947. They were under orders from the Ministry of Defence to organise a camp in Keevil for civilian occupation after demobilisation. This they did, renovating a small chapel into which a new altar had been built. At the end of that year Chaplain Joseph Czerniecki S.D.B. arrived and set about organising the spiritual side of life in the camp. In 1948 the camp was taken over by the National Assistance Board, and the task of re-uniting the ex-servicemen with their families, who had been separated from them and scattered throughout the world during the war, began.

In the 1950s people at the camp began moving into their own homes and finding work and by 1957 Fr. Czerniecki and the rest of the camp had moved. An old pub and land in Waterworks Road was purchased, becoming the property of the Polish community, and so gradually the Polish Mass Centre and Club was formed. The community still keeps alive its tradition and culture.

Since the War the parish has developed through the pastoral work of its parish priests, and in 1968 Bradford-on-Avon, which had been looked after from Trowbridge, became a parish in its own right.

Westbury: St. Bernadette

For many years the few Catholics who lived in Westbury had to depend on getting to Mass in Trowbridge on Sundays, initially by pony and trap, and latterly by special coach. Eventually the question of a church in Westbury was raised and money collected for that purpose. The foundation stone was laid by Bishop Lee in July 1938. He had just returned from Lourdes and resolved to name the church after St. Bernadette. During the Second World War Catholic prisoners of war were allowed to attend Mass at St. Bernadette under guard. For some time American troops were also stationed nearby and the church and congregation frequently benefited from their traditional generosity.

K.McG.

Tuffley, Gloucestershire: Church of the English Martyrs

Tuffley is one of the four parishes divided out of the parish of St. Peter Gloucester in recent years. Mass was said regularly there from 1943, at first in the skittle alley of the Northfield Hotel. In 1947 an American army

Warminster: Ursuline Convent chapel

hut in Southfield Road was bought for £15, and for thirty years served as
a chapel, served from St. Peter. It was dedicated to the English Martyrs.
Thereafter Mass was said in the Anglican church of St. George, Tuffley.
The present church in Tuffley Lane, designed as a church hall as a compromise for want of funds, was consecrated in 1985. By 1993 Mass attendance was over 300.

J.A.F.

Wardour, Wiltshire: All Saints: See Tisbury and Wardour

Warminster, Wiltshire: St. George

Until 1900 the nearest place for Warminster Catholics to attend Mass had
been Frome. In that year Mr. and Mrs. Tisseman moved to 'Torwood', 24
Boreham Road, and made their home available for monthly Mass. This
arrangement continued until the arrival of the Ursuline Sisters in 1907. It
was on 8 December 1906 that *The Warminster and Westbury Journal* informed
its readers that 'the mansion in East Street (now 'Yard Court') is to be
taken on lease by ladies of the Ursuline Order'. The convent chapel, a
small hut in the grounds, served the needs of the local Catholics. The
sisters called their house 'St. George's Convent' in an effort to identify with

their host country. They opened a school for girls which remained until 1919 when the sisters were able to return to France from where they had been expelled because of the anti-clerical laws. Several of the sisters lie buried in the Minster churchyard.

Following the departure of the Ursulines, local Catholics were able to attend Mass at Sutton Veny where large numbers of Australian and New Zealand (ANZAC) troops were stationed. When the camp closed Canon (later Bishop) Lee obtained the use of an old army hut near the railway station as a Mass centre while he sought a site for a more permanent building. Mr. Tisseman eventually found the site on which the church stands today. The original church built in 1921/22 consisted of what is now the nave. On 13 April 1922 Bishop Burton opened the church but it remained without a resident priest for sixteen years, being served from Frome, nine miles away. In 1938 the building was enlarged by the addition of two transepts, the sanctuary being 'pushed back' to its present position. The presbytery was built in that same year and Fr. Donal O'Connell was appointed first parish priest. Forty years later, on the occasion of the re-ordering of the sanctuary, the church was consecrated on its patronal feast by Bishop Alexander.

Warminster is distinctive in its close association with the armed forces and as there were many Catholics serving in the army, it followed that St. George's would be closely involved too. The prosperity that the garrison began to bring to the town in 1937 coincided with the establishment of the parish. In the 1940s the generosity of the American garrison at Sutton Veny helped enormously in clearing the debt on the church. Fr. (later Mgr.) Joseph Sutton, parish priest during the War, was also a stand-in chaplain to the United States Air Force base there. He liked to recall that the troops 'because they were nearer to death were always ready to go to the sacraments'. Thirty Masses were offered by service chaplains preparing to leave for the D-Day invasion. The congregation expanded during and after the War, and numbers have remained constant, averaging 300 in Mass attendance.

In 1970 the parish, under the leadership of Fr. Nicholas McCarthy, realised its ambition of having its own primary school. Unfortunately one night in March 1974 it suffered almost complete destruction at the hands of an arsonist. The school was rebuilt in 1975 with the help of an appeal to which many in the town generously contributed. Recent years have seen considerable additions to the building.

In 1982 a narthex was added to the church, the sacristy was enlarged and at the same time linked to the parish hall. These improvements marked the Pope's visit to this country, an event which was celebrated by the placing of a commemorative plaque, fashioned in stone from the former high altar, in the wall near the entrance.

Warminster received its second community of sisters when the Salvatorians arrived, in August 1973, from Abbots Langley in Hertfordshire and opened a convent near the church at 37 Boreham Road. Their ministry in the parish has involved teaching, nursing and visiting. Leaving in 1982 they returned eight years later to reside at 9c Boreham Road.

K.McG.

Warmley: See Bristol: Our Lady of Lourdes

Watchet, Somerset: Served from Minehead

Wellington, Somerset: St. John Fisher

From the early to mid-seventeenth century a recusant family, the Porters, lived at Old Court, Mantle Street. Through the English Mission in Rome, they secured the services of Fr. James Jenison S.J. Officially known as the gardener and handyman, if soldiers came looking for priests, he would escape via a tunnel under what is now the town's playing field, to re-emerge in Home Farm (now the Court Nursing Home). No further Catholic priests served in Wellington until 1941. Before the present church opened Mass was celebrated in the former town hall by a priest from Taunton. Taunton's Catholic community collected money for a Wellington mission from about the mid-1930s.

In 1936 the Popham Almshouses were vacated, the residents being moved to a new site in Victoria Street. It was bought by the Catholic community and converted to form the present church. The architect responsible for the conversion, John Willman, reportedly did the work free of charge. The church was opened by Bishop Lee in March 1937 and certified as a place of meeting for religious worship 26 November 1940.

The church occupies the site of the original building planned as an almshouse by the foundation of Sir John Popham, Lord Chief Justice of England, in 1594 (Popham owned a large mansion nearby). The original almshouse was built about 1606, and rebuilt in 1833, apparently to a design inspired by old Blundells School, Tiverton. About 1964 considerable restoration work was carried out on the main buildings. These included the removal of the chimneys and the creation of the parish room. In 1990 major repairs were carried out to the roof and this was followed in 1996 by the installation of a new ceiling. The roof repairs were paid for with part of a generous bequest by a parishioner, the late Mary Morris.

From 1937–1941 St. John Fisher was served from Taunton. The parish priest at Taunton for some forty years (c. 1930 to 1967) was Mgr. Provost Richard Iles. The first priest in charge at Wellington was Fr. Ninian O'Connor, however, in the interim, visiting priests included Fr. Francis Kelly S.J. who officiated at the first marriage in the church, 25 November 1941.

Cothay Manor

No history of St. John Fisher parish would be complete without a reference to Cothay Manor, near the village of Greenham. Once described as 'the most perfect small fifteenth century house that survives in the Kingdom', it was owned from 1947 to 1972 by Mrs. Vera Astley-Rushton, whose husband was a descendant of the original feudal overlord of Cothay. She was the first Catholic to live there since the Bluetts in 1588. Mrs. Aston-Rushton opened an oratory and the first Catholic Mass since the reformation was celebrated there by Archbishop Thomas Roberts S.J. in 1953. For a number of years the house was the venue for days of recollection, and a number of well-known priests held days there including Archbishop Roberts, Mgr. Vernon Johnson, Rev. Alfonso Zulueta and others. Cothay was also the venue for the parish's annual Corpus Christi procession from 1956 until 1968.

Another notable venue in the parish was *Bindon House*, near the village of Langford Budville. As *St. Monica's Priory*, it was the Assumptionist novitiate from 1947 until about 1950. Bindon was a former grange of the pre-Reformation Minchin Buckland Priory, Durston (originally founded as an Augustinian house).

Wiveliscombe: St. Richard

Wiveliscombe was for some years a separate parish with its own priest. Catholics originally met wherever they could find an available room. This reputedly included hired rooms in local public houses, and for a while, a room in the town hall chambers. A mission was started there by Bishop Lee in 1942, the priest serving the community being Fr. (later Canon) Ronald McDonald. A church dedicated to St. Richard was opened above a shop in Silver Street on 26 July in that year with the priest living in the adjoining house. In 1953 an architect's and surveyor's report mentioned the poor state of both church and presbytery, and the poor condition of the church was again raised in 1960. At some point around this time concern about the strength of the floor led to the church being moved from the first floor to the ground floor to occupy what is now a newsagent's shop. News that the buildings might have to be demolished for road widening gave the parish the incentive to look for a new site. Parishioners therefore set about raising the money for a new building. At this time the diocese owned a site of one and a half acres, but this was zoned for industrial use. In 1965 outline planning permission was granted for this land to be developed industrially, and the following year the diocese sold part of it for £2,300.

Meanwhile a possible venue was found at 34 Church Street. This comprised a detached house, and an adjoining property belonging to B.J. Langdon and Sons, egg and poultry packers, which could be demolished. Negotiations resulted in a price of £8,000. The new church was opened by Bishop Rudderham in 1967. During the intervening period Mass was held in the house, which had become the presbytery.

On the retirement of Fr. Henry Formosa, in 1973, St. Richard's became the responsibility of the parish priest at Wellington. The following year the presbytery was sold for £14,000. Also at this time some land at the front of the property was sold for road widening. One resulting quirk of history is that St. Richard's has never benefited from a mains water supply. When Fr. Formosa lived next door the expense of piping water to the church was seen as unnecessary, as it could be obtained so easily from the presbytery. After the sale of the house this left the problem of water having to be imported for services and other functions – a disadvantage that has yet to be rectified.

C.A. Ralls

Wells, Somerset: SS. Joseph and Teresa

In the seventeenth and eighteenth centuries Wells was one of the places served by the Jesuits. Fr. John Scudamore S.J. who died at Bristol in 1778 was missioner in the district for a time.

In 1835 there were about thirty Catholics in Wells and the nearest priest was at Shepton Mallet. Bishop Clifford wished to set up a mission in this Cathedral city, so he invited a Carmelite community, originally from Lanherne, to come to Wells. He found a house with suitable grounds called The Vista in Chamberlain Street (now no. 11) and arranged to buy it for them. He celebrated the first Mass in the new convent on 16 July 1875. Shortly afterwards they opened a Catholic school on that portion of land which extended into Union Street. Initially this caused some consternation in the city though, eventually, many Protestants were happy to send their children there. However, the school went into decline as Bishop Clifford confided in his diary:

Wells: Corpus Christi procession in 1916

June 26 1883 – Wells school – Fr. Butcher having received notice from the Educational Department that an Inspector will be sent to examine if the school will pass for **Efficiency**; has replied that school closes on Thursday – it will not be opened again – there is only one Catholic child. The rest are children refused admission to other schools – no competent teacher – and no funds.

(Fr. Joseph Butcher had been a Rosminian working in the Cardiff mission but had transferred to Clifton as a secular priest in 1882.)

The convent chapel, opened on 17 October 1877, served the mission until the erection of the present church. Built in the grounds of the convent, the building (designed by Charles Hansom) consisted of no more than the present nave. It was built at the expense of John Mercer, a nephew of one of the nuns. In 1888 it was enlarged by the addition of the current sanctuary, with a choir for the nuns leading off to the left through the usual Carmelite grille (where there is now a large arch). Two years later the debt was paid off and the church consecrated on 31 July 1890. A contemporary writer commented: 'a notable feature of the interior is the handsome altar and reredos of stone and coloured marbles designed by Canon Scoles'.

In the early part of the twentieth century there was an annual Corpus Christi procession through the streets of the city. For many years the church was served by the convent chaplain. In 1924 the nuns bought 5 Chamberlain Street as a presbytery and gave it to the diocese in November 1947.

In 1876 the Apostolic Nuns (afterwards the Tertiaries of St. Teresa) came from Wardour to Wells with the object of running the mission school. They purchased a house in Priory Road where they established a school and also made altar breads. They left in 1879 but returned in 1887 when Bishop Clifford purchased for them 22 Chamberlain Street. The nuns eked out a meagre existence but finally departed in 1936.

In 1972, owing to dwindling numbers, the Carmelite nuns were also obliged to leave Wells. The parish school, which moved into a new building in Lovers Walk in 1975, is popular with Catholics and non-Catholics alike, and another new classroom is to be built as soon as funds permit.

M.McC. and J.A.H.

West Harptree: St. Mary C. of E.: Served from Chew Magna

Westbury, Wiltshire: St. Bernadette: Served from Trowbridge

Weston-super-Mare, Somerset: Corpus Christi

The first recorded instance of a Catholic presence in the town dates from 1806 when a Franciscan, Fr. O'Farrell, preached at a cottage in the High Street. Later in the century the town began to develop as a Victorian holiday resort and the Catholic population increased. By 1858 the parish church of St. Joseph in Camp Road was completed with Fr. William Pippet as the first priest in charge. As time went by St. Joseph's church became too small to accommodate the growing Catholic community.

In 1898 the La Retraite Sisters opened their first school in Quarry Road, and despite many initial setbacks, eventually succeeded in providing an educational system for the children of the parish. The school moved to Carlton Street where it was used as a Mass centre. In 1921 a simple chapel was erected in Carlton Street and given the title of Corpus Christi. As in so many instances throughout the diocese a new parish began to emerge from a Mass centre. Only two months after the opening of the Mass centre a site was being considered for a possible school and church, and land was soon purchased in Ellenborough Park South. Within the decade the congregation who attended the original Mass centre in Carlton Street had moved to their new parish church of Corpus Christi. The church was opened in 1929, one hundred years after the Catholic Emancipation Act, and was consecrated in 1934 by Bishop Lee. The new building owes a great deal to the energy and foresight of Mgr. Canon Lyons.

Weston-super-Mare:
Corpus Christi

In 1936 the Poor Servants of the Mother of God bought a house in Oldmixon. Their work was with mentally handicapped girls and women. It ended in 1974 when an acute lack of vocations forced the sisters to close their convent at Oldmixon which had housed sixty patients. The 1930s witnessed a rapid expansion of the Catholic population in Weston. In 1938 a new church was built at **Milton** and dedicated to **Our Lady of Lourdes**. This was served by the clergy of Corpus Christi until 1964 when it became a separate parish.

In 1942 Corpus Christi church had a narrow escape when a time bomb dropped in the grounds and had to be defused.

In 1962 Fr. (later Mgr.) Joseph Leahy had the new school built and purchased Ellenborough Park from the Council for the school children's recreation ground. In the mid-1970s, to improve the social life of the parish, Fr. (now Canon) William Ryan had the parish hall built next to the church.

In 1972 the La Retraite sisters were obliged to close their school and convent in South Road, but they are still active in parish work and their retreat team operates from Walliscote Road. In 1996 the Sisters of Mercy arrived at Stanhope Road.

K.McG.

Weston-super-Mare, Somerset: St. Joseph

At the beginning of the nineteenth century Weston-super-Mare was a small community of farmers and fishermen. In the five decades from 1800 to 1850 the original population of 163 had increased to 4,000. The main cause was tourism, which is still the town's primary industry. The first record of a Catholic presence dates from 1806, when a Franciscan, Fr. O'Farrell, preached at a cottage in the High Street. The town developed as a popular Victorian holiday resort and during the summer months Jesuit priests came on Sundays and Holydays to say Mass in the Assembly Rooms in Regent Street which later became the Railway Hotel.

In 1855 the foundation stone of St. Joseph's church in Camp Road was laid by Bishop Clifford. By 1858 the parish church of St. Joseph was complete. The first priest-in-charge was Fr. William Pippet. There appears to have been some local hostility in the early years for the records show that Fr. Pippet had to write to the Chairman of the Petty Sessions to complain that 'services were being interrupted by parties who behaved in a most unseemly manner'. The Chairman's response was swift. He told the police 'to look to their duty' and issued the general warning that anyone interfering with the services of any denomination 'would receive the full severity of the law'.

The new mission made rapid progress. Twenty-four people made their Easter duties in 1859: and by 1865 the number had risen to fifty-nine. Gradually the local prejudice against the Catholics broke down due mainly to a succession of outstanding parish priests. Canon Maurice Power served for sixteen years, Fr. John Bouvier for twenty years and Canon Eustace Barron, the former Administrator of the Pro-Cathedral, also served for twenty years until his death in 1916.

In 1898 the La Retraite Sisters opened a school in Quarry Road. In the beginning it was a stern test of faith and perseverance for the sisters. In addition to being pelted with mud by local roughs, only one pupil arrived for class on the first day. However, their faith was rewarded and the numbers began to grow steadily. The school moved to Carlton Street where it was used as a Mass centre.

As time went by St. Joseph's church became too small to accommodate the increasing Catholic population and in 1921 a small chapel was opened in Carlton Street and given the title of **Corpus Christi**. This eventually grew into the present parish of Corpus Christi in Ellenborough Park South where the church was opened in 1929 and consecrated in 1934 by Bishop Lee.

A painting *The Adoration of the Shepherds* once thought to be by Pittoni (1687–1767), but now regarded as Flemish, used to hang in the church. It is now on the south wall of the chancel in St. Catharine, Chipping Campden.

The parish hall was opened and blessed by Bishop Alexander in February 1999.

V.A.

Weston-super-Mare, Somerset: Our Lady of Lourdes

Following a gift of land in Baytree Road from Daniel Cotter, a simple wooden building was erected in 1923. This, the first Catholic chapel in the Milton area, was dedicated to Our Lady of Lourdes and the first Mass was celebrated on 29 June 1923.

In 1933 more land was bought for £560. On it the present church was built in Gothic style of Taunton Vale cream bricks with firestone facing. It was completed in 1938 at a cost of about £4,000 and held 300 people. It was served by the priests of Corpus Christi church until 1964 when Fr. (now Canon) William O'Callaghan became its first parish priest. The church was consecrated in February 1978 by Bishop Alexander, parish priest from 1965 to 1972.

Fr. Michael O'Sullivan succeeded him at a time when Milton and Worle had expanded greatly and, to meet this expansion, a new side chapel and sacristy were added in 1976. The reorganisation of the sanctuary and the decoration of the church was completed in 1977. In 1992 a small hall to accommodate up to thirty people was built off the sacristy.

Over the years the leaded windows deteriorated and in 1988 one of the larger windows was replaced by stained glass depicting St. Thomas More, St. Margaret Clitherow and St. Cuthbert Mayne. In 1995 seven of the smaller windows were replaced with white cathedral and Flemish glass, four with crosses in yellow. The following year a large stained glass window depicting the Holy Family was fitted in the Lady Chapel. A pipe organ was purchased from St. Peter's (Anglican) church, Burnham-on-Sea and installed in 1978. A new presbytery was built in the church grounds in 1982.

The original wooden chapel was used for various parish activities until 1970 when it was replaced by the parish hall which was paid for by a bequest from a parishioner.

Edith Whatling

Whaddon, Wiltshire: The Holy Family: Served from Salisbury St. Osmund

Whitchurch: See Bristol St. Bernadette

Williton, Somerset: See Watchet and Minehead

Wilton, Wiltshire: St. Edith: Served from Salisbury St. Gregory

Wincanton, Somerset: SS. Luke and Teresa

The origin of St. Luke's is closely connected with the Catholic church which existed at Bonham until the beginning of this century. Since the time of the Reformation the few Catholics in Wincanton looked to Bonham as their place of worship and the earliest record of Mass being celebrated at Wincanton is 1881. In May of that year Fr. William Cotham S.J. and brother of the chaplain at Bonham, celebrated Mass at the home of Thomas Clementina in North Street. It seems likely that there was a nucleus of a congregation in Wincanton, because negotiations were soon afoot to establish a Mass centre in the town. Acorn House in South Street was purchased, and it was here, on St. Luke's Day in 1881 that the mission was formally established. Meanwhile, Bishop Clifford had approached the Father General of the Carmelites (Discalced) to discuss the possible taking over of the mission. The result was that the first Carmelites, under Fr. Edward Sharples, arrived on 21 December 1882. In 1888 a new priory was built, and in 1907 the Community turned their attention to the building of a new church to replace St. Luke's hall which had served the congregation for over a quarter of a century. The result was the present Gothic building with its twin towers rising seventy feet to give a panoramic view of the surrounding countryside. There are six stained glass windows: two of which depict the patrons of the priory church; St. Luke and St. Teresa; two depict St. Peter and St. Paul; one depicts the parents of the Blessed Virgin Mary; the last St. George and St. Martin of Tours. The last named was the gift of the British Red Cross Society as a token of their appreciation for the use of the priory as a hospital during the First World War.

In connection with the original mission a school was built in Market Place in 1884 and transferred the following year to North Street. In 1891 the Ursulines from Swansea arrived to take charge of the school. From 1961 to 1973 the nuns of the Company of Mary were in charge of a private primary school at Touthill House. This school became a voluntary-aided infant and junior Catholic school in 1976 under the supervision of the Sisters of Christian Instruction (St. Gildas).

In 1995 the Carmelites departed after a century or more of pastoral care during which the spiritual and social life of the parish flourished. Our Lady's school is no longer under the direction of the Sisters of Christian Instruction, although they are still an influential presence in the parish. The school was taken over by the diocese as a pastoral retreat and conference centre under the direction of Deacon David Wakefield.

Mere: St. Mary

For some years the Catholics at Mere were looked after by the Benedictines serving the Bonham mission, but in July 1942 the Diocesan Trustees purchased two plots of land in Boars Lane for £100. In August 1944 part of the land was let for twenty-one years to the Wiltshire County Council, the Council covenanting to erect a hut for use as a school canteen. In 1946 the church of St. Mary was built and for three years it was served by the chaplains at St. Mary's Convent, Shaftesbury, although the convent is in the parish of Tisbury. More recently Mere was served from Wincanton, then by a priest from Warminster, then in 1971 it reverted to Wincanton.

Since 1969 Mass has been celebrated in the Anglican church of St. John the Evangelist at **Milborne Port**, which is one of the most southerly areas of the diocese being on the Somerset/Dorset border.

Sisters of Jesus Crucified, St. John's Priory, Castle Cary

The Congregation was founded in France in the early 1930s when several ladies felt that certain infirmities and illnesses were a bar to religious life in other orders. This was certainly a revolutionary idea since each member is sick or handicapped in some way. The Rule selected is that of

Wincanton: former Bonham chapel

St. Benedict, in which the Divine Office takes up a large part of the day, but the sisters send out bulletins for the deaf and blind, and are involved in the education of the mentally handicapped as well as pastoral and retreat work.

A small congregation came to Castle Cary in 1959 and Mass was celebrated at the Priory until they left in 1996, since when it has been said in the Anglican church of St. Andrew.

Bonham

The small manor of Bonham originally belonged to the family of that name; an Editha Bonham was Abbess of Shaftesbury from 1441 to 1460. The manor afterwards came into the possession of the Stourton family. Edward, the twelfth Earl, sold off most of the family estates in Dorset and Wiltshire but retained the manor and established a priest in charge. Charles Philip, sixteenth Lord Stourton, sold this property in 1785 to Henry Hoare of Stourhead but especially reserved quarters for a priest and a chapel for Catholic use. The proximity of Wardour points to the existence of a long-established Catholic community at Bonham. *Return of Papists* (1767) states the Parish of Stourton (Bonham) had 107 Catholics living within its boundaries, the principal trades being husbandry and spinning. Bishop Walmesley, O.S.B., Vicar Apostolic of the Western District, administered confirmation at Bonham in 1772 and 1781 and he also paid a visit in 1788.

Bonham features in a fascinating entry in the journal kept by Rev. John Skinner, Vicar of Camerton 1803–1834:

> *1824 Tuesday January 4* '. . . Lord Arundel showed me the chapel attached to the house, which seemed in a very dilapidated state: I find it is in contemplation to build a new one'.

To this he adds his personal reflections regarding the moves then afoot which led to the granting of Catholic Emancipation in 1829:

> 'If all Catholics were as devoid of bigotry as Lord Arundel there would be nothing to fear, indeed, not only that, but a union might be effected without the smallest difficulty, for I have not yet heard an opinion fall from his lips which the most orthodox might not agree in: this cannot be termed art or management in a man of his Lordship's rank, although it might bear that appearance in a Jesuit. I am decidedly against the Catholic claims, taken as a political measure; still, where there are such liberal-minded men who are excluded from a participation of what the most worthless and irreligious actually do enjoy, it then assumes rather an injurious appearance. The priest at Bonham takes pupils; we saw several children on the premises, who receive instruction, some as preparatory, I suppose, to the ministry. Let us calmly ask the question, Are not these likely to become as good citizens and subjects as the puritanical levelling Methodists and Presbyterians?'
>
> (*Journal of a Somerset Rector 1803–1834* p. 259)

Bonham is distinctive for its rural 'English Catholic' character and composition. The whole congregation was said to be English and this would seem to be attested by an incident in 1850. In September of that year four parishioners wrote to the Bishop to complain about the Rector – a Benedictine from Downside. The signatures were: J. Shepherd, D. Matthew, V. Sindrey and J. Withey. On 2 October a further eighty-three parishioners – all with English names – wrote to the Bishop to disassociate themselves from the complaint.

Numbers seem to have remained stable throughout the middle decades of the nineteenth century. In 1858 there were about 100 Catholics residing chiefly at Bonham, Gaspar, Stourton, Zeals and Whitecross and in the same year twenty children were confirmed at Bonham. The *Somerset and Wiltshire Journal*, (28 October 1871) carried the following news item: 'The Roman Catholic School at Bonham, Stourton, was opened on Tuesday last by a tea, followed by a ball in the evening. The band of the eighth Wilts Rifles was in attendance. On Wednesday the children were treated to a tea'. The school has since closed although the building still stands in the village.

143 people signed an address of loyalty to Pope Pius IX in 1877 and the number of Easter communicants was seventy. The last two decades of the century seem to have witnessed a decline in numbers, with rural farming communities being adversely affected by the economic slumps and changes in agricultural methods that occurred during these times. By 1902 the Rector was writing that 'the receipts from the congregation do not cover the expenses of the services'. In 1954 Bishop Rudderham was forced, because of a shortage of clergy, to close the mission.

On 25 June 1993 Bishop Alexander blessed a Garden of Remembrance at Bonham Manor House. The plot had been generously donated by Stuart and Xenia Ponting so that, in the event of their moving elsewhere, at least part of the land would always be in Catholic hands. They have since left the area. Chris and Penny Deverill, whose family have long-standing links with Bonham, carried out the practical work of moving and arranging the headstones of those buried there. The Garden is worth a visit as the last reminder of a small sector of 'old Catholic' England.

J.A.H.

Winchcombe, Gloucestershire: St. Nicholas

The Catholic faith returned to Winchcombe in the late nineteenth century in circumstances almost unique in this country, when Mr. and Mrs. Stuart Foster, the Catholic owners of Postlip Hall, undertook the restoration ('severe' in Verey's view) of the chapel of St. James the Great in its grounds. St. James's, a twelfth-century building, had been served from Winchcombe Abbey until the Reformation, when it became derelict. With its consecration in 1891 it became only the third ancient church in this country to be reconciled to the Faith (another example from the very different climate of recent times is at Cricklade).

About the turn of the century several ambitious plans were mooted for Winchcombe. Mrs. Forster had hopes of building a Cistercian monastery there, and there was a suggestion that Postlip Hall should become a hospice for priests. It seems that in 1899 plans were well advanced for building a chapel to the designs of William Lunn, the architect of Chipping Campden church. They came to nothing, and in 1910 Mrs. Forster left Postlip for nearby Cleeve Hill, where she converted the chapel in her house 'Petra' for the use of the local Catholic population. Postlip Hall was sold in 1915 with assurances as to the future of the chapel building.

The Winchcombe mission was initiated in the same year 1915: the last to be established in the diocese before the end of the missionary status of

Winchcombe: former presbytery

the country. Early in the First World War Fr. Wilfred Palmer was given authority to build a chapel there for the thirty Catholics in Winchcombe, and also for the Belgian refugees there. The disused buildings of the Chandos grammar school were adapted, and the church of St. Nicholas opened in that year. The first Mass to be celebrated there was a requiem for Mrs. Forster who died tragically at her home. Fr. Bede Griffiths made his first Communion as a Catholic there. In 1955 the church was extended to incorporate a Lady Chapel and sacristy, and a new presbytery built. This followed the demolition of the former presbytery, a medieval half-timber house. The architect was Peter Falconer who has done much work for the Catholic church in post-war years. The church now has a stone slated roof and bellcote.

In 1948 the nearby Toddington manor, which once belonged to the Sudeley family, was acquired by the Irish Christian Brothers, who established it as their English Provincial residence and as their novitiate and scholasticate. When they left in the late 1950s the fittings of the chapel went to Winchcombe church.

A striking event in the recent history of Winchcombe parish was the ordination as deacon of Peter Doran in the Anglican parish church of St. Peter, made necessary because St. Nicholas's was too small. St. Peter's is

Winchcombe: Postlip, St. James's pre-Reformation chapel

one of the great wool churches of the Cotswolds and the last time it found Catholic use the monks of Winchcombe were still serving Postlip.

When Winchcombe church was opened in 1915 St. James's again became disused and neglected. In 1990 a group, the Friends of Saint James's Chapel, was established with the aim of again restoring it to become a place of pilgrimage and prayer. They met with a major success in 1994 when they attracted a grant of £25,000 from English Heritage. A yearly Mass has been said there for some time. In 1995 Fr. Richard Barton, who had played a leading part in establishing the Friends, said Mass there shortly after his ordination.

                                                                    J.A.F.

Withywood: See Bristol: St. Pius X

Wiveliscombe, Somerset: St. Richard: Served from Wellington

Woodchester, Gloucestershire: Our Lady of the Annunciation

The concentration of Catholic interests in Woodchester and its vicinity followed the arrival of the wealthy convert William Leigh who bought the estate of Woodchester Park in 1845. It was his intention to build a Gothic church to be served by a religious community, and on Cardinal Wiseman's advice the Passionists, led by Blessed Dominic Barberi, were invited to

Woodchester. They arrived in the next year and took up temporary accommodation in nearby Nailsworth, later moving to St. Mary's Hill House. In the same year priory and church of Our Lady of the Annunciation were begun. Originally Pugin had been commissioned as architect, but after drawing up plans asked to be excused, stipulating that no one should use them. Nevertheless the church, built by Charles Francis Hansom, is in a characteristically Puginesque Decorated style. It was consecrated in 1849. In the following year the Passionists left and were replaced on Leigh's invitation by the Dominicans, who were to remain there for nearly 120 years. Leigh's original stipulations reflect a more spacious age: not less than three priests there, a good day school for boys to be maintained, a priest to celebrate Mass in Leigh's private chapel, and Masses to be said for him and his family *in perpetuum*. The Priory was completed in 1853. It became the headquarters of the Order in England, and also its novitiate. Consequently many of the most notable figures of English Catholicism were at Woodchester, among them the future Cardinal Bourne, Vincent McNabb, Bede Jarrett, and R. H. Benson, the convert son of an Archbishop of Canterbury. The priory also had associations with well-known laymen: Matthew Bridges the hymnologist and J. M. Capes, who when in Anglican orders had been rector of Bridgwater and was to edit *The Rambler*, the organ of liberal Catholic thought in England. He played a part in the arrival of

Woodchester: Priory, proposed design including chapter house

the Franciscan nuns in the parish. The priory, having become uninhabit-
able, was closed in 1966 and its buildings demolished in 1970. The friars
who remained went to St. Mary's Hill House (which is now the presbytery).
They continued to serve Woodchester parish until 1985 when it became
the pastoral responsibility of the diocese of Clifton, Father Michael Jones-
Frank being appointed the first diocesan parish priest. Extensive restoration work on the Priory Church was completed in 1989.

St. Thomas More and St. John Fisher, Box, Rodmarton

For some sixty years from 1931 a mission was served from Woodchester at
Box. It began on the initiative of six local Catholics, with Mass in a room in
the Box Institute. Land was then bought, and a chapel built, through the gen-
erosity of Mrs. Johnson of Woodchester. It opened in 1936, and was known as
Hampton Court chapel. By 1953 the average attendance at Mass was forty.
It continued to be served from Woodchester until it closed in 1992.

Convent of the Immaculate Conception

The enclosed nuns of the Third Order of St. Francis became established at
Taunton early in the nineteenth century. In 1860 Bishop Clifford, to whom
the jurisdiction of the convent had been resigned by the Order, decided
that a daughter house should be established. Woodchester was chosen
because of the Dominican presence there, the house Summerwells was
bought from Capes, and extensions, including the chapel, were made by
Hansom. Further additions were made by Canon Scoles and the convent
was completed in 1869. In the earlier days of the convent an orphanage
and a primary school were associated with it. When changing conditions
made these unnecessary their buildings were adapted for a guest house,
which functioned until 1973. After the Second Vatican Council the
Woodchester nuns, and those of the mother house in Berkshire, decided to
become Poor Clares, the Second Order of St. Francis. They were joined at
Woodchester by three members of the Berkshire community. The most
important secular activity of the community is now the making of altar
breads. Some five million are made and despatched each year.

                                                              J.A.F.

Wootton Bassett, Wiltshire: The Sacred Heart

There is reputed to be a priest's hiding hole in the Manor House at Wootton Bassett. This little town, now a dormitory for Swindon, used to be a

'rotten borough' sending two members to Parliament from the fifteenth century until the Reform Bill of 1831.

Before the Second World War there were only a few Catholics in the town. Three families are known to have kept the faith since the Reformation, attending Mass at Malmesbury and (later) at Holy Rood, Swindon. Mass was also celebrated at Great Wood Farm, home of the Collingbourne family.

In 1941 there was an influx of Catholic servicemen and, more significantly, a party of schoolchildren with their teacher, Mrs. Hamilton, and an elderly priest from the Westminster Archdiocese. They had been evacuated from the Angel Islington in London and were mainly of Italian descent. The priest was billeted at the Cross Keys Inn, which at the time was run by a Catholic family. Mass was celebrated at the Inn and at the teacher's lodgings. The priest suffered a stroke not long after his arrival in the town and was replaced from Westminster by Father Maher.

A Mass centre was officially constituted in 1942. After the departure of the evacuees in 1945 it was served for the next thirty-two years from Holy Rood – surely some kind of a record. A hut at the local cricket ground, then a room at the Cross Keys followed by an outbuilding on the Manor Estate – the location of the new church – were used as the Mass centre.

The anticipated growth of Wootton Bassett led to work being started on a church in 1952. It was completed the following year and on Christmas Eve the first Mass was celebrated by Fr. (now Canon) Jeremiah O'Brien, the senior assistant at Holy Rood. For many years to come a priest from Holy Rood would say Mass first at **Wroughton** and then at **Wootton Bassett**. Afterwards he would enjoy the hospitality of Mr. and Mrs. Aylard in the adjoining house. In 1967 Wootton Bassett became a parish in its own right with Fr. Michael Roche as first parish priest.

The Sisters of Marie Réparatrice established a convent in 1978 using two cottages belonging to the church. In 1989 the sisters were recalled from the parish as part of the order's reorganisation.

During the late 1980s moves were made to redevelop the overall site but these had to be abandoned owing to problems of access. In 1990 a fresh attempt was made to solve problems of a different kind resulting from deterioration of the grounds and buildings. On 6 January 1992 work was started on yet another church with access from the main road. Land not required by the church was sold and now accommodates a home for the elderly.

The first Mass in the new building was celebrated on 5 December 1992 and the church was subsequently consecrated by Bishop Alexander on 21 February 1995. In May of that year the Sunday morning Mass was broadcast nationwide, live, by ITV.

Based on an account by Tony Guilfoyle

Wotton-under-Edge, Gloucestershire: Holy Cross

During the First World War, and for a time afterwards, Mass was celebrated in Wotton by the Dominicans of Woodchester, but after the war numbers fell to four or five, and in 1920 the Provincial, Fr. Hugh Pope, had to tell the Bishop that problems of transport made it impracticable for them to continue for so small a congregation.

In the 1940s Mass was again celebrated at Wotton, in the Boys' Club, served from Thornbury. Then a retired teacher, Miss Wells, wished to do something for the church in memory of her close friend Miss Ward. She gave the money needed to acquire, at a bargain price, a building, then in use as the Liberal Club, which had previously been part of Old Town Mill, built in 1817. At the time the ground floor was a garage and the church was established on the first floor. It was opened in 1953, dedicated to Holy Cross, perhaps in recognition of the medieval community of the Brothers of the Cross at nearby Kingswood. Wotton was still served from Thornbury until a conveyance, on generous terms, of the adjacent property made a presbytery possible. In 1982 the church was thoroughly rebuilt at a cost of £42,000. The church is now on the ground floor. Its decor effectively introduces a modern idiom into its shell of early nineteenth century stone.

For nearly fifty years the Daughters of the Cross, later to be the Sisters of Christ, played an important part in the life of the parish. They came from Portsmouth in 1940 and established a temporary school for evacuees. After leaving Wotton for a time they returned with the intention of establishing their novitiate there, but finally left in 1987. They established a catechetics centre in the parish which still flourishes.

In 1998 Wotton saw the first Mass since pre-Reformation days in the medieval parish church when a Catholic wedding outran the capacity of Holy Cross. Wotton is served by Society of the Divine Saviour – the Salvatorians – a society of priests, brothers and sisters who take on anything 'which the charity of Christ might inspire'.

J.A.F.

Wroughton, Wiltshire: St. Joseph

Only fifteen years after the apparitions to St. Bernadette, a chapel at Wroughton was dedicated to Our Lady of Lourdes. It was probably one of the earliest examples of this dedication anywhere in Europe. The chapel which was opened and blessed by Bishop Clifford on 5 July 1873 was built by W. W. Codrington and stood within his estate at Wroughton house. A contemporary account in *The Tablet* noted: 'It will hold about sixty persons and is open to the public. It is built in the early decorated style from the designs of A. J. C. Scoles, Esq. a son of the late J. J. Scoles, Esq. who is also the architect of the new church at Prior Park. The stone carving is by Mr. G. Porter, sculptor, of Bath, and the glass and fittings have been supplied by Messrs. Thomas Orr & Co. of Baker Street, London.' (12 July 1873). The Codringtons were a Wroughton family, pillars of the Church of England. Indeed many members of the family are buried in the parish church.

In 1882 the new residents at Wroughton House, Mr. and Mrs. Ferdinand Eyre, accompanied by Mrs. Eyre's mother, the Dowager Lady Bedingfield, entertained some 140 children from Holy Rood School, Swindon. They had walked the four miles in procession, led by the Swindon Town Band. It must have been a splendid occasion as there were not only sports for the children but also 'several open-air choruses by Weber, Rossini and Mendelssohn' sung by the members of the St. Cecilias' Society. The children were similarly entertained on other occasions.

Mass was said each week by the priest from Swindon. This ceased in 1885 to be resumed with an occasional celebration in 1887. All these arrangements apparently came to an end in 1891.

In 1950 a chapel dedicated to St. Mary and St. Camillus was opened in the R.A.F. Hospital (later re-named The Princess Alexandra Hospital) at Wroughton. In those days it was served by the chaplain at the R.A.F. Station, Yatesbury.

In 1953 Canon John Noonan of Holy Rood, Swindon opened no fewer than three churches within the area covered by his expanding parish. One was at East Swindon (St. Mary), the others at Wootton Bassett (The Sacred Heart) and Wroughton (St. Joseph). The design of all these churches was functional and almost identical, the idea being that in the fullness of time, when population growth would call for something more spacious, the original church would revert to being the parish hall. Although growth did take place at Wroughton, today the same building still serves as a church. However, in August 1960 a farm building at the rear, known as Barcelona House, received three sisters of the Presentation Order from Bicester. Initially two of them taught at Holy Rood School. The accommodation was always seen as temporary and in 1964 they opened a convent in the newly established parish of Holy Family in Marlowe Avenue, Park North, Swindon.

Wroughton continued to be served by the clergy of Holy Rood, and on the death of Canon Michael Fitzpatrick in December 1962, Canon (later Mgr.) Joseph Leahy was appointed to take his place. He entered into negotiations with another religious order, the Missionary Servants of the Holy Ghost, with a view to their moving into the vacated property. This they did, and while retaining their convent at Lawrence Weston in Bristol, they decided to build an imposing mother house at Wroughton. This was opened in September 1969. The architect was Gerard P. O'Brien of Ivor Day and O'Brien, of Bristol. The outside cladding around the building is cut from local stone from South Cerney. Inside the chapel, the altar area is faced with black granite. The normal number of sisters in community is ten.

St. Joseph was given the status of a parish in 1969. Mgr. George Pitt, the first priest, had served as a chaplain in the Royal Navy rising to the rank of principal chaplain in 1963. After the surrender of Japan in 1945 he had been one of the first to witness at first hand the terrible devastation caused by the atom bombs at Hiroshima and Nagasaki.

J.A.H.

Yate, Gloucestershire: St. Paul: Served from Chipping Sodbury

Yatton, Somerset: SS. Dunstan and Anthony: Served from Clevedon

Yeovil, Somerset: The Holy Ghost

In 1887 there were six Catholic families in Yeovil. From time to time they had unsuccessfully petitioned Bishop Clifford to send them a priest. During April of that year the newly-appointed editor of the *Western Chronicle* came to live in the town. His name was Charles Gatty, and he was a convert who became a prominent Catholic spokesman in the political life of the time. Before long he had persuaded the Bishop to make it possible for Mass to be heard once more in the town. This was in Charles Gatty's own drawing room at 137 Hendford Hill. Thus the first Mass to be celebrated in Yeovil since the Reformation was on Sunday 13 November 1887 and was attended by a congregation of sixteen people. The celebrant was Fr. E. M. Badger from the Carmelite mission at Wincanton and the server was Edmund Talbot, later to become Viscount Adair of Derwent. So great was the initial interest that within six months the expanding congregation had outgrown Gatty's drawing room and under his direction he had rented the chantry opposite St. John's church. A contemporary account in *The Talbot* stated:

> 'The building, which has until lately been used for the Yeovil Charity School, was originally a chantry, built on to the west end of the parish church. As most of the charities in this district became educational centres in the sixteenth century, so this Yeovil Chantry became the Yeovil Free School. Some thirty years ago the chantry was removed from the end of the church to where it now stands, and the school being in abeyance, the building has been hired for the

Yeovil: Holy Ghost, high altar (1899)

use of Catholics, and makes a very pretty chapel. The carved stone corbels from the old chantry still support the present roof, and two niches and a piscina in carved Ham Hill stone occupy the same places in the new chantry as they did in the old'.

Large numbers of non-Catholics now attended Mass; and the baptismal registers show that by 1889 there had been twenty-six conversions to the Faith. Eventually the Bishop agreed to make a permanent appointment which resulted in the transfer of Fr. (later Canon) Alexander Scoles from Bridgwater. The opening of the chantry for Mass, together with the interest of non-Catholics, excited strong anti-Catholic feelings in some sections of the local community. This feeling was exacerbated by public meetings in the town hall which were organised by visiting speakers. Windows in the chantry were smashed by local roughs, but the hostility gradually abated, helped by the tolerant attitude of influential local people.

   Fr. Scoles was noteworthy for his talents as an architect and planner. He soon purchased land for a presbytery and church. The church of The Holy Ghost was opened on Whit Sunday 1899. Four years later the Missionaries of St. Francis de Sales assumed responsibility for the parish which still remains in their pastoral care today. Like some other parishes in the diocese, educational development was helped by refugee nuns and sisters from the anti-clerical laws in France. In 1907 Fr. Louis Valluet invited the Sisters of St. Gildas de Bois to open a parish school. In the following year the sisters opened a convent and school close to the church. In September 1907 Fr. Valluet left Yeovil for Devizes and was succeeded by Fr. Joseph Antonioz. This priest was to spend twenty-six years in Yeovil during which time the congregation increased to 300.

   During the First World War Yeovil looked after the needs of large numbers of Belgian refugees. A large schoolroom was built in **South Petherton** with the aid and co-operation of the local vicar. Following this period another increase in numbers in the **Crewkerne** area warranted a separate church and parish which came into existence in the 1930s. In 1986 South Petherton celebrated its silver jubilee, and today several hundred people attend Mass in Yeovil and Petherton. In 1971 the convent school became 'voluntary aided' and the Sisters of St. Gildas still serve the parish.

K.McG.

Yeovilton, Somerset: H.M.S. Heron, R.N. Air Station, Our Lady and St. Augustine.

The Royal Naval Air Station at Yeovilton was commissioned in 1940 and the Church of St. Augustine was built around this time. It served for many years as the Fleet Air Arm Memorial Church.

During the war a Nissan hut was provided as a Catholic Mass centre and this was later replaced by another temporary building. When the Memorial Church was moved to St. Bartholomew's in Yeovilton village in 1993 the Catholic church of Our Lady Queen of Peace acquired St. Augustine's. On 26 June 1994 the Bishop of the Forces, Francis Walmsley, consecrated the church and it was renamed Our Lady and St. Augustine's Roman Catholic Church. The main front window represents Christ the Redeemer standing on the world and the windows on each side represent the various trades of the Royal Navy.

At the time of writing (Dec 1998) the church is served by an officiating chaplain who is also chaplain at nearby Leweston School at Sherborne in Dorset. The congregation is approximately 350 Catholics.

V.A.

CHAPTER FIVE

Catholic Education and the Diocese of Clifton: a brief history

Introduction

When the diocese of Clifton was founded in 1850, a substantial amount of missionary and educational work had already been in progress in its constituent counties of Wiltshire, Somerset and Gloucestershire. These previous efforts laid the necessary groundwork for the schools and colleges we have in the diocese today. Catholic education in Clifton diocese is an integral part of the national story of the struggle for Catholic education. This national story is a long, complex and gripping account of how English Catholics clung tenaciously to their Faith against heavy odds. It goes on to tell of the ways in which they handed on this precious heritage to succeeding generations through formal and informal schooling. The first phase begins with the Elizabethan Act of Supremacy (1559) and the succeeding legal restraints that forbade Catholic education in any form. Thus began a 'Catholic Resistance' by means of wandering schoolmasters, secret schools and the founding of schools and colleges on the Continent. Over the years these schools and colleges would send many priests and teachers back to England to instruct English Catholics in their Faith.

The next phase could be said to begin in the closing decades of the eighteenth century. There was the growth of a more tolerant attitude towards Catholics and a gradual repealing of the laws that forbade them to build schools for Catholic children. In 1778 the first Catholic Relief Act was passed. Catholics were allowed to own landed property; and the lifelong imprisonment for keeping a Catholic school was abolished. This Act was followed by the Gordon Riots (No Popery Riots) which destroyed the newly-built Catholic chapel in Bath. In 1791 a second Relief Act was passed. Those who took the prescribed oath were freed from the statutes of recusancy and the demands of the Act of Supremacy; Catholic worship and schools were tolerated; and certain posts in the legal and military professions were opened to Catholics. In 1793 Irish Catholics were admitted to Trinity College Dublin, and there is evidence that a number of English Catholics took advantage of this concession. However, the universities of Oxford and Cambridge remained closed to them – and would remain so for the next hundred years. The Emancipation Act of 1829 enabled Catholics to re-enter parliament and make their voices heard in the government and administration of the State. An education system was necessary if they were to benefit from the restoration of their civil rights. But how was this system to be achieved? The majority of Catholics were poor and demoralised. They had no school buildings worthy of the name; and they had no teachers. These national problems applied to Clifton in special ways, as we shall see.

Catholics, Education and the State

The public emergence of the Church after Catholic Emancipation was most visible in her attempts to provide education for the poor and needy. Both the Catholic Church and the State were soon to be faced with a school population problem on a scale not encountered before. There was an explosion in the child population as large numbers of poor and destitute Irish people tried to escape from the Great Famine of 1847. It must be remembered that there were no local authorities as we know them today. The existing rudimentary services were soon swamped by a population movement that baffled – and frightened – the contemporary authorities and administrators. The State was not directly involved in providing education for the poor. In 1833 it had grudgingly allocated funds to be distributed according to need by two large voluntary societies. These were: The National Society, representing Anglican interests; and the British and Foreign School Society which represented the Nonconformists. The needs of Catholics were not taken into account.

Thus our story begins with the founding, in 1847, of the Catholic Poor School Committee to compete for government aid with the aforementioned religious bodies. This was an important milestone in Catholic, social, and political progress. It brought bishops, priests and laity into formal committee contact with the government of the time. In the past, Catholics had tended to keep their heads down in political matters; now they were negotiating for their rights according to the democratic procedures of the day. There were many problems to be solved. The State was not convinced that education should be provided for out of the public purse. Religious educa-

tion was a matter for the different denominations themselves. There was
no sharp distinction between religious and secular education such as exists
today. The beginnings of a State system were to come many years later.

The Catholic Poor School Committee

There was a lot for the Catholic Poor School Committee to do; and time
was of the essence. So this new Committee settled down to the urgent tasks
of evaluating claims and providing a system of inspection to ensure that
government money was properly spent. It can be seen from the Committee's Minutes and reports that the members for Clifton Mission were well
to the fore in starting schools in what was to become the new diocese.
Clifton's representatives were: Mr. J. Clifford of Cannington and Father
W. Vaughan from the Church of the Holy Apostles, Clifton – later, Bishop
of Plymouth. In 1848 the Clifton Mission was given a grant for the conversion of part of the crypt to make it into a schoolroom. There was a grant
of £100 for the boys' school and £70 for the girls' school. The purpose of
these grants was to help with school equipment. Buildings and staff salaries
were the responsibility of the particular mission. The adaptation of the
crypt marks a recognisable stage in the history of Catholic schools which
is known as 'the school chapel' period. This makeshift arrangement
occurred at different times and in different places and many readers may
recall such dual-purpose buildings.

In 1850 came the new diocese of Clifton, and as we move along the
decade of the 1850s we find documentary evidence of grants for Chipping
Campden £10; St. Mary-on-the-Quay £50; St. Nicholas, Pennywell Road
£50; Bedminster Mission £30; and Chippenham coming away with a grant
£50. Under the special heading of 'Support Grants' Salisbury obtained a
grant of £10. At the latter end of the decade there were grants for Bristol,
Dighton Street £30; Gloucester £30; Bridgwater £50 – and the princely
sum of £1 for Fairford. The Committee took several factors into account
when allocating funds: among these were the existing resources of the mission; the urgency of the need for the school and the state of existing buildings. Gradually, throughout the century, the components of a Catholic education system were moving into place. An educational system needs pupils;
there was no shortage of needy pupils waiting to benefit from the system.
Strongly present too were the energetic hearts and minds of the clergy and
the laity as they ingeniously adapted for school use a disparate array of
buildings, from urban garrets to rural cowsheds. But other essential components were missing. There was the chronic lack of funds, there was an
acute shortage of teaching materials and there was only the rudiments of

a teaching curriculum. Most importantly of all there was a lack of teachers, and of those who teach teachers. There was no teaching profession that we would recognise today. Such a profession would have to, as it were, 'raise itself by its own bootstraps'.

Towards a teaching profession for Catholics

Four years before the founding of the diocese the State introduced what was called: 'the pupil–teacher system'. This system derived from the Lancasterian or monitorial system which was a popular method of mass education in the first half of the nineteenth century. One schoolmaster, aided by boys (monitors), taught large numbers of pupils by breaking the subject matter to be taught into question and answer units. The staple of this method was the teaching of reading, writing and arithmetic; or as they were more humorously known: 'Readin', Ritin' and 'Rithmetic'. – the three R's. Pupil teachers evolved from those monitors who showed aptitude and ability and wished to become teachers.

The procedure was as follows. Up to the age of 15 years they assisted the schoolmaster or schoolmistress as 'monitors' by supervising small groups of children. At the age of 15, subject to a successful interview with the Inspectorate, they were admitted as pupil-teachers at a small salary to enable them to stay at school. This salary was £25 a year for boys and £20 a year for girls. If progress was satisfactory the pupil-teacher went on to one of the new 'Queen's Colleges' which had been set up for the training of teachers. An outcome of this scheme was the founding of Catholic training colleges. In the course of time some of these would be widely regarded as 'models of good practice'. The work of the Catholic Poor School Committee included the sponsoring of three teacher-training colleges; one for men at Hammersmith, West London (later Strawberry Hill) and two for women in Liverpool and Roehampton. The men's college was the oldest, founded at Brook Green, Hammersmith in 1850. The two colleges for women were: Our Lady's College, Mount Pleasant, Liverpool, staffed by the Sisters of Notre Dame de Namur and Digby Stuart College in Roehampton which was run by the Sisters of the Society of the Sacred Heart.

Pupil-teachers were a means of providing money for the school as their salaries were paid by the government and not out of school funds. More importantly, the Catholic Poor School Committee gave funding priority to those schools training pupil-teachers. Occasionally there were accusations of exploitation and 'cheap labour'; and sometimes, inexperienced pupil-teachers had to hold the fort in difficult situations.

The logbook of Holy Cross School, Bristol, tells of a time when the

schoolmistress was absent with a serious illness and the school was super-
vised by two pupil-teachers. However, Her Majesty's Inspectorate were not
pleased and threatened to stop the school grant unless qualified staff were
appointed. To prevent abuses of the system and to ensure proper supervision the government made the rule of only two pupil-teachers to one certi-
ficated teacher. The School Committee Reports show that although the
inspection procedures were strict they could also be benevolent and helpful.
They tell of teachers coping with squalid physical conditions, lack of teaching resources and, sometimes, problems in class control. Although these
reports are written in bland 'officialese' we can easily decode their meaning. In 1851 Bath, St. John had eighty boys on the register. They had a
'trained teacher' and the 'required set books'. The Inspectors' report was
that the 'school was satisfactory'. School textbooks were expensive and few
poor families would have had the necessary spare money to buy them. Poor
overcrowded Bristol, St. Joseph had 130 boys on the register. The
Inspectors were sympathetic. The 'imperfect organisation' was excused by
the obvious need for better accommodation'. Not unlike schools today, an
external authoritative complaint will often spur the management to action.
The following year St. Joseph's had 'an improved building'.

Curriculum and Teaching Methods

School organisation and teaching methods went through several stages in
the nineteenth century. Many features remained until well into the twentieth century; indeed many new ideas and innovations show their nineteenth
century roots. Initially, the schoolroom was a large barnlike structure with
high windows. Around fixed positions marked on the walls stood the
children in semi-circular drafts of tens and twelves. The intended focus of
their attention was a chart suspended from a peg, or a nail, in the wall.
The monitor or pupil-teacher pointed to a word or number and the pupils
responded singly, or in a 'group chant' to the question posed by the
monitor. Gradually the better-off schools acquired blackboards. The next
stage came with the arrangement of pupils seated in rows on long benches.
Later, desks were added for the teaching of writing. This pattern of classroom teaching remained in use for many years especially in the poorer
schools.

The agreed basics were reading, writing and arithmetic, together with
needlework for girls. These subjects were taught by the rote method, a
technique that used the constant repetition of facts to commit them to
memory. Textbooks were scarce and expensive. However, the mindless
repetition of facts can have drawbacks. One School Committee inspection

report tells of a school where the children 'chanted' the names of the capital cities of certain foreign countries and could produce the names in pat form when asked. All went well until the Inspector asked the location of these cities relative to England. The pupils were confused. It seems that the school was unaware of the use of maps in teaching geography. It is likely, too, that the school could not afford them.

Victorian schools devoted a great deal of energy to the teaching of reading. Sandtrays and slates were most frequently used for the beginners to teach them letter formation. The teaching sequence proceeded by the spelling and pronunciation of syllables reinforced and clinched by constant repetition and dictation. Basically it was the mechanical art of rendering syllables into sounds and then forming simple words such as LON-DON'. Repetition was the key. These methods were gradually refined as time passed and gradually evolved into what we know as the 'Look and Say' and the Phonics method. The former relies on giving the complete sentence to establish the meaning of a word; the latter method on breaking the word into sound units. Methods of teaching reading were just as contentious then as they are today. The teaching of writing posed problems of a different kind. It needed special equipment and a comfortable seating space for the pupil to co-ordinate hand and eye. After elementary letter formation the pupils proceeded to 'headline copies' where they attempted letter designs and forms after the manner of the style being taught.

The ability to copy a letter in a clear and legible hand was a valued occupational skill in an age before photocopying. In Salisbury St. Osmund's we read of the introduction of 'Johnson's Vertical Hand' in 1896. The more advanced pupils went on to 'write from dictation' usually from selected passages of prose, to give them an idea of the various sentence formations. Arithmetic progressed through number recognition exemplified by use with objects. After addition and subtraction came that famous nineteenth century learning activity: the multiplication tables. The Inspectors' reports worried continually about 'proficiency in arithmetic'. It was a skill highly valued in a commercial nation. The teaching of needlework was graded with factory precision as the lesson sequence progressed though 'hemming' 'buttonholing' and on to the more elaborate stages of embroidery. This was not the total learning experience. The more enterprising schools went beyond this narrow utilitarian syllabus whenever they could, and taught drill, poetry recitation, music and singing.

However, if the State was going to pay for public elementary education, it was only right that it should seek value for public money. This it did by specifying what we would now call a 'core curriculum' without anything else that might be regarded as frivolous or unnecessary. In 1863 the infamous

'payment by results' was established. This system made the school grant
dependent on the performance of the children in reading, writing and
arithmetic, with needlework for girls. An added requirement was the ful-
filment of a minimum number of attendances. The most casual perusal of
any school logbook for the period will show the deep anxiety felt by school
managements on the attendance problem. The truancy rate tended to be
high in the poorer Catholic schools. Parents could see little point in sending
children to school when they could contribute to the family income. The
1880 Education Act required unconditional attendance between the ages
of five and ten years, with exemptions 'on the grounds of proven efficiency'
for those between ten and thirteen years. As one might guess this law was
not easy to implement. In 1893 the State tried again. The minimum age
was raised to eleven and, in 1899, to thirteen years of age. In 1891 elementary schooling became (for the most part) free; though school logbooks
and anecdotal evidence tell of the collection of 'school pennies' for many
decades afterwards.

After some time, and many protests, the severities of the Revised Code
were lessened. The work of elementary schools was divided into six 'Standards'. Pupils, usually, began Standard 1 at the age of six, and, given
normal attainment and progression, passed through the other Standards
year by year. We can get some idea of the expected attainment in Religious
Instruction by glancing at the requirements for Standard Four in 1870:

> 'By heart, the whole of the Catechism. Correct knowledge of the main services
> of the Church and their significance. The Miracles and Parables of Our Lord.
> The Sermon on the Mount. Bible history down to the building of the Temple
> of Solomon, with a general knowledge of Kings, Prophets and the Captivity of
> Babylon.'

The pupils would also learn by heart the Lord's Prayer, The Hail Mary,
Glory Be, and the Apostles Creed. There seems to have been the occasional
problem in getting the children to take part in the liturgy. The parish
priest, as school manager, had the task of getting the children to attend
Mass. In the logbooks of St. Mary on the Quay the problem changes from
'bad' to 'reasonably satisfactory' in the last decades of the nineteenth century. However, one must add a cautionary note to the effect that schools
varied a great deal depending on local physical and social circumstances.

In 1898 the *Catechism of Christian Doctrine* was published. This was to be
known to generations of Catholics as the 'Penny Catechism'. This publication differs from the present-day catechism in that it relied on 'question
and answer'. There is strong evidence that the teaching intention was to
be 'word perfect' in giving the required answer. Paraphrasing or giving the

gist of the answer in one's own words was frowned upon. It is possible that inexperienced teachers were nervous of departing from the text when they prepared pupils for a more thorough examination by the parish priest.

Religious instruction and contemporary attitudes

Existing records of syllabuses in religious instruction show that there was much solid subject matter to be digested. We shall never know the extent to which the pupils understood what they were being taught although we may reasonably assume that the basic religious principles became more meaningful as they encountered the problems of later life. The curricula of Catholic schools were more or less a private matter for Catholics until the passing of the famous 1870 Education Act. Now the public became more aware that they were paying for what was taught in Catholic schools. Feelings of suspicion fed by centuries of hostile propaganda were readily orchestrated by the Protestant Alliance, a hostile ultra-Protestant organisation. They argued that a Protestant people were being asked to pay for 'spreading Romish sedition'. This group, which had strong allies in Parliament, took strong exception to certain passages in the history textbooks used in Catholic schools. They singled out for special comment the treatment of Elizabeth I as illegitimate.

Linked with this was the controversial way in which the origins of the Church of England were described and explained to children. Catholic school teaching about Queen Victoria's ancestors was perversely construed as disloyalty to the Queen herself. But the Protestant Alliance had another, and more substantial, objection which originated in a loosely-drafted section of the 1870 Act. This particular section was designed to ensure that public money was not spent giving religious instruction 'peculiar to any denomination' except at 'the time set apart for the purpose'. But such is the nature of the Catholic school that it is difficult to seal off religious instruction from other more secular subjects. There was an accusation that the children were taught writing by making them transcribe the Hail Mary. The religious environment of the school gave offence as well. When the Catholic Poor School Society first gave a grant to a school it also gave that school a statue of Our Lady as protectress. The prominence of this gift, together with other statues, was a further cause for complaint. This problem was aggravated when Catholic schools had Protestant children on their rolls. This was true of a number of Clifton parishes, for example, Minehead and Frome.

There was much more of this hostility throughout the nineteenth century, and into the twentieth, when the cry was: 'Now we have Rome on the

rates'. A specimen of one the many accusations included the statement that
the 'Roman Catholic Church teaches that the Bible is a hateful thing' – a
standard smear from the folklore of British anti-Catholicism. However wild
and silly these accusations may seem to us now, they were taken seriously
by many influential people of that time. Many of the schools as we shall
see were founded by religious congregations of women. 'Anti-conventism'
was rife, and was often nurtured by the newly-emerging tabloid press.
There were tales of children and novices being 'imprisoned' and the fate
of Protestant children was too terrible to be imagined. Local opinion was
often inflamed; and schools in parishes such as Taunton and Weston-super-
Mare felt this hostility from time to time.

Special educational and social needs

The steady inflow of poor and pauper Irish immigrants from the 1840s
onwards increased the numbers of British Catholics, but it also brought
huge pastoral problems for the severely understaffed Catholic clergy. In
1886 the Catholic Directory estimated a Catholic population of 1.5 million,
this was roughly three times the estimated population in 1850 when the
Catholic dioceses were founded. This figure may be an underestimate. It is
reasonably probable that thousands of Irish immigrants were swallowed up
in the expanding urban slums without contact with a Catholic church or
school. We know from contemporary social reports of the morally and physically degrading effects of these slums and that these conditions did not
begin to improve until the end of the century. Irish Catholics were at the
bottom of the social pyramid, a condition which made them figure prominently among the prison population of the time. The welfare of destitute
and orphaned Catholic children was a problem on a national scale and as
such had to be addressed by collective action on the part of the hierarchy.
This was eventually done when Cardinal Vaughan founded the Crusade of
Rescue in 1899. The bishops faced several problems. In addition to the
usual 'drift' and 'leakage' among both immigrant and 'settled' Irish, they
had to negotiate with the procedures of the police courts and the workhouse
system. No less difficult were the non-Catholic welfare agencies. These
usually stipulated a Protestant upbringing for the children under their care.
Catholic children formed a large proportion of the child beggars and 'street
arabs' who came before the magistrates. In most cases there was a Protestant missionary present. Frequently, because there was no Catholic agency
present, the children were given over to the care of non-Catholic homes.
This failure had to be remedied. By the late 1890s matters improved. Some
non-Catholic homes, such as Dr. Barnardo's, agreed that Catholic welfare

agencies would be notified when Catholic children were presented to them for care.

Such was the historical background against which the Clifton diocese had to plan for its special schools. In 1854 the Reformatory Schools Act enabled religious organisations to open schools for those children who had already been committed to prison. This eased the old difficulty of getting access to Catholic children in penal institutions in order to instruct them in their faith. In 1850 Bishop Hendren had bought a site at Arno's Vale on the Brislington Road to provide for a Catholic cemetery. Part of this site was used to build the convent of the Good Shepherd which housed the Reformatory. It was here that the Good Shepherd Sisters educated 'youthful criminals of the Romish faith' – as a local newspaper put it. The Salisbury Mission responded to this urgent social need through the generosity of Lady Herbert of Lea, a recent convert. She established a school for destitute girls who would be, in the modern phrase, 'at risk'. This school was run by the Sisters of Charity and was a notably advanced school for its time. The regime was strict and the training course was broad and flexible. The girls were received at the age of six and taught household skills to fit them for employment when they left.

In addition to the usual needlework, the syllabus included a thorough course in baking and dairying. Both institutions had stories to tell – stories that give illuminating images to the social conditions of the time. In 1896, in an appeal to subscribers, we have St. Elizabeth's telling of 'little girls who survive by running errands and at night sleep under the doors and dry arches'. The Good Shepherd Sisters reported the rescue of 'Ellen Welch, a travelling pickpocket who begs most piteously not to be sent back to Liverpool gaol'. Ellen was thirteen years old.

These examples indicate the social problems against which the diocese struggled as clergy and religious tried to cope with an increasing number of destitute children. At Cannington an industrial school was founded in 1869 and was later, in 1920, moved to Prior Park. Lack of money was an ever-present problem and the administrative authorities who disbursed the money reflected the attitudes of their time. In their view the waifs, strays and the destitute were morally flawed. Their plight was a consequence of moral weakness. The normal Treasury Grant was five shillings per child for schools of this type. In 1853 the Clifton orphanage kept by the Sisters of Penance contained twenty-eight children of whom twelve were kept entirely on charitable subscriptions raised by the Sisters. This sector of educational provision overlapped with what later came to be known as 'adult education'. In Bristol, the parish of St. Nicholas ran a 'night school' for boys. In 1860 the Franciscan Sisters at Taunton started a foundation at Woodchester where they ran an orphanage and a 'night school' for girls. Some of these 'night schools' were linked to what was known as 'the half-time system'.

When, in the later nineteenth century, the government tried to impose compulsory attendance it had to allow for the dire financial necessity of child labour in very poor families. Children could make up the required hours of attendance by going to 'night school'. The logbooks of St. Mary-on-the-Quay show the difficulties in keeping the school grant as the number of 'half-timers' began to rise. This often happened during periods of economic depression, and was a particular problem for rural schools. The 'half-time system' was abolished in 1918, but the welfare needs of the poor persisted. In another specialist education area the Dominican Sisters of St. Rose's Special School have been educating physically handicapped girls. They have been in Stroud since 1912, and the diocese is deeply indebted to their work.

Catholics and the Dual System

What was known as the dual system started in 1870 and has continued in various forms into our own century. Under this arrangement a 'voluntary system' was left to compete with the State's own system which was organised through its own local instruments: the School Boards. This arrangement brought Catholics and Anglicans into partnership with the State. Some Catholics welcomed this new system; other Catholics saw the State schools as a rival system against which they would have to compete with the odds loaded against them. It was a contest that Catholics could not afford to lose. Those voluntary schools that did not reach 'required standard' would be closed and their places given to the School Boards. A wide geographical area and scattered clusters of popoulation made Clifton's Catholic schools particularly vulnerable. Sometimes, their numbers were barely enough to warrant separate provision. This problem seems not to have applied to Bristol, which was one of the first cities to elect a School Board. A prominent member of the Board was Canon W. J. Clarke who exercised a strong influence on its decisions and fought the Clifton corner when necessary. Despite the best Catholic efforts it became obvious, as the century drew to a close, that the Voluntary Schools could not survive without financial help on a large scale.

In 1897 the government made an attempt to help. The proposal was to make a grant of five shillings for every pupil in attendance. The administration of this new grant entailed the setting up of Voluntary Schools Associations, that is combinations of voluntary schools in different dioceses through which the government would distribute the grant money. For this purpose, Clifton combined with the diocese of Newport. The Minute Books of their meetings give some idea of the problems they faced in distributing the money, as well as the names of the schools which applied. If we take the year 1898 as an example, we find grants for Clifton, Park Place; Bristol, St. Mary-on-the-Quay; Bristol, St. Nicholas, Pennywell Road; Gloucester, St. Peter; Chipping Campden, St. Catherine; Cheltenham, St. Gregory; Bishopston, St. Bonaventure; Painswick; Beeches Green; Bath, St. John; Stratton on the Fosse, St. Benedict; Taunton, St. George; Wells RC School; Devizes St. Joseph; Malmesbury, St. Joseph; Salisbury, St. Osmund; Swindon, Holy Rood; Kemerton, St. Benet; Woodchester, St. Dominic and Wardour. Wardour received nothing; the others came away with grants ranging from £30 to £70. There were two major resolutions. Voluntary contributions must be kept up: they were perceived to be slipping; and preference would be given to those schools with pupil teachers. There was a lengthy discussion on the government of Nympsfield School – a story which was become something of a saga. The Board of Education refused to recognise it; this recognition was to come many years later.

Two years after the diocese had celebrated its first fifty years a more favourable arrangement was introduced in the form of the Education Act of 1902. The School Boards were abolished, and Local Education Authorities were formed. Rate-aid was extended to Voluntary Schools. There were, of course, certain concessions to be made in school government. One third of the managers were to be appointed by the Local Education Authority. On a very practical matter: the new arrangement had a beneficial effect on the salaries of Catholic teachers. In 1901 the newly-qualified headmaster of a Catholic school received an average of £130 per annum. His opposite number in the Board School received £175. By 1906 each received the same salary. A fully-qualified assistant mistress in a Catholic School received £58 per annum; her opposite number in the Board School received £85. By 1906 each received a salary of £114 per annum. Although there was a sufficiency of Catholic women teachers, there was a noticeable scarcity in the recruitment of Catholic men to the profession which was not remedied until after the First World War.

Looking back from the vantage point provided by the 1902 Education Act, the previous fifty years show a steady advance reflecting the efforts of a great many people. Wealthy Catholics and wealthy converts often provided initiative and resources in building churches and schools. Woodchester owes a great deal to William Leigh. The Reverend John Moore Capes, a convert clergyman, founded a school at Bridgwater. Dr. George Case, another convert, used his personal fortune to rescue the struggling church and school at Gloucester. Captain Dewell resigned his commission to found a school at Malmesbury. The French émigré clergy were a distinctive part of the Clifton progress in the nineteenth century. The parish entry for Salisbury tells of the hard work and enterprise of the Abbé Bégin. There was the Abbé Bouvier at Bridgwater. When he arrived there in 1871 he found that the forty or so Catholics at Highbridge included many children without instruction. The Abbé hit upon a plan to bring the Highbridge children to school in Bridgwater. He negotiated with the recently-opened railway to bring the children back and forth at the rate of three pennies a day: the earliest instance of commuter school children in the diocese.

There were instances of expansion and contraction. By the end of the century the school at Salisbury was bursting at the seams. Swindon, a text-book example of rapid population growth, had gone in seventy years from a population of 1300 to a population of 45,000 in 1900. In 1888 Holy Rood school was erected in Groundwell Road. Swindon was to challenge the wisdom and ingenuity of school builders and planners for the remainder of the new century. On the debit side Frome was in decline and an attempt in 1880 to found a school in Trowbridge foundered through lack of support. Bonham is another poignant example. It had a thriving community in the 1880s. By the end of the century Bonham had declined to the level where the congregation could no longer support a priest. Clifton diocese was vulnerable to population movements, whether caused by economic depression or the movement of military garrisons, as in the case of Trowbridge.

University and Secondary Studies

During the nineteenth century the social structure of British Catholicism reflected overlapping groups with differing aspirations and different views on education. The 'respectable poor' the destitute and the artisan classes have already been mentioned. There were also, the 'Old English' Catholics, the recusant families and the Catholic gentry. There was a growing Catholic professional and commercial class in the larger cities, particularly in London. There were the 'new converts' from the Church of England many of whom came from a university background. Although Catholic Emancipation allowed English Catholics back into political and civic life the universities of Oxford and Cambridge were closed to them because of the required religious tests. In the penal times Catholic families who could afford to, sent their sons – and daughters – to colleges on the continent. Now they felt they would rather send them to colleges where they would be educated with their social equals. The University of London had been founded in 1835 and, soon after, Stonyhurst, St. Edmund's and Prior Park were affiliated colleges and re-organised their courses to comply with the

London graduation requirements. There was one important point about the new University of London; no religious tests were required. Indeed, there is anecdotal evidence of nuns attending lectures at University College in their habits; seated, according to rule, at the back of the lecture room. As the century progressed Catholics were able to attend colleges such as Owen's College, Manchester, and Durham, and the civic university colleges such as Bristol and Exeter. Such is a sketch of the background against which the 'Catholic University' question took place.

A substantial amount of thinking and planning on this theme had been going on even before Clifton diocese was founded. The idea for a Catholic University was a continuing and major presence in the active mind of Peter Augustine Baines, Vicar Apostolic of the Western District. Bishop Baines was strongly of the view that Downside should be a centre of higher studies for both laity and clergy. It appears that Downside resisted this view, and Bishop Baines, after lengthy and complex negotiations, purchased Prior Park, near Bath. And Prior Park was to figure prominently in the history of education in the Clifton diocese. He persuaded a group of Ampleforth monks to join him in setting up the nucleus of a Catholic university. In 1840 Prior Park was affiliated to London University and students were able to register for matriculation and bachelor of arts degrees. Bishop Baines died in 1843 and although the college struggled on until 1856 it had begun to drift away from its original objectives, and it was in financial difficulties. In 1867 the college was re-opened by Bishop Clifford and the 'Catholic University' idea was mooted again. This idea was much discussed among Catholics of the time, and was most famously espoused by Cardinal John Henry Newman. Unfortunately for Prior Park there were plans for a similar institution at Kensington, in the diocese of Westminster.

This competition among Catholic colleges was seen by many influential Catholics as a waste of scarce resources. Not only was the student market small and undefined; there was also a scarcity of teachers who would be members of an academically acceptable professoriate. However, the national position remained unsatisfactory, even after Oxford and Cambridge had relinquished religious tests. Rome, through the Congregation de Propaganda Fide, forbade entry to Catholics. Many converts, who were becoming increasingly influential, continued to press for admission to a system that had nurtured them.

Chief among the protagonists for change was Bishop Clifford who contended that Catholics would never be an influence in the cultural and religious life of the nation until they were allowed to study at the ancient universities of Oxford and Cambridge. Cardinal Manning took a contrary view arguing that Oxford, in particular, was a centre of secular rationalism and religious indifference, both dangerous to the faith of young Catholics. Nevertheless, some Catholic parents chose to send their children to these universities despite being forbidden by Rome. Others applied to their bishops for special permission to do so. It was all becoming a muddle, and it looked as though Rome's prohibitions were being honoured more in the breach than in the observance. The emergent civic universities gave no problems regarding attendance by Catholics. The change eventually came in 1895 in the pontificate of Leo XIII. Certain safeguards were insisted upon by Rome, chief of which was the appointment of a resident chaplain who would be obliged to give regular 'conferences' on the Faith to the undergraduates.

These conferences gave rise to some important publications on Catholic apologetics. The conferences of Father Joseph Rickaby were subsequently published under the title, *The Lord is my light* (1915); and those of Monsignor Ronald Knox under the title, *In soft garments* (1942). It is interesting to note that the first chaplain to be appointed was from the diocese of Clifton. He was Monsignor Charles Kennard whose portrait still hangs in the chaplaincy at Oxford.

Because of the social history of British Catholicism only a very small proportion of Catholics went to university until the 1950s. The growth of access to secondary education and the government policy of 'equality of opportunity' were influential in increasing the presence of Catholic students in higher and further education. A predominantly secular and academic environment provided the Church with a new pastoral challenge of a special kind. The diocesan response is witnessed in the chaplaincies at the Universities of Bath, Bristol, and the West of England.

In the last decade of the nineteenth century there developed a strong national interest in providing an elementary education that would go beyond the statutory requirements. Scientific and technical knowledge was expanding, and, consequently, the pupils needed more education and training beyond the official school-leaving age.

On 2 June 1896 Brother J. T. Hayes of the Irish Christian Brothers arrived in Bristol. His purpose was to set up a system of post-elementary education for Catholic boys. Brother Hayes had come at the behest of Bishop Brownlow (Bishop Clifford's successor) following negotiations which had started four years earlier. Brother Hayes bought No. 9 Berkeley Square for £900. Thus the Irish Christian Brothers began their long association with Bristol and Prior Park. Looking back, it was a daring stroke to invite the Irish Christian Brothers to a city such as Bristol with its strong Protestant traditions. They were an able and competent teaching order with a strong belief in 'muscular Catholicism'; but they were also known for strong

Mgr. Canon Arthur Kennard: courtesy the Catholic Chaplaincy, Oxford University

views on Irish Home Rule – a contentious issue at the time. Contemporary records indicate that their arrival did cause some ripples of unease; yet their work once begun started to go from strength to strength. There were sixty boys on the roll in the first month. In 1897 the Bristol Education Committee recognised the new 'Christian Brothers College' for the holding

of Junior City Scholarships. The invitation was warmly welcomed and
developed. In 1902, of the six available scholarships for boys, four were
won by what later came to be known as St. Brendan's College.

Prior Park appears to have provided a recurring administrative and
financial headache for the diocese. Bishop Brownlow was unable to finance
Prior Park from his private means as his more wealthy predecessor had
done. To prevent the school from closing he asked the Irish Christian
Brothers to take it over. This they promptly did; but, at their own request,
for a trial period of seven years. This seven years happened to expire
between the death of Bishop Brownlow and the appointment of Bishop
Burton in 1902. Some of the Clifton clergy persuaded the new bishop to
refuse to extend the lease; and Prior Park was once again the Diocesan
School. But two years later, at Easter 1904 Bishop Burton, alarmed at the
huge running costs, decided to close Prior Park again. Thus the premises
remained vacant until the War Office took over the building from from
1914 to 1919. The story will be resumed later.

Back at St. Brendan's the register of fathers' occupations show that the
new school served tradespeople as well as professionals. This reflected the
growing national interest in secondary education with a strong technolo-
gical component. The range of academic and technical aspirations is shown
in the curriculum content. There was Latin, Greek and mathematics; there
was also technical drawing, science and bookkeeping. Technical instruction
was becoming of increasing national concern as politicians feared that Britain was falling behind the major European nations.

Facing the challenges of change

One of the most outstanding features of the diocese's response to the forces
of social and educational change was the zeal and vision of the religious
congregations of women. It would be difficult to overestimate their contribution to the development of Clifton's schools. Some came for short periods
and then moved on to other fields; other bore the heat and burden of the
day from the founding of the diocese to the latter decades of this century;
others, as numbers dwindled, moved from the classroom to the active pastorate as parish sisters and catechists. The complete story of their contribution to Catholic education has yet to be told.

In 1858 the Congregation of La Sainte Union des Sacres Coeurs (LSU)
were invited by the Benedictines to Bath. Their humble beginnings in that
city were embodied in the faith and activities of three determined Sisters.
A school of 600 pupils was to crown their centenary year. The Diocesan
Yearbook of 1999 attests the presence of their Pastoral and Book Centre.

In the following decade the Sisters of St. Joseph of Annecy founded a school in Devizes. Twenty years later the Sisters were educating the Catholic children of Malmesbury. The La Retraite Sisters were at Burnham-on-Sea in 1887 whence they spread throughout the diocese. The Sisters of the Daughters of Charity of St. Paul went to teach in Wardour in 1887. In 1891 the Ursulines arrived at Wincanton from Swansea to take charge of the school. In 1898 the Sisters of Charity of St. Louis established themselves at Minehead. They took in laundry to finance their school. In the same year the La Retraite Sisters established themselves at Weston-super-Mare. In 1904 they were at Clevedon. From here they were to depart in 1924 to take over St. Joseph's Academy for Young Ladies at Clifton. For many decades they would educate Catholic girls in Bristol. The Congregation of the Poor Servants of the Mother of God are still involved in teaching and parish work. They came to Holyrood School, Swindon in 1922. In 1939 they founded St. Margaret's School, Chippenham and are still involved with St. Mary's Primary School in that town. In Gloucester they have taught at St. Peter's School since 1939. From 1939 to 1972 they ran St. Michael's Convent School as an independent primary school.

The story of the famous Franciscan convent at Taunton may be consulted in the entry for that place. It is the story of how the Community of the Third Order of St. Francis came to Taunton to escape death or imprisonment in the French Revolution. On the run from the revolutionaries the Sisters disguised themselves in secular dress, slept in farmsheds, saying their prayers in the straw before being smuggled on to a coal barge bound for Rotterdam. The redoubtable courage of Mother Gertrude Weld and the sympathy of George III enabled them to bring their rosaries and breviaries past the customs when such items were forbidden. This was half a century before the diocese was founded. The Sisters began their long association with Taunton when they started a school: 'for teaching Catholic female children from poor homes to write and cast accounts'. Many secular histories of education cite the Franciscan Convent at Taunton for its contribution to the education of women – an innovation that was strange in early nineteenth-century England.

The first decade of the new century brought radical changes in national education policy. One of these was a growing concern for the health and physical welfare of children. The 'cleanliness inspection' began to figure in school logbooks and inspectors reports. Remedial action needed a national administrative structure.

In 1902 Local Education Authorities were formed. There was a growing feeling that the State should take some responsibility for the physical welfare and nutrition of school pupils. In 1908 local authorities were empowered to levy a halfpenny in the pound for the provision of school meals. This School Meals Service continued until 1980. As in many other welfare matters the convent schools were ahead of the State in providing food for the poorer children. The first decade of the century was an active phase in school development. In 1908 the Sisters of the Saviour and the Blessed Virgin came to Shepton Mallet and opened a boarding and day school for girls. Across the Channel in France there was government perse-cution of religious orders and congregations. Many came to England; and English Catholic education derived the benefit of their help and educa-tional vision. The Ursulines came to Warminster as refugees in 1907. They started a school for girls which, after an initial period of suspicion, beame very popular with the locals. To express their gratitude to the English nation the Sisters adopted St. George as their patron saint. The Sisters returned to France in 1919 and their patronal choice was adopted by the newly-founded parish which bears his name.

In the same decade the Sisters of St. Louis were active at Frome and La Sainte Union had founded a school at Portishead. As might be expected the First World War greatly retarded diocesan development and depleted the male teaching staff in many schools. In 1918 the school leaving age was raised to 14 years of age. Secondary education was beginning to assume a more coherent shape. The School Certificate was introduced in 1917 designed to be taken at the end of a four-year course of study, usually at 16. Two years later the Higher Certificate was introduced, requiring two further years of study. These two innovations greatly altered school organis-ation at both secondary and elementary levels. St. Brendan's College began to expand and re-direct its activities. In 1919 the Irish Christian Brothers returned to Prior Park to supervise the Industrial School. Meanwhile, the boarders' accommodation at Clifton – now the convent attached to St. Mary's hospital – was closed and the boarders moved to Prior Park in 1924. The Ursulines maintained their girls' school at Cheltenham from 1912 to 1931. In 1919 the convent of St. Gildas, Chard was founded. It was to serve the diocese for seventy years. In the 1930s the Salesians opened a school for disadvantaged boys at Newent. In 1935 the Sisters of La Sainte Union replaced the Ursulines at Cheltenham. In the following year the Sisters of Mercy founded a boarding school at Clevedon, and just before the outbreak of the Second World War the Sisters of the Poor Handmaids of Jesus Christ began their ministrations in Cirencester.

It is an interesting fact that despite the economic depression between the wars there was a great deal of thinking and planning on education. There was a series of government reports which were later to be influential in the way we think about education. The diocese was not idle. In 1938

Bishop Lee approached the Bristol Education Committee in connection with the 'proposed re-organisation of Catholic schools in Bristol'. He asked for grant of 75% of the cost of providing the sites and the buildings. Bristol Education Committee agreed subject to certain conditions. Needless to say there was a large body of opinion opposed to the payment of such a grant 'to one denomination'. Then came the Second World War and the debate was postponed to another age and another time.

The Last Fifty Years

'Severe frost. No buses running. Not one child arrived at school.'

This terse entry from the logbook of Wardour School dated 5 March 1947 speaks volumes regarding the acute shortages, the lack of heating, and the dreadful weather in those years immediately after the war. Nonetheless, it was the era of post-war reforms in education. Access to secondary education was to be a right open to all, regardless of social background. In 1944 the primary school replaced the elementary school, and in 1947 the school leaving age was raised to 15 years. The effect of this measure on school accommodation can be readily imagined when we realise that in 1940 the Irish Christian Brothers were desperately seeking accommodation for the 500 boys in their Clifton school. The evacuation of children during the war had already placed heavy demands on existing school facilities in many places in the diocese. Sometimes the children and their families stayed on to form new school communities requiring extra provision. The provision of 'temporary' huts tended to become 'permanent'. In the political sphere there was the introduction of the 'eleven plus' test for entry into selective secondary schools. In 1951 the General Certificate of Education replaced the School Certificate. The teaching force was still depleted after the war. All these reforms were benign in intent; but their implementation was a constant worry for the impoverished resources of clergy, teachers and parents.

The diocese's building stock was in bad repair, cramped and impoverished, many buildings were unsuitable for the demands imposed by new curricula, particularly in physical education and the sciences.

The 'parish levy' to pay for schools was an extra load on struggling parishes. Then there was 'the bulge'. Many readers will remember that picturesque description of the growing demand for school places resulting from the increase in the birthrate after the war. It brought a shortage of teachers, overcrowded classrooms, temporary huts, and as the 'bulge' moved on it left abandoned school premises. There were other problems. Many Catholics were unhappy with the social philosophy behind the 1944

Education Act with its confident segregation of children into three broad levels of aptitude: secondary, secondary technical and grammar. For example, Salisbury had no Catholic secondary school. When the Act raised the leaving age to fifteen, St. Osmund's had to absorb 'the bulge' until St. Joseph's was built and ready for occupation – some twenty years later.

In 1944 Bristol had two direct grant grammar schools: La Retraite and St. Brendan's. They received a 'direct grant' from the central authority and reserved a proportion of places for children of local primary schools. The diocesan response to the shortage of places was to develop St. Patrick's, Redfield into an 'all age' school. The extra accommodation was provided by huts and temporary buildings – an expedient common at the time. All Catholic children in Bristol were transferred to St. Patrick's for their final compulsory year of schooling. St. Thomas More's school was completed in 1954 at an overall cost of £150,000, of which the diocese paid twenty-five per cent. This took some of the strain off St. Patrick's. However, the Clifton Diocesan Catholic Schools Commission, founded in 1949, had a formidable task ahead. The Committee had to liaise with local authorities, an activity requiring considerable diplomatic and financial skills. In 1958 came St. Bernadette, Whitchurch, as a three-form entry school providing 450 places. But demand still outstripped supply.

The 1960s brought a surge in the diocesan building programme. In 1964 the first Catholic school on Salisbury Plain was opened to provide for the Catholics of Amesbury and the surrounding districts. In the following year the famous circular 10/65 was issued by the Department of Education. This influential document requested local authorities to submit re-organisation plans. It was hoped that voluntary schools would be integrated into the new comprehensive structure as part of government policy. A further proposal was even more contentious: this was a plan for a two-tiered comprehensive system, covering an age-range of 11–16 years combined with a sixth-form college for pupils of 16 years and over. The resulting 'hiving off' effect would cause difficulties both administrative and educational. Many feared that the sixth-form colleges would drain away talent from where it was most needed. There was considerable debate within the diocese for many years on this topic.

There were different patterns of response and different ways of re-grouping within the diocese. We have seen how Salisbury tackled the problem. St. Edward, Cheltenham, provides another instance. In 1939 the original property was purchased by La Sainte Union Convent, and twenty years later it passed to the Carmelites. St. Edward's was originally two schools: Whitefriars was the boys' school situated in Ashley Road; and Charlton Park accommodated the girls on the present site. The schools merged and became co-educational in 1987, resulting in a Junior, Middle and Senior School system. This changed in 1995 and now the school had kindergarten and junior pupils at Ashley Road, and the 11 year olds on the present site.

In 1969 Bishop Rudderham published his decision to re-organise Bristol's Catholic secondary schools by establishing a Sixth Form College on the site of La Retraite school. The remaining five schools were to become 11–16 comprehensives. This was not acceptable, and an alternative scheme was drawn up. The Christian Brothers wished St. Brendan's to remain a direct grant grammar school. St. Bede's and St. Thomas More's to be mixed; St. Brendan's to be boys only and St. Bernadette's to be girls only. The Christian Brothers were reluctant to conduct a mixed school. At this point further complications arose. An alternative scheme was drawn up by a group representing the views of St Brendan's and La Retraite. This paper was submitted to the Bishop five months after his original statement. This second proposal involved the rationalising of existing sixth form facilities with a view to facilitating the interchange of all Catholic secondary school pupils within the area.

The debate continued through to 1971 when a new proposal was turned down by Margaret Thatcher, then Minister of Education. She was not convinced by the proposal to establish a Sixth Form College on the La Retraite site. In her view it was not a wise use of existing educational and material resources. A new factor was introduced with the change in local government areas. Hitherto, the planners had concentrated on Bristol as a singular entity. The new county of Avon brought Bath into the equation. There existed in Bath two Catholic schools: an independent girls' convent school, La Sainte Union; and a three-form entry school, Cardinal Newman's. With fee increases and falling numbers the convent school was assessing its future seriously. The general decline in pupil numbers was also significant at Cardinal Newman's School which existed uneasily alongside the county's comprehensive system.

Planning for the future

In February 1976 the Diocesan Schools Commission issued a pamphlet detailing the future of Catholic education within the diocese. It urged a non-selective system and recommended the government policy on direct-grant schools. The planned time scale gives an indication of the urgency of the planners, teachers and clergy. A new 11–16 school was to be opened in Bath in September 1979; the two direct – grant schools in Bristol were to be phased out in the same year. A new Sixth Form College was to be built in Bristol in 1982 or 1983 at the latest. Eventually, the Christian Brothers were persuaded that a Sixth Form College within the state system was the only alternative to the school being taken over. But there was still the task of selling the new structures to Catholic parents, many of whom had strong ideas on current trends in education, coupled with a strong sense of loyalty to those schools about to be merged. It seems that the most strenuous opposition came from the parents of St. Bede's. After many meetings and exchanges of letters the position in Bath and Bristol became stabilised. Swindon was, to some extent, slightly ahead of the game in 'going comprehensive'. In 1964 the Swindon Education Committee decided that its area would be re-organised on a comprehensive system to come into effect in 1965. The outcome was the amalgamation of St. Joseph's and a previously planned St. John Bosco school to become an all-through comprehensive 11–18 establishment on two sites. St. Joseph's Comprehensive School became fully operative in January 1966 – the first all-through comprehensive school in the Clifton diocese, and in Wiltshire. Even as the school started with a nominal roll of 858, it was predicted that it would have to plan to house a population of over 1500 pupils.

The national picture was becoming clearer and firmer; indeed, the 1976 Act attempted to make comprehensive the only permitted form of state-maintained secondary education. But, as we have seen earlier, education and politics are even intertwined. The 1976 Act was repealed in 1979 after the election of a Conservative government. Nonetheless, by 1988 comprehensive schools were providing for 86% of the pupils in England, and this, more or less, reflects the position in Clifton. In Bath we had St. Gregory's; in Bristol, St. Bernadette's, St. Bede's and St. Thomas More's. Within the same frame we have St. Joseph's, Salisbury; St. Benedict's, Cheltenham and St. Augustine's, Trowbridge. It looks as though the once controversial idea of the Sixth Form College now commands a wider acceptance. In 1991 Sixth Form Colleges were removed from local authority control and St. Brendan's, now a Sixth Form College, celebrated its centenary in 1996. St. Peter's High School, Gloucester and St. Augustine's, Trowbridge, have Sixth Form Centres.

Then came the year 1988 and the landmark of the Education Reform Act. It is still too early to assess its effect on the relationship between Catholic parishes and their schools. This Act created Grant Maintained Schools which can 'opt out' of local authority control and receive finance direct from the Department of Education. Most of all, the Act was dedicated to 'parent power' and encouraged parental involvement at all levels.

Summary and retrospect

This brief account of such a tangled history must of necessity be sparingly selective. The reader is urged to flesh out the bare bones by reference to the parish histories and the bibliographies provided. I hope that it shows that the range, quality and commitment of Clifton's schools is the legacy of the enduring faith, unremitting toil and Christian vision of our Catholic ancestors. As in most accounts of human achievement, the records we have used tell us of those who were 'mentioned in dispatches' in some shape or form. But the innumerable parents, catechists, nuns, teachers, clergy, all those who raised funds, wrestled with government legislation, attended meetings, instructed children in dilapidated schools – these are known only to God. In this year we can look back from a special vantage point at the continued development of education in the diocese. Some schools have vanished, or have been merged; but some lines of continuity remain. Downside needs little or no introduction in the history of Catholic education; and where Bishop Baines once dreamed of a 'Catholic University', the new school of Prior Park flourishes. It has been a long haul since the days of the 'school chapel', the converted shed and the resourceful nuns and sisters taking in laundry to get 'start-up' money for their schools.

In the history of the curriculum our story began with barefoot children chanting their lessons by rote. As time passed the 'chalk and talk' method yielded to 'discovery learning', and examinations gave way to course-work. Then came information technology with computer-aided instruction and the Internet. Discussions on the aims and philosophy of education became full of the language of the market place. Parents and pupils became consumers and teachers became 'managers of learning resources'. In 1992 Her Majesty's Inspectorate was replaced by OFSTED: the Office for Standards in Education. The diocese's sixty maintained schools educated approximately nineteen thousand children during the year 1997. The majority of these schools have governors appointed by the Trustees. Governors, staff and parents are charged with the responsibility to preserve and develop their Catholic nature. During that year of 1997, twenty-one schools received OFSTED inspections which reported favourably on their spiritual, moral and academic well-being, as well as the close collaboration with their parishes. We have noted the culture of opposition in which our Catholic schools began. Most heartening for the future is the ecumenical approach to Christian education of which there are many examples. One may suffice to give the idea. St. Augustine's of Taunton is a joint Anglican-Catholic foundation involving

Clifton and the Anglican Diocese of Bath and Wells. The aims of this innovative school may be put forward as a blueprint for the future: 'To create a community in which the concept of Christianity as a living Faith will pervade all aspects of school life and activities'.

Kevin McGarry

CHAPTER SIX

The Diocese of Clifton 1850–2000
A Personal View by J. A. Harding

1850–1900

English Catholic history in the first half of the nineteenth century is dominated by the Irish potato famine. The failure of this essential crop had occurred on several occasions in the first three decades of the century but had its most devastating effects in the years 1845 to 1847. It is estimated that some 1,000,000 people died and that approximately the same number emigrated and went to the U.S.A. and were to become forbears of Presidents Kennedy and Reagan and of many others who now comprise the influential Irish lobby in American politics. A substantial number came to the British Isles making their entry at, and often settling in, the great ports and their immediate hinterland. Liverpool and Bristol were clearly the desired havens of many.

The dire poverty of these thousands – amounting to total distitution – cannot be exaggerated as the following news item in the *Bristol Mercury* so graphically describes.

> 'Last week a schooner named the *Shannon*, 126 tons, McDonnell master, from Cork, came into this port with a cargo consisting of 113 Irish paupers, 90 sheep, 18 horses and 19 lambs . . . On "rummaging" the vessel . . . Mr Davis (tide surveyor) stated . . . that a scene of the most squalid misery presented itself, and that the horrible stench which arose from the filth caused by the passengers was sufficient to engender the most loathsome disease; he had never met with anything so dreadful in the whole course of his experience. Several of the passengers were scarcely able to walk, owing to the state of debility to which they had been reduced through want of food, and from other causes . . .'

(16 June 1849)

St. Nicholas of Tolentino in the heart of Bristol was one of the missions

founded specifically to provide for the spiritual and material needs of so
many. Founded in 1848 it had been built from the pennies of the poor.
Others settled in the mission of St. Mary-on-the-Quay, while the Church
of the Twelve Apostles (later the Pro-Cathedral), Clifton was seen as the
natural home of Oxford converts and of other well-to-do gentry.

Such dire poverty brought with it, or was aggravated by, the excesses
of drink. Letters to the local press made the point with unsympathetic
candour and there can be no doubt that while the numbers of the Catholic
community were boosted by the shamrock invasion, the converse was that
it added to the already hostile perceptions held by the Protestant majority.

Simmering anti-Catholic feeling had always been a fact of life, albeit
just below the surface, and it took only one individual like the firebrand
Lord George Gordon to set in motion a trail of hatred and destruction. The
incendiary attack (1780) on the newly erected Catholic chapel in Bath
proves the point, reinforced half a century later by the Bristol Riots (1831)
which, although different in inspiration – the refusal of the Lords to pass
the Reform Bill – nevertheless showed how a fanatical mob can vent its
rage in matters political as well as religious. On this occasion the Bishop
of Bristol's palace was destroyed and much credit was given in the press to
Fathers Francis Edgeworth O.S.F. and Patrick O'Ferrell, O.S.F. for their
efforts in calming the situation.

Such was the already fevered brow of John Bull when the announcement
was made by Pope Pius IX in September 1850, that he was to re-establish
the Catholic Hierarchy of England and Wales. An archbishopric was to be
established at Westminster with twelve dioceses to be created elsewhere,
including the diocese of Clifton (comprising the counties of Glos, Wilts and
Somerset). Public meetings were called in Bristol, Cheltenham, Salisbury
and elsewhere to protest against the so-called Papal Aggression.

A vigorous exchange of letters appeared in the correspondence columns
of both the national and local press. Many of the participants were clergy-
men and some of the arguments used were of a highly technical (i.e. scriptural and theological) nature. Cruder forms of abuse, however, were never
far away as is shown from the following letter written by W. C. which
appeared in the *The Bristol Times*.

> Sir – Yesterday, on my return home over Durdham Downs, my attention was
> suddenly attracted by two persons coming towards me, the one a youth about
> 18 years of age evidently of respectable appearance, the other a priest or
> Jesuit habited in the usual garb of that class of evil spirits now prowling about
> all over England, like wolves in sheeps' clothing, seeking whom they can
> devour. In passing me, I heard the ghostly man exclaim, in a foreign accent,
> 'They are enemies of God and man.' The Jesuit or priest had placed his fangs

in an excited manner on the youth, who appeared rather desirous of disengaging himself from the grasp of the unwelcome expounder of the religious opinions which he sought to inculcate . . . in this way he continued his denunciations, calculated to frighten the youth into an acquiescence in his doctrines, in the style of the highwayman propounding his alternative, "Your purse or your life." "Turn Roman Catholic or prepare for eternal perdition . . ."

(15 May 1852)

Throughout this period, and even from before the restoration of the Hierarchy, there had been an almost lurid curiosity amongst the general public concerning the phenomenon of Catholic monasteries and, more especially, convents. The enclosure of nuns was seen as the symbol of a giant effort by the Church of Rome to hide something essentially mysterious and even immoral. For its part the press did not hesitate to fan the flame of such suspicions and yet, in a rather curious way, almost invariably showed a deep respect for the postulant or novice as she took the veil and dedicated herself to a life of prayer away from the world. The number of Protestants who attended such ceremonies was frequently commented upon. Sometimes, however, amusing phrases crept into the account as when *The Bristol Mercury* spoke of the habits being 'fumigated with incense' (23 January 1847). Nor could the same writer resist the titillating phrase when he told his readers that one of the candidates was 'said to be possessed of a handsome fortune.' Three years later a ceremony took place in the convent of St. Catherine of Siena, Clifton. Under the heading 'Popery at Clifton' the young lady was said to be 'possessed of more than ordinary personal attraction' (*The Bristol Mercury*, 21 September 1850).

The local reporting of these events pales into insignificance when compared with the public notoriety heaped upon the diocese in the Talbot Case (1851). Miss Augusta Talbot, niece of the Earl of Shrewsbury, stood to inherit £85,000. As an orphan of nineteen years she had been placed in the charge of a guardian, Fr. Thomas Doyle, who obtained a place for her at The Lodge, attached to the Franciscan Convent in Taunton. As someone who needed protection she was admitted as a 'temporary postulant' although she had no intention of becoming a nun. Her stepfather brought a case against both the Rev. Mother and her confessor (Bishop Hendren) alleging the abduction of Augusta. Meanwhile *The Times*, *Punch* and the national press generally joined in the hue and cry. The church authorities were portrayed as manipulative, seeking to lay their hands on the wealth of a candidate who, by taking a vow of poverty, would be handing over all her earthly possessions to the religious order she was seeking to join. Even the Lord Chancellor visited the Lodge to see the situation at first hand.

Eventually the case in Chancery went against the stepfather, and Fr. Doyle continued to be her guardian. Shortly afterwards Augusta left and married Lord Edward Howard. Gratitude, not hostility, was Augusta's sentiment towards the convent that had befriended her and over the years she sent a number of gifts to mark her appreciation.

Mercifully there was another side to this national picture of religious tribal warfare. For some time serious attempts had been made to reach a genuine understanding of the scriptural, theological and ecclesial issues on which Protestants and Catholics took such a contrasting stance. The most celebrated of these attempts was the Discussion which took place at Downside in February and March 1834 on 'The Rule of Faith' and 'The Sacrifice of the Mass'. Two ministers represented the Protestant tradition while the Catholic side was put by Dom Thomas Brown OSB (later Bishop of Newport & Menevia), Father T.M. MacDonnell (a noted controversialist) and Fr. Edgeworth (missioner at Bristol). An authenticated Report was published two years later. It contains about five hundred pages of closely reasoned argument – an achievement which pre-dates the better-known Malines conversations by nearly a century.

On the national level, too, there was an attempt at mutual understanding. The *Association for Promoting the Unity of Christendom* (APUC) had also begun in the 1830s and its unofficial leader on the Catholic side was Ambrose Phillipps de Lisle. An inveterate optimist he felt that his hand had been strengthened when Bishop Clifford, a relative by marriage, was persuaded to join their ranks. For a while the movement flourished until membership from the Catholic side was prohibited by Rome on the grounds that it favoured indifferentism.

Another arm in this aspect of the Church's apostolate was the *Clifton Tracts*. First published in 1851 they were a forerunner of the Catholic Truth Society pamphlets and aimed at least to remove misunderstanding and to correct the grosser accusations made about the teaching of the Church. The *Tracts* were written both by born Catholics such as William Austin Gillow and by converts from Anglicanism such as James Spencer Northcote. Originally published by the Society of St. Vincent de Paul, of which the Clifton conference is one of the oldest in the country, it is interesting to note that they were subsequently published in the U.S.A. There were even *Clifton Tales*, e.g. *Joe Baker; or The One Church*. This was by another convert, Mrs. Gertrude Parsons, a deeply religious woman who, 'having no children, devoted her leisure . . . to supplying the want of Catholic stories' (Gillow).

Bishop Hendren, who since 1848 had been Vicar Apostolic of the Western District, was chosen as the first Bishop of Clifton. The progression was not as inevitable as it might seem because he was in fact totally against the continued ownership of the flagship property of Prior Park, – a spectacular pile dominating the fashionable city of Bath. In this Hendren antagonised many to such an extent that his continued tenure of Clifton became virtually impossible. After only nine months he was transferred to the still vacant see of Nottingham.

His successor at Clifton was Thomas Burgess – an unlikely appointment as at an earlier period he had been Bishop Baines's lieutenant in trying to create an episcopal residence and seminary at Prior Park. Baines had overreached himself to a serious extent and the resulting debt had crippled not only the Western District but also its successor, the fledgling diocese of Clifton. After three years the diocese was vacant yet again, Burgess having succumbed to the burden of debt which he had manfully tried to clear (1854).

Clifton's plight came to the attention of Pope Pius IX who blocked the appointment of a new bishop until the financial trauma facing the impoverished flock had been effectively cured. Archbishop George Errington, astute and unbending – and perhaps for that reason not a good choice to assist Cardinal Wiseman at Westminster – offered his services as Administrator so as to ensure that financially the diocese was placed on an even keel. This he did during the years 1855 and 1856 and then submitted a report to the Pope to say that Clifton was now ready to receive a new bishop.

William Clifford, the second son of Lord Clifford of Chudleigh, was the personal choice of the Pope and was consecrated by him in the Sistine Chapel on 15th February 1857. At the age of thirty-three he was the youngest Catholic bishop since the Reformation. Throughout his thirty-six years as bishop he used his personal wealth in a variety of ways, especially in embellishing the Pro-Cathedral at Clifton. Although an aristocrat he was nevertheless a 'man of the people'. One early gesture that was particularly well received was that he chose to be enthroned on the feast of St. Patrick.

Meanwhile priests throughout the diocese struggled to make ends meet. One such was Fr. James Clark. Writing in *The Tablet* in January 1859 he pleaded:

> 'Will any one refuse to assist this poor mission in its struggle for the holy cause of raising for itself a little temple in which its God may be truthfully adored? The work will be commenced next month or the month following. But we have not the means . . . Will no one, then, lend us a helping hand? Good, generous-hearted Catholics, did you know our distress. I am sure you could not refuse what we so earnestly beg of you . . .'

He followed this appeal with at least six other begging letters. Incredibly

Archbishop George
Errington

the 'poor mission' referred to was at Swindon – now often described as 'the fastest growing town in Europe'.

In due course Bishop Clifford became a member of various local historical and archaeological societies and through these learned bodies he established links with clergy of other Faiths. He corresponded with Lord Arthur Hervey, Bishop of Bath and Wells, and Prebendary W.H. Jones, the antiquary who was responsible for the excavation of the Saxon church at Bradford-on-Avon.

Unlike other holders of his office both before and since, Clifford was also a figure on the international stage. At the First Vatican Council he spoke in favour of a Universal Catechism but earned disapproval in some quarters for his reservations regarding the proposed definition of papal infallibility. However, when the dogma was defined he loyally accepted it – although with over fifty others he had absented himself from the final vote – but much of what he said regarding the importance of the college of bishops was enshrined a century later in the thinking of the Second Vatican Council. At home he argued over many years, in particular against Manning, in favour of Catholics being allowed to go to Oxford and Cambridge.

The strength of High Church ritualism in the ranks of the Church of England was a major feature of this period. Frome in particular, but also Bristol (Holy Nativity, Knowle and All Saints, Clifton) were centres noted throughout the land, and ensuing controversy, not only in the courts but also even in occasional civil disorder in the Somerset market town, was never far from the headlines. A number of Anglo-Catholics were received into the Church by Bishop Clifford among whom was the vicar of Longbridge Deverill, Lord Charles Thynne (uncle of the Marquess of Bath). Branded by the press 'A lordly pervert' he was subsequently ordained priest (1885).

Although he came from the ranks of the aristocracy, Clifford did not neglect the needs of the poor. He was vigilant in overseeing the work of the Good Shepherd nuns in the Reformatory at Arnos Vale, Bristol. He had dealings with the Home Office on their behalf and answered criticisms in the press (1861) referring to a case of alleged maladministration. Again, in its early years (1878 and 1879) the Industrial School at Cannington had received an unfavourable report. Clifford saw to it that problems were rectified and informed the local press of this through a letter from his secretary.

Work among the poor continued elsewhere. In the north of the diocese, at Cheltenham, the Sisters of Nazareth opened a home and within days went to the local workhouse and 'brought back with them blind and paralysed' (1884), while in the south, at Salisbury, we find the Sisters of Charity opening a soup kitchen and serving 300–400 poor people a week during the harsh winter of 1888.

William Clifford was universally mourned when he died in 1893. What is interesting about the list of three names *(terna)* put forward to succeed him is that they were all converts. The man chosen was William Brownlow, a convert of Newman and at the time of his appointment Vicar General of Plymouth. His main contribution to scholarship was as joint author with Northcote of *Roma Sotterranea* (1869), a study of the catacombs at Rome based on the excavations in the 1820s carried out by Count De Rossi. The work was of considerable doctrinal importance because it showed by an examination of the paintings and inscriptions of these underground cemeteries, how the teachings and liturgical practices of the Catholic Church today are exemplified in the beliefs and devotions – in particular, prayers for the dead – of the Early Church.

Three local events are to be noted from Brownlow's seven years as Bishop of the diocese. The first was the inauguration of the first Catholic pilgrimage to Glastonbury. This took place on 12 September 1895 when the pilgrims climbed to the top of the Tor. Two years later the Anglicans followed with a pilgrimage to the Abbey grounds (3 August 1897). Secondly there was a rather sharp controversy with the Bishop of Bristol (Dr. George Forrest Browne) on the true succession of the ancient hierarchy in these islands. In about 1883 lists of incumbents first began to appear in Anglican parish churches, purporting to show at the local level continuity of succession – a move which received the wholehearted support of Dr. Edward White Benson, Archbishop of Canterbury (1883–1896). Differences remain to this day but happily the anniversary of St. Augustine's arrival was celebrated in 1997 in a manner far less adversarial than it was in the correspondence columns of a century ago. The third notable event of Brownlow's episcopate was when in 1900 St. Gregory's Priory at Downside, founded in 1814, was accorded abbatial status together with Douai (then still on the continent) and Ampleforth.

1900–1950

George Charles Burton – he changed his second name to Ambrose on his appointment in 1902 – became the fifth bishop of Clifton. The year after his arrival he moved the episcopal residence and the diocesan archives from the Pro-Cathedral House to Prior Park, Bath (8 September 1903) but returned to Bristol the following year. Noted as a classicist, an example of his Latin style may be seen in the epitaphs he composed for the tombs of Bishop Walmesley and Bishop Baines in Downside Abbey. The couplet for the former nuns:

> Inclyta me genuit Lancastria, Roma sacravit,
> Quas colui rapiunt denique Sulis Aquae.

which one versatile translator has rendered as:

> A proud Lancastrian born, ordained in Rome,
> Bath waters bore me from my earthly home.

(*South Western Catholic History* No 8, 1990, p. 40)

But events abroad of a far greater importance had already begun to unfold and were to have a profound influence on the life and history of the diocese. As with the Revolution just over a century before, France was again to be the epicentre. Anti-clericalism had been gaining ground and had

Salisbury: St. Osmund,
Martin, Trappist chapel
of Our Lady of Paradise

reached its climax in the Law of Associations (1901). This had put the
French church in a straitjacket of restrictions including the prohibition
of the wearing the religious habit in public. The cause of education was
particularly badly hit with the closure of 132 religious houses and no fewer
than 13,904 religious schools. 'It's an ill wind . . .' and these sad events in
France again helped to breathe new life into the Catholic community on
this side of the channel. Convents were opened (e.g. the Ursulines in Warminster, 1907) and even a Trappist monastery at Martin, seven miles south
west of Salisbury.

The First World War broke out in August 1914, and before the end of
the year a number of Belgian refugees had come to find refuge in Bristol

and Wiltshire. Bishop Burton, Canon Lee and the Catholic Women's
League distinguished themselves in the way that practical help was made
available by the Church and many other bodies. The War devastated the
male population of this country and war memorials everywhere bear witness to the thousands who lost their lives. Letters from the French Mother
Superior at Warminster to Bishop Burton describe how the young soldiers
from the nearby army camp on Salisbury Plain would come to pray before
the Blessed Sacrament exposed in the little iron chapel before leaving to
meet certain death in the trenches of the Somme. Apart from the human
tragedy, society also suffered a severe demographic imbalance between the
sexes which was to last for more than a generation.

In his public utterances Burton showed himself a staunch patriot. He
did not go as far as Dr. Arthur Winnington-Ingram, Bishop of London
(1902–1939), who at a mass rally called for British soldiers to:

> '. . . band in a great crusade to kill Germans. To kill the good as well as the
> bad, to kill the young men as well as the old, to kill them lest the civilisation
> of the world should itself be killed.'
>   (*Canterbury Tales*, broadcast Channel 4 March 1997, Transcript 1, p. 12)

Burton did, however, state privately in 1917: 'I am quite prepared to
denounce Germans and Pacifists and Conscientious Objectors . . .'

One sad – though, within its own context, understandable – feature of
the time was the lack of co-operation in worship between Catholics and
other churches. Memorial services, dedications and the like were eschewed
by the bishops because, as Rome saw it, it gave rise to indifferentism ('one
religion is as good as another'). Thus we see Bishop Burton in the letter
just quoted, while willing to share a public platform to protest was not
willing to share it to worship. It was a view which saw a sudden reversal at
the Second Vatican Council but Burton, not unnaturally, was a child of his
time who for all his breadth of learning was very much in the mould of the
institutions where he had been trained in late 19th century Rome. The
Code of Canon Law (1918) enforced such views.

The re-establishment of the Hierarchy in 1850 had not meant a complete regularisation of church structures in England and Wales. It was not
until St. Pius X's *Sapienti Consillio* in 1908 that supervision by the Congregation of Propaganda (responsible for the missions) ceased; nor was it
until the code of canon law was enacted ten years later that proper parish
structures were established in this country. This explains why even after
1850 priests continued to add 'missionary apostolic' or 'missionary rector'
to their signatures in church registers.

In 1914 twelve Benedictine monks from the Anglican community of

Caldey made their submission to the Catholic Church. Eventually a new home was found for them in a mansion on the slopes of the Cotswolds. The property, which had once belonged to the Abbots of Gloucester, was given to the monks by Mr. Dyer Edwardes. Initially (1925) both Bishop Burton and the cathedral chapter had grave misgivings about the undertaking but in time these were resolved and the monks took up residence in their present location in December 1928.

Bishop Burton died in February 1931 and was succeeded almost a year later by his Vicar General, William Lee. Although not an intellectual he was entirely the man for the task and his great achievement of buying land and building schools and churches did much to prosper the ecclesial life of the diocese of Clifton. Eighty-one places of worship – albeit some temporary to meet a particular need – was no mean achievement for a reign that lasted less than seventeen years.

In the early 1930s people were much troubled by the political Left/Right divide, particularly as exemplified in the Spanish Civil War (1936–39). Most in the Church's hierarchy opted for the Right – as Lee did for Franco – although the Church had been careful to condemn the extremes of both political creeds as Pius XI had done in uncompromising terms in *Divini Redemptoris* (on Atheistic Communion) and *Mit Brennender Sorge* (on National Socialism).

Research into the persecution of the Jews in Germany even before the Second World War has brought to light the achievements of a Catholic baptised (1884) at St. Joseph's, Bridgwater and brought up in Highbridge. Frank Foley was an MI6 agent working in passport control in Berlin who, risking his own safety, saved the lives of some ten thousand Jews. The achievements of this hitherto unsung hero of the diocese who as a young man wanted to become a priest have been chronicled in a recently published biography, prompting moves among the Jewish authorities to confer on him their highest accolade, the title 'Righteous of the Nations'.

Architecture as well as books reflect the spirit of an age. It would be hard to imagine a more British-Raj inspired building than H.S. Goodhart-Rendel's design for Prinknash Abbey. Started in 1937, it was later abandoned because of the cost although the crypt was partly completed and houses the church that we see today. Lutyens's discarded design for Liverpool Cathedral was of the same genre. In the same year Prinknash Priory was raised to the status of an Abbey.

The Second World War, with its aerial bombardment, brought with it problems that were quite unprecedented. Bomb damage was sustained in many places including Painswick, St. John's, Bath and Holy Cross, Bedminster, Bristol. Father Timothy Sheridan was killed and Father Francis

Meegan and Father John O'Donnell were injured. The Good Shepherd
Convent at Arnos Vale was severely damaged on the night of 2nd January
1941 and it was Bishop Lee who secured a safe haven for them at Eagle
House, Bathford. So worried were the civil authorities that a plan was put
into operation to evacuate children from the great cities to other (safer)
parts of the country. Lee's Diaries indicate his untiring efforts to safeguard
the interests of the evacuees and on a number of occasions he visited them
at Exmouth and other locations. Prisoner of War Camps also received visits
from him.

During the war moves were already afoot to provide universal secondary
education when peace was restored. An extremely anti-Catholic address
was delivered in the House during a debate on 25th February 1944. The
hapless Labour M.P. was Alexander Walkden representing the constituency
of Bristol South. Within days his agent was summoned to Bishop's House
when Lee (as he noted in his diary) 'explained to him our position and
what would be necessary for me to do if the Party did not speak on the
matter'. Days later the local association duly issued a statement disassociat-
ing itself from the views of its M.P. At Bishop Lee's funeral in September,
1948, a telegram was read from Chuter Ede, Home Secretary who had
previously worked with R. A. Butler, praising the late bishop: 'He had an
intimate acquaintance with the problems of schools in the poorest districts
and his loss will be mourned outside your own communion'.

One noticeable feature of diocesan life in the years immediately following the war was the boys' camps, organised in the main by Dr. Francis
Grimshaw. At that time great emphasis was placed on Youth (e.g. Young
Christian Workers) – a policy which was also mirrored in the thinking of
the government of the day which raised the school leaving age and (albeit
for other reasons) introduced conscription to the armed forces.

Another feature has been the erection of parishes for refugees from
behind (what used to be) the Iron Curtain who have settled in this country.
The Ukrainians have their own church in Gloucester. The Poles, too, have
a church in Bristol (the former Arley Chapel) and a centre in Swindon.

1950–1975

Joseph Rudderham succeeded in 1949, his name having been put forward,
it was said, by Dr. Grimshaw who had been his contemporary as a student
in Rome and was now Bishop of Plymouth. The new bishop carried forward
the education programme conceived by his predecessor within the frame-
work of the 1944 Act and over the years secondary modern schools were
opened in Bristol, Gloucester, Swindon and Bath.

A notable event took place just six years into Bishop Rudderham's episcopate. A contemporary account of the Clifton Diocesan Religious Vocations Exhibition, held in September 1955, reads like a passage from the
gospel: 'So great was the crowd which poured into the Victoria Rooms,
Clifton, the largest hall available for such a function, that every foot of
space was occupied and the throng overflowed into the surrounding cor-
ridors.'

The numbers were certainly impressive although ultimately the success
of such events is known only to God. What is significant, however, is the
venue, for it was here only a hundred years before that strident denunciations were being made of 'Papal Aggression' and of the alleged priestcraft
of the Church of Rome.

Catholics in the 1950s witnessed for the first time the celebration of
Mass in the evening. For many it meant greater flexibility in their weekend
leisure time table. On the other hand it led almost inevitably to the decline
and eventual demise of a well-loved Sunday institution: devotions, sermon
and Benediction. Other casualties were to follow. In the early 1960s proces-
sions along the public highway in honour of the Blessed Sacrament, as in
Swindon, or of Our Lady, succumbed to the pressure of ever-increasing
traffic. Nor was the 'flickering altar of television' (as Archbishop Murphy
of Cardiff once described it) without its impact. Indeed, in a perverse sort
of way one might argue that both these all-consuming phenomena – the
car and the television set – were as much instrumental in bringing about
change in the life of the average parish as the liturgical decrees that were
soon to emanate from the Second Vatican Council.

In truth life was becoming ever more comfortable. No better example
of this can be found than in the matter of fast days when only one meal is
allowed and flesh meat forbidden. At this period in the 1960s the number
was four; today (2000) it is only two (Ash Wednesday and Good Friday).
This should be contrasted with the *sixty-five* fast days imposed by the Vicars
Apostolic on Catholics living in the poverty-stricken England of Charles
Dickens:

> The forty days of Lent: the Ember Days (12): the Vigils of Whit Sunday, of SS
> Peter & Paul, the Assumption, All Saints, and Christmas: the Wednesdays and
> Fridays in Advent.
>
> (The Catholic Directory, 1842, p. iii)

Not unexpectedly ecumenical endeavour during the years prior to the
opening of the Council was non-existent. To one enquirer who asked the
bishop whether he ever had any contact with the Bishop of Bristol, Rudderham replied, 'Only to send his mail on to him'.

The Second Vatican Council lasted from 1962 to 1965. Unlike Bishop Clifford a century before, Rudderham took no active part in the plenary sessions. This is hardly surprising bearing in mind the vast increase in the number of bishops and abbots entitled to take part from 679 in 1869 to 2,322 at the end of 1965. Furthermore while Bishop Rudderham had other qualities, intellectually he was no match of Clifford.

Although by temperament a conservative, he loyally put into effect the liturgical and other provisions of the Council. The council of priests (to advise the bishop), parish councils (optional) and the ordination of (married) men to the permanent diaconate (1973) bear witness to this. Indeed, profound changes were now taking place in the everyday life of parishes. Most notable of these was the celebration of Mass and the sacraments in English and the refashioning of the ceremonies of Holy Week, building on the work of renewal begun by Pope Pius XII. In the early 1960s Christian Stewardship or 'planned giving' became a feature in the life of most practising Catholics.

Knowledge of the Latin tongue, once a prerequisite in candidates for the priesthood, has all but disappeared among the clergy of fifty years or under. The education system in this country, and elsewhere, focussed almost exclusively on what were perceived to be 'the interests of industry' and abandoned this valuable tool in the training of language and thought. To guess the meaning of Latin from derived words in French or Spanish is, of course, of limited use as it ignores the fact that in Latin it is word endings which determine the meaning of a phrase or sentence. With the breviary in English thus becoming a necessity the opportunity was seized to conduct a complete overhaul of the church's official prayer – something advocated by Bishop Clifford a century before as part of an address at the First Vatican Council on the Life of the Clergy, but achieved with only partial success under Pope St. Pius X (1903–1914) – with the inclusion where possible of extracts from the writings of the saint whose feast was being celebrated. The result has been an outstanding success. Many lay people now recite the Office in private or in common.

At about this time church music took a new direction, all the more interesting when seen in the context of what had gone before. Indeed in the last century and a half, like church interiors, it had passed through a variety of fashionable expressions. In the 1840s and later decades operatic arias with music by Mozart, Haydn and Hummell – so prominent in church services at Clifton and Trenchard Street – eventually gave way under Pope St. Pius X to a greater use of plainchant, coupled with *The Westminster Hymnal* and its diet of much-loved but almost exclusively Catholic hymns. After the Second Vatican Council English Catholics were introduced not

only to the hitherto neglected masterpieces of the Wesleys and other Protestant hymnologists, but also to rhythmic creations by a new breed of Catholic composers who had but recently burst upon the scene. For some Catholics the advent of the guitar into liturgical worship symbolised the
'opening of the windows' approach of Pope John while for others it signified
the arrival of pop culture within the very portals of all that was holy. Significantly young and old were to be found in both camps.

In the last quarter of a century this has led, in part, to a feature of
parish life that is curiously redolent of the Church of England in the eighteenth century. Each Sunday Catholics are to be found crossing parish
boundaries in pursuit of that particular brand of churchmanship – Gregorian or guitar – that most appeals to them. Growth in car ownership, of
course, makes this easy and, given the upward social mobility of a growing
number of Catholics, some feel that where they worship makes a statement
not just about themselves but about their perception of the Faith.

Humanae Vitae (1968), in which Pope Paul VI re-affirmed the church's
traditional opposition to artificial birth control, proved to be a watershed
in the life of the Church. It was said that the Vatican was taken by surprise
at the extent of the opposition, voiced at all levels, particularly in the correspondence columns of *The Times*. Publicly there was some debate in Clifton, notably in the press, but the trauma suffered elsewhere in terms of
open intellectual revolt in the ranks of the clergy did not materialise here.
However, at this time, some priests did defect though not necessarily
because of the encyclical. With hindsight the number involved cannot be
ignored as one factor giving rise to the present day shortage of diocesan
clergy.

What one writer has described as 'the unbuttoning of the nation'
occurred during the 1960s. 'The pill' epitomised a new way of thinking
amongst the young and those not yet in middle age, particularly in sexual
mores, and there are many who with hindsight would date the fall off in
the number of those going to Confession not only to the availability of this
universal placebo, but also to the widespread dissent regarding the morality
of its use. It is not merely in politics that public disagreement can weaken
the party line.

But the balance sheet was not all negative. Concern for the Third World
became a real motivating power in the lives of the young, and numerous
sponsored efforts in aid of the Catholic Fund for Overseas Development
(CAFOD) redeemed what otherwise might seem an unmitigated pursuit of
hedonism, so often excoriated by Malcolm Muggeridge. Support for the
work of Mother Teresa of Calcutta, the adopting of various projects in
Africa and South America, the sacrifice of holidays in order to take sick

and handicapped children to Lourdes (HCPT) – these and many other endeavours with the young at the forefront helped to create a new optimism and a new awareness of shared humanity. This too was the inspiration behind a trickle of diocesan priests opting to work in Peru, Brazil and other parts of South America.

In April 1973, a significant step forward was taken in ecumenical dialogue and understanding with the holding of the South-West Ecumenical Congress. Study papers had been prepared and discussed for months before, and during the congress delegates attended simultaneous conferences on eight different topics at centres throughout Bristol. The climax of the event came at the Colston Hall when some two thousand people assembled to hear Dr. Ramsey, the Archbishop of Canterbury, Cardinal Suenens, the Primate of Belgium, and others speak on the theme 'The Future of the Christian Church'. A second congress was held in 1976. The charismatic movement, a new phenomenon in modern devotional life, though with a pedigree going back to sacred scripture itself, was one of the subjects discussed.

Clifton Cathedral took the place of the Pro-Cathedral as the mother church of the diocese on 29 June 1973. Visited shortly afterwards by H.M. the Queen it is a building which incorporated all the latest liturgical ideas. Unfortunately, because of the devaluation of the pound, various economies of style, particularly on the exterior and in the size of the presbytery, had to be introduced. The fact that the site of the Pro-Cathedral remained unsold did not help matters. Nevertheless most observers have pronounced it a success. Some critics, it is true, have described it when empty as being little different from a concert hall. This is unfair, and on Maundy Thursday, when the bishop is surrounded by his priests and people, the building can then be seen and judged in its proper context as the home of the Church of Clifton at worship.

1975–2000

Dr. Mervyn Alexander was ordained auxiliary bishop to Bishop Rudderham in 1972 and succeeded him in December 1974. Like Bishop Lee he was a priest of this diocese but in episcopal style he was far removed from the rather bullish manner of his two immediate predecessors. He continued the reforms of Second Vatican Council and his time as bishop was marked by a number of meetings with both clergy and laity to open up still further the channels of communication – *The Clifton Chronicle, Catholic Voice* and *Clifton Catholic News* all appeared in successive decades – to affirm the role of the laity and to emphasise the importance of social issues in the ministry of the Church. The work of CAFOD, the setting up of a Justice and Peace commission and the bishop's visits to the clergy working in South America underline this fact. Latterly the bishop came to be known as 'Bishop Mervyn', a style of address already used in the Church of England. His involvement with the young – visiting their camps and taking part in sponsored walks – subtly points to the contrast with the previous quarter century.

In 1976 a further and definitive stage was reached in the reorganisation of education in Bristol. A decision was taken to create a Catholic VI Form College at Brislington – one of the first in the country – on the site of the school run by the Irish Christian Brothers. Soon afterwards the Brothers withdrew having since 1896 played a major part in the education of boys first at Berkeley Square, Clifton and then, since 1961, at Brislington.

Churches continued to be re-ordered although sadly, when examples of Anti-Victorian Philistinism did occur, it was countered all too late by the setting up of a Department of Art and Architecture. Diocesan commissions, and what were described as 'Diocesan Services' burgeoned. Members of both sexes were encouraged to become readers at Mass and special ministers of Holy Communion. Family Fast Days, Penitential services, particularly those organised on a deanery level during Lent, and healing services became a familiar feature of modern day parish life.

The visit of the Holy Father in 1982 caused great excitement and many people travelled either to Coventry or to Cardiff to witness an event so utterly unthinkable in the days when his predecessor Pope Pius IX (1846–1878) was being burnt in effigy.

A controversy arose over the Diocesan Youth Service which caused some bitterness, but this was overshadowed in the mid and late 1990s by a far wider debate on the issue of allowing the Neo-Catechumenate to continue to work in the diocese. Founded by Kiko Arguello and enjoying papal approval it was nevertheless perceived by some as both elitist and divisive of parish life. A panel of three was set up by the bishop to investigate and to take evidence from both sides in what was becoming an increasingly bitter dispute. Three parishes in particular were involved – in Gloucester, Cheltenham and Bristol. The panel's findings included the following: 'We do not conclude that each P.P. has caused any individual harm but we do conclude that the methods of the NC Way have done so' (II, v, V, g). Not unnaturally the national press showed great interest in these happenings, not least *The Guardian* which read into the report's 'unexpectedly strong conclusions ... a direct challenge to the Vatican' (8 November 1996). It was indeed a sad episode, especially as it came on the eve of the bishop's episcopal silver jubilee.

Taking a broader view of the last century and a half one notices a
contraction in land and property owned in particular by religious communities no longer able to sustain a sufficient number of vocations to make
such large undertakings viable. On the other hand greater co-operation
with secular and other religious bodies has resulted in a more open-ended
witness by the Church. Links with various housing charities, the Samarit-
ans and drug awareness schemes and, quite strikingly, the opening of Walsingham House, a drug and alcohol rehabilitation centre – unique in this
country: all of these point both to new problems and to new perspectives
at the end of the twentieth century.

The life-style of the clergy is another area where change is undoubtedly
discernible. Until the 1960s clerical dress was *de rigueur*, but with the
relaxations of that era came a more hirsute body of men, loyal and yet
more critical of the Church and not slow to say so in the media. Criticism
of the Holy Father is not unknown.

Clergy conferences are now less formal. In the past they had resembled
the teaching curriculum in Napoleon's schools with subjects for discussion
already decided by 'central government'. Sadly there is an almost universal
ignorance of the Latin tongue and on occasions a scarcely veiled disdain
for anything pre-conciliar. The other side of the equation must be seen in
a greater willingness to be involved in social issues and to make common
cause with others in combating the wrongs of society. A good example of
this is The Communities Organised for a Greater Bristol (COGB) which
defines itself as 'a confederation of community groups – mainly, but not
exclusively, Christian – committed to acting responsibly in the public area
for the common good'.

Longevity in the ranks of the diocesan clergy reflects a trend in society
at large. (Today there are over 10,000 people in Britain aged 100–plus.)
Strikingly the first edition of the *Clifton Diocesan Year Book*, published in
1951, does not list a single priest out of the 115 clergy of the diocese as
being fifty or more years ordained whereas in 1999 the figure is 27 out of
a total of 149. Conversely there are fewer younger clergy today than there
were half a century ago.

Honours have proliferated, a fact which is explained (although only in
part) by former members of the chapter living long enough to go into
retirement. Today an unprecedented twenty priests have the title 'canon'.
Among the laity recipients of papal awards – virtually unheard of in 1950 –
are to be found in most parishes.

Vandalism, which ranks as one of the great social scourges of the day,
has resulted in many churches being kept locked during the hours of daylight. Private visits to the Blessed Sacrament, already on the wane, have

suffered in city and in rural churches alike. A growing number of parishes have abandoned Midnight Mass in favour of a Mass on Christmas Eve. Again, crime against the person is cited as the reason.

More informal dress is common amongst religious as well, sisters often being barely recognisable as such with little more than a cross on a necklace to signify their calling. Saints' names have been abandoned in favour of Father or Sister (and first name).

The vocation of parish sister has proved very beneficial to parish life. In a ministry which is both varied and flexible she provides a focal point particularly in those districts where there is only one priest. In his absence there are still occasions when people need someone to whom they can turn for comfort or to make arrangements for a christening or funeral or merely to issue a certificate. The tradition of hospital visiting and catechetical instruction continues to be a high priority for sister and priest alike.

The laity, too, are noticeably more articulate and less likely to accept an *ipse dixit* of prelate or priest. Numerous courses are available to them in theology, catechetics and, more recently, feminist issues. There is now some limited demand for the ordination of women to the priesthood, and one of the annual features of Maundy Thursday at Clifton Cathedral is a clutch of women and men silently proclaiming, 'The Church is all the poorer in not recognising the gifts of women'.

Conversely it was because of this (and other) issues that sixteen former Church of England clergy had by the end of 1998 embarked on their journey to Rome and been ordained as priests of the Clifton diocese. Some of them are married men whose Catholic ordination by English bishops during a concessionary period lasting four years was authorised by Pope John-Paul II. These, when working in parishes, are known as 'associate pastors'. Their presence has gone some way to alleviate the shortage of diocesan clergy but at national level (e.g. in letters to *The Tablet*) their recognised marital status continues to rankle with those celibate clergy who left the ministry in order to marry but are being denied the possibility of resuming their priestly duties.

Cohabitation, either before marriage or indeed without any intention of marriage, appears to be commonplace. Petitions for nullity brought before the Diocesan Marriage Tribunal, at one time rising inexorably, have undergone a decline with 'conscience' being perceived by many as supplanting due juridical process by the Church. This, however, is but part of a larger picture. In its *Annual Report* for 1995 the Government Office of National Statistics stated that in the U.K. there was a dramatic drop in the number of first time marriages from 221,927 to 166,418 over the ten year period between 1985 and 1995.

Sadly the Catholic community is not immune from such trends. In a news item on the Report *The Universe* noted that 'the number of couples giving the same address when getting married at a civil ceremony hit an all time high of 80 per cent' (26 July 1998). This underlines one of the new challenges faced by the parish priest of today – 'new' because the illegitimacy of fifty years ago was seldom the result of actual cohabitation.

The diocese of Clifton has its fair share of interesting buildings. Pugin (St. Osmund, Salisbury); Hansom (St. John, Bath, and St. Joseph, Weston-super-Mare); Canon A. J. C. Scoles (St. John the Baptist, Trowbridge; and Holy Ghost, Yeovil); Doran Webb (Holy Rood, Swindon) have adorned both urban and rural settings with their creations. Even a medieval chapel (Postlip near Winchcombe) and church (St. Mary, Cricklade) are once again the setting for the Mass.

In style there could be no greater contrast than that between the classical lines of Prior Park chapel (completed 1882) and the tent-like St. Bernadette (1968) at Whitchurch, Bristol. Anglicans are sharing their churches with us in Stockwood, Bristol, West Harptree, Somerset and elsewhere, while in Wilton Catholics worship in the same building as the Methodists and the members of the United Reformed Church.

No fewer than six bishops for other dioceses have come from the ranks of the Clifton diocesan clergy:

William Vaughan	Bishop of Plymouth 1855–1902
Ferdinand English	Archbishop of Port of Spain, Trinidad 1860–1862
Edmund Knight	Bishop of Shrewsbury 1882–1895
Michael McGrath	Bishop of Menevia 1935–1940
	Archbishop of Cardiff 1940–1961
Francis Grimshaw	Bishop of Plymouth 1947–1954
	Archbishop of Birmingham 1954–1965
Crispian Hollis	Auxiliary Bishop of Birmingham 1987–1988
	Bishop of Portsmouth 1988–

Conspicuous among several appointments of religious from the diocese was

Basil Christopher Butler O.S.B.	Auxiliary Bishop of Westminster 1966–1986

In the two General Councils our diocese has played its part through the words of Bishop Clifford and Abbot Butler. In the year 2000 we find it in less triumphalist mood than it was fifty years before. Today apathy has replaced the hostility of 1850.

At first sight the priest with a 'bleeper' in his hand ready to respond to a hospital sick call and the bishop issuing a press release on a fax machine would seem to be a far cry from the Irish immigrants arriving penniless in a cattle boat in the port of Bristol. And yet, *mirabile dictu*, it *is* the same Church, it *is* the same diocese of Clifton.

* * * * *

DIOCESAN STATISTICS
1850–2000

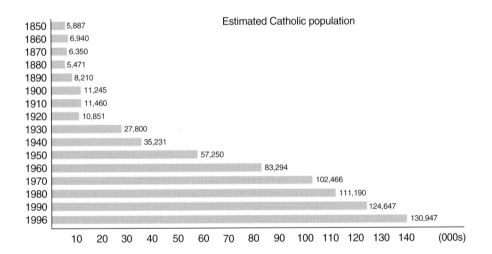

Estimated Catholic population

Year	Population
1850	5,887
1860	6,940
1870	6.350
1880	5,471
1890	8,210
1900	11,245
1910	11,460
1920	10,851
1930	27,800
1940	35,231
1950	57,250
1960	83,294
1970	102,466
1980	111,190
1990	124,647
1996	130,947

10 20 30 40 50 60 70 80 90 100 110 120 130 140 (000s)

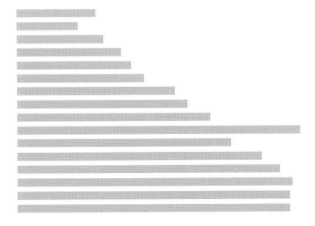

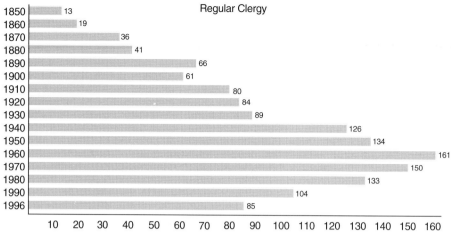

Regular Clergy

Year	Value
1850	13
1860	19
1870	36
1880	41
1890	66
1900	61
1910	80
1920	84
1930	89
1940	126
1950	134
1960	161
1970	150
1980	133
1990	104
1996	85

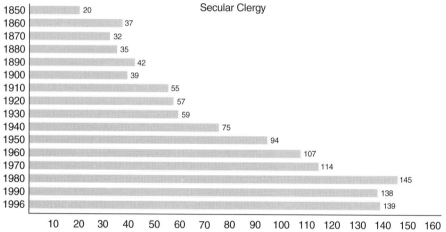

Secular Clergy

Year	Value
1850	20
1860	37
1870	32
1880	35
1890	42
1900	39
1910	55
1920	57
1930	59
1940	75
1950	94
1960	107
1970	114
1980	145
1990	138
1996	139

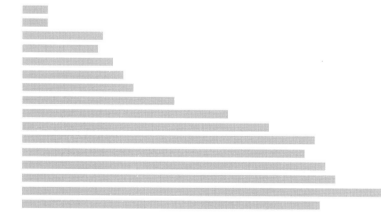

Appendix 1

Vicars Apostolic

The first bishop to be appointed after the Reformation had charge of the whole of England and Wales.

William Bishop	1623–1624
Richard Smith	1625–1655
No appointment made until 1685	
John Leyburne	1685–1688

In 1688 Pope Blessed Innocent XI divided England and Wales into four districts or vicariates: London, Midland, Northern and Western. Wales was part of the Western District.

Vicars Apostolic of the Western District

Philip Michael Ellis O.S.B.	1688–1705
No appointment made until 1713	
Matthew Prichard O.S.F.	1713–1750
Laurence York O.S.B.	1750–1770
Charles Walmesley O.S.B.	1770–1797
Gregory William Sharrock O.S.B.	1798–1808
Bernadine Peter Collingridge O.S.F.	1809–1829
Peter Augustine Baines O.S.B.	1829–1840

In 1840 the number of districts was increased to eight. Wales was given its own Vicar Apostolic.

Peter Augustine Baines O.S.B.	1840–1843
Charles Michael Baggs	1843–1845
William Bernard Ullathorne O.S.B.	1846–1848
Joseph William Hendren O.S.F.	1848–1850

The diocese of Clifton, with Bishop Hendren as its first bishop, came into being in 1850 with the restoration of the Hierarchy by Pope Pius IX. The remaining part of the Western District (Dorset, Devon and Cornwall) became the diocese of Plymouth.

Appendix 2

Popes

Pius IX (Mastai-Ferretti)	1846–1878
Leo XIII (Pecci)	1878–1903
St Pius X (Sarto)	1903–1914
Benedict XV (della Chiesa)	1914–1922
Pius XI (Ratti)	1922–1939
Pius XII (Pacelli)	1939–1958
John XXIII (Roncalli)	1958–1963
Paul VI (Montini)	1963–1978
John-Paul I (Luciani)	1978
John-Paul II (Wojtyla)	1978–

Archbishops of Westminster

Cardinal Nicholas Wiseman	1850–1865
Cardinal Henry Edward Manning	1865–1892
Cardinal Herbert Vaughan	1892–1903
Cardinal Francis Bourne	1903–1935
Cardinal Arthur Hinsley	1935–1943
Cardinal Bernard Griffin	1943–1956
Cardinal William Godfrey	1956–1963
Cardinal John Carmel Heenan	1963–1975
Cardinal George Basil Hume, OSB	1976–1999

Bishops of Clifton

Joseph William Hendren, OSF	1850–1851
Thomas Burgess	1851–1854
George Errington* Titular Archbishop of Trebizond	1855–1857
William Joseph Hugh Clifford	1857–1893
William Robert Brownlow	1893–1901
George Ambrose Burton	1902–1931
William Lee	1932–1948
Joseph Edward Rudderham	1949–1974
Mervyn Alban Alexander	1974–

*Apostolic Administrator of Clifton

Appendix 3

The Bishops' Residences

Bishop Walmesley O.S.B.

Until 1780 (Gordon Riots) Lodged at the Bell Tree House, Bath.
He also spent much time at Woollas Hall on Bredon Hill, with his friends, the Handfords.
After 1780 Between 1780 and 1786 the Bell Tree property was rebuilt, but in February 1786 the new O.S.B. incumbent, Jerome Digby, refused to have Walmesley as a lodger and asked him to leave.
The bishop then took up residence at 8 Chapel Row (which has been identified as being in Queen Square). He was in this house in 1790 and presumably died there (1797).
(Acknowledgements to Abbot Geoffrey Scott O.S.B. of Douai for this information)

Bishop Sharrock O.S.B.

1780–1809 at 13 St. James Square.

Bishop Collingridge O.S.F.

1808–1812 at Miss Jones's Boarding House, High Street, Chepstow. (The bishop used to refer to his two attic rooms as his 'palace'.)
1812–1818 at the Franciscan Convent, Taunton Lodge, Taunton.
1818–1829 at the Court House, Cannington.

Bishop Baines

1823 Pierrepoint Place, Bath.
1824–1830 Bathampton Manor, near Bath.
1830–1843 Prior Park, Bath.

Bishop Baggs

1844–1845 Prior Park, Bath.

Bishop Ullathorne O.S.B.

1846–1847 7 King's Square, Bristol.
1847–1848 22 Meridian Place, Clifton.

Bishop Hendren O.S.F.

1848–1851 22 Meridian Place, Clifton. (Bishop Hendren was responsible for building the presbytery at the Pro-Cathedral. After his retirement in 1852 he lived at the convent at Taunton Lodge, where he died in 1866.)

Bishop Burgess

1851–1854 22 Meridian Place, Clifton.

Archbishop Errington (Administrator)

1855–1857 22 Meridian Place, Clifton.

Bishop Clifford

1857–1891 22 Meridian Place, Clifton. After the death of the President of Prior Park, Mgr. Edward Williams, the bishop lived at Prior Park from 1891 until his death in 1893.

Bishop Brownlow

1894–1901 22 Meridian Place, Clifton.

Bishop Burton

1902–1903 22 Meridian Place, Clifton.
1903–1904 Prior Park, Bath.
1904–1931 St. Ambrose, North Road, Leigh Woods, Bristol. All the subsequent Bishops of Clifton have resided there. From 1972 to 1974, when he was auxiliary bishop, Dr. Mervyn Alexander lived at St. John's Presbytery, South Parade, Bath.

St. Ambrose, Leigh Woods, Bristol

On leaving Prior Park in 1904, Bishop Burton was told of a house, suitable as an episcopal residence, at Leigh Woods, Bristol. Miss Georgina Braham of Weston-super-Mare had already indicated to him her intention to benefit the Bishop of Clifton after her death and so on Holy Saturday Burton visited her and asked for her promised help to be brought forward so as to enable him to purchase the property. The £3,000 – which the local parish priest, Canon Barron, strenuously argued had already been promised for the purchase of a disused Baptist chapel in Weston – was duly forwarded and the transaction was concluded. A plaque in Latin on the wall of the bishop's private chapel recalls the generosity of the benefactress.

Originally called 'Wootton Lodge' and then 'Barscobe' the house had belonged to William Hain who in a will dated 14 May 1892 bequeathed it to his housekeeper, Mary Jane Ancrum. In 1904 the occupier was Col. McLellan. On his moving out the bishop and his secretary took up residence and set up the diocesan office. (There is an apocryphal story suggesting that the house once belonged to someone involved in the construction of the nearby Suspension Bridge. For this reason he called it 'Suspension House' – a name which the new occupier, Burton, was determined to change remarking, so it was alleged, that no priest would wish to visit his bishop at such an ominous address.)

Bishop Burton, a classicist, was a great admirer of Saint Ambrose (c 340–397). Not only did he try to emulate his Latin style but on his appointment he actually assumed his name. As if to underline this *pietas* he re-named the episcopal residence 'St. Ambrose'.

In the dining room there are portraits of all the Vicars Apostolic, except Bishop Sharrock whose portrait was probably never painted, and of the Bishops of Clifton. Photographs of the latter are reproduced in this book.

J.C & J.A.H.

Appendix 4

Diocesan Synods

1.	Bishop Burgess	14 December 1853	Pro-Cathedral
2.	Bishop Clifford	1 June 1864	Pro-Cathedral
3.	Bishop Clifford	8 July 1875	Pro-Cathedral
4.	Bishop Clifford	*date not known*	Pro-Cathedral
5.	Bishop Brownlow	5 October 1897	Pro-Cathedral
6.	Bishop Rudderham	25 October 1955	Pro-Cathedral
7.	Bishop Alexander	8 December 1988	Clifton Cathedral

Appendix 5

The Clifton Mission and (later) Parish

Administrators and Parish Priests

1842	Francis Edgeworth OFM
1844–1847	Thomas McDonnell
1847–1855	William Vaughan
1855–1856	Frederick Neve
1856–1857	Ferdinand English
1857–1863	Frederick Neve
1863–1872	John Bonomi
1872–1873	John Clarke
1873–1878	Frederick Neve
1878–1894	John Clarke
1894–1898	Eustace Barron
1898–1904	Arthur Russell
1904–1910	David O'Brien
1910–1932	William Lee
1932–1962	Patrick Long
1962–1981	Thomas Hughes
1981–1987	Crispian Hollis
1987–1997	Gabriel Leyden
1997	William Mitchell

Appendix 6

The Pro Cathedral

The present whereabouts of various items and furnishings which were dispersed when the church was finally closed in June 1973.

High Altar *mensa* (since 1998)
Paschal candlestick
Votive candle stand
Liturgical books (Mgr. C. Parfitt)
	Saint Saviour's House
	  (Society of St. Pius X)
	  St Agnes Avenue
	  Knowle, Bristol

Stained glass windows	Holy Cross Church
	  Bedminster, Bristol
	St. Patrick's Church
	  Redfield, Bristol.

Visitation window
Clifford window, Bishop's chapel
  Pro-Cathedral House
	Saints Peter & Paul School
	  Aberdeen Road, Redland
	  Bristol.

Statue of Saint Peter	St. Peter's Church, Swindon
Medieval Trinity Altar (part)	St. Nicholas Church Museum, Baldwin Street, Bristol.

Statue of Our Lady (left of
  sanctuary)
	Saints Peter & Paul
	  School

Statue of Sacred Heart (right of
  sanctuary)
	Little Sisters of the Poor
	  Cotham, Bristol.

Brass (shortened) Bells (clock) Tabernacle (high altar)	Clifton Cathedral

Big Six Candlesticks	Athelhampton Hall
	  nr. Dorchester, Dorset.
	  (Residence of Sir Robert Cook,
	  M.P. for Bristol West).

Benches (sanctuary)	St. Bernadette Church Whitchurch, Bristol.

Organ, console	St Mark's Church
	  (Church of England)
	  Swindon

Lions (south porch) { Saints Peter & Paul School (playground)

Marble pillars (south porch)

On end with capital;
Entrance to 6 Mornington Road Clifton, Bristol.

Two gargoyles from St. Catherine's Hall

Saints Peter & Paul School.

Appendix 7

Cemeteries and Churchyards

(This list does not include Catholic sections in public cemeteries)

BATH	Perrymead cemetery, Ralph Allen Drive.
BECKFORD	In the grounds of the Manor House.
BONHAM	Unmarked graves in the grounds of the House. Headstones in the Garden of Remembrance.
BRIDGWATER	St. Joseph's cemetery, Gordon Terrace (old church)
BRISTOL	Holy Souls, Arnos Vale, Bath Road, Brislington.
BROWNSHILL	St. Mary's churchyard, St. Mary's Way.
BURNHAM-ON-SEA	La Retraite Sisters cemetery, Rosewood Avenue, (adjacent to the playing field of St. Joseph Primary School).
CANNINGTON	Unmarked graves. Headstones against the wall of the 'Nuns Garden' in the Somerset College of Agriculture and Horticulture.
CHIPPING CAMPDEN	Cemetery, Hoo Lane.
DEVIZES	Churchyard adjacent to the church.
DOWNSIDE	In the grounds of the monastery.
FAIRFORD	Churchyard adjacent to the church.
GLOUCESTER	Cemetery, Tredworth Road.
KEMERTON	Churchyard adjacent to the church.
LECHLADE	In the grounds of the Manor House.
NYMPSFIELD	Churchyard adjacent to the church.
PRINKNASH	In the grounds of the monastery.
SALISBURY	Churchyard adjacent to St. Osmund.
STRATTON-ON-THE-FOSSE	Churchyard adjacent to St. Benedict.

WARDOUR   Cemetery half a mile from the Chapel (on the Tisbury-Semley Road).

WOODCHESTER   1) Churchyard adjacent to the Church of the Annunciation,

                                    2) In the grounds of the Convent of the Poor Clares.

Notes

1) Some of the places listed above are now full.
2) *Cheltenham*: In the 1840s and 1850s many Catholics were buried in the church-yard adjoining the Passionist Church at Broadway, Worcestershire.
3) *Shepton Mallet*: Bodies of nuns from Sales House, at one time buried beneath the old church, were later exhumed.
4) *Stroud*: In the mid 1970s bodies of the sisters from St. Rose's Convent were transferred to Woodchester churchyard.

Appendix 8

The progress of Catholicism in Wiltshire in the late eighteenth century

Bishop Walmesley (Vicar Apostolic 1770-1797) has left records of several of his visitations after 1780, and we discover him administering confirmation — though never it seems in the winter months, on account no doubt, of the difficult conditions of the roads and the hazards of travel — in every part of his Vicariate. In 1781 we find him in Dorset, Wiltshire and Glouces-ter; in June of the following year he is in Wales, while the year 1786 sees him at places as far apart as Bristol and Holywell, and during the next two years he is in Wiltshire again.

His visit to the county in 1781 took in Bonham, where he found a con-gregation of 'upward of 100 men, women and children' and confirmed eighteen or nineteen persons; Salisbury, where eleven were confirmed, there being 'between 40 and 50 communicants, but fluctuating as strangers come and go,' and Wardour, of which the Bishop records, surely with pro-found satisfaction, 'I confirmed there 82 persons on the 17 of June, 1781. The congregation increases there by converts and now (1781) consists in the whole of about 540'.

He visited Wardour again on 1 October 1787, confirming sixty-one per-sons, and Salisbury and Bonham in the following July, confirming nine and twenty-eight respectively, and finding that the Bonham congregation had risen to 'at least 150 in the whole'. There seems little doubt that the Catholic population of Wiltshire was increasing and even Bishop Walmes-ley's cautious and pessimistic temper must have conceded that the outlook

was in this respect perceptibly brighter than when he had first arrived ι
the Western District more than thirty years before.

(J. Anthony Williams, Catholic Recusancy in Wiltshire
1660-1791, pages 138–140)

BIBLIOGRAPHY

A Local Bibliography

In the compilation of this work we are deeply indebted to oral and written sources too numerous to mention. The following is a select list of the published and unpublished sources which are relevant to the pre-history and history of Clifton Diocese.

Anglin, D. The early history of the Bristol School Board 1871–91. (1971). Unpubl.

Anson, P. *The Benedictines of Caldey.* (1944)

Antonioz, J. *The Catholic Church of the Holy Ghost, Yeovil.* (1928)

Appleby, C. *A history of St. Dominic's Catholic parish, Dursley.* (1998)

Atthill, R. The Catholic Church at Shortwood 1795–1883. *South Western Catholic History*, 2, 1984

Badeni, J. [Countess]. *St. Aldhelm's Catholic Church Malmsbury.* Nd.

Barton, R. *St. Gregory's Cheltenham: development of the parish to 1916.* (1987)

Bellenger, D. A. Ed. *Fathers in Faith: the Western District 1688–1988.* (1991)

Bellenger, D. A. Ed. *A pictorial history of Downside.* (1998)

Berry, R. *A history of the convent in Taunton.* (1988)

Bourne, M. *His mercy is from age to age: the story of the Sisters of St. Joseph of Annecy.* (1983)

Bradshaw, J. *God gave the increase: Thornbury, Christ the King.* Nd.

Brooke, C. [and others] *David Knowles remembered.* (1991)

Bryan, T. *St. Nicholas of Tolentino Church 1848–95.* (1995)

Caraman, P. *Wardour: a short history.* (1984)

Cashman, J. Old Prior Park: the final years, 1843–56. *Recusant History*, 23 (1) 1996.

Cashman, J. A question of obedience: Bishop Baines and the Cannington community. *South Western Catholic History*, 14, 1996.

Catholic Poor School Committee. Minutes. 1847–

Champ, J. F. Priesthood and politics: the turbulent career of Thomas McDonnell 1792–1869. *Recusant History*, 18 (3) 1997.

Clark, A & R. *The Church of St. Gregory the Great, Cheltenham.* (1977)

Clifford, H. *The House of Clifford.* (1987)

Clifton Catholic Diocesan School Commission. Minutes.

Coggles, A. B. *The history of St. Mary's Parish, Chippenham 1855–98.* (1998)

Collins, C. *St. Benet's Church, Kemerton: a brief history 1843–93.* (1993)

Cooke, V. *La Retraite High School Clifton 1924–82.* (1983)

Corpus Christi Church, Weston-Super-Mare. *Jubilee 1929–79.* (1980)

Darby, J. *The Diocese of Clifton 1850–1950: a centenary souvenir.* (1950)

Davis, F. [and others] *The Shepton Mallet story.* (1968)

Dockery, J. *The Church of the Immaculate Conception, Clevedon.* (1987)

Dockery, J. B. *Collingridge: a Franciscan contribution to Catholic Emancipation.* (1954)

Dove, C. *The story of Nympsfield.* (1987)

Drumm, W. *Bridgwater's Catholic past.* (1997)

English, J. *The history of the English family in Bath.* (1995)

English Martyrs. [Church of], Chard. *A parish history, written by parishioners.* (1995)

Fitzgerald-Lombard, C. *A guide to Downside Abbey.* (1981)

Gloucestershire and North Avon Catholic History Society. *Journal.*

Grimshaw, J. Sketch of the rise and progress of the Highbridge Mission to 1913. Unpubl.

Hankins, K. *In My Father's House: St. Mary-on-the-Quay* . . . (1995)

Harding, J. A. *1300 years: a history of the Catholic Church in Warminster.* (1980)

Harvey, P. The Catholic Church and secondary education in Bristol. (1980) Unpubl.

Hicks, B. *Hugh Edmund Ford: first Abbot of Downside.* (1947)

Hollingsbee, V. *St. Augustine of Canterbury, Matson 1962–1988.* Nd.

Holy Rood Church. *Swindon's Catholic Church: its origins and growth.* (1978)

Howard, J. *The Poor Servants of the Mother of God.* Nd.

Howell, B. S. The formative years of Catholic boys' secondary education in Bristol 1890–1918. (1975) Unpubl.

Johnson, T. *Tapestry: a history of the Catholic Faith in the Trowbridge area* (1979). *See also* St John the Baptist, Trowbridge.

Kerby, M. *The parish of St. Gerard Majella, Knowle.* Nd.

Knowles, D. *Cardinal Gasquet as an historian.* (1962)

Knox, R. The Centenary of the Hierarchy: II. *Occasional Sermons* (1960).

Lawrence, B. Dom Philip Powell (1594–1646). *South Western Catholic History,* 4 1986.

Leslie, S. (Ed.) *The letters of Herbert Cardinal Vaughan to Lady Herbert of Lea.* (1942)

Leslie, S. The missing letters of Cardinal Vaughan to Lady Herbert of Lea. *Dublin Review* 220 Autumn, 1947.

Little, B. Tensions in Trenchard Street: the Bristol Cause 1829–47. *South Western Catholic History* 3, 1985.

Merrifield, B. *Kingswood Catholic Parish* (1996)

Miller, D. *History of the Church of the Sacred Heart, Minehead: centenary year.* (1986)

Murch, J. *Biographical sketches of Bath celebrities.* (1893)

Murphy, E. *History of St. Lawrence's Church, Chipping Sodbury.* (1988)

Murphy, F. *St. Bernard's Catholic Church, Shirehampton 1902–92.* (1993)

Murray, M. Beginnings of the mission at Shepton Mallet 1765–1865. *South Western Catholic History,* 8 (1990)

Nazareth House, Cheltenham. *Souvenir brochure 1957–82.* (1983)

Oliver, G. *Collections illustrating the history of the Catholic religion* . . . (1857)

slow, P. The Minehead Mission a hundred years ago. *South Western Catholic His-ory*, 7 (1989)

ur Lady of Victories Catholic Church, Cinderford. *Golden Jubilee brochure*. Nd.

)ur Lady Queen of the Apostles, Cheddar. *The story of our church*. (1990)

Pierce, A. *Sacred Heart Church Cheltenham: Silver Jubilee 1957–82*. (1983)

Prinknash Abbey. *The story of Prinknash from time immemorial to the present day*.

Rees, D. *Bishop Butler 1902–86*. (1987)

Roche, J. *The history of Prior Park and its founder Bishop Baines*. (1933)

Roche, W. *Holy Family Church, Swindon 1962–87*. (1988)

Rudden, J. *Our Lady and St. Kenelm, Stow on the Wold*. (1985)

St. Brendan's Sixth Form College. *Centenary year 1896–1996*. 91996)

St. Gregory's Cheltenham. *Development of the parish to 1916*. (1987)

St. John the Baptist, Trowbridge. *Tapestry: the story continues 1990–96*. (1997)

St. Joseph's, Ilminster. *see English Martyrs, Chard*.

St. Joseph's Church, Littleton Pannell. *Great oaks from little acorns grow*. (1987)

St. Joseph's Catholic Church, Bridgwater. *History 1882–1982*. (1982)

St. Michael Archangel. *Short history of Catholicism in Tetbury*. Nd.

St. Osmund, Salisbury. *St. Osmund's and Catholic Salisbury: a short history*. (1998)

St. Peter's, Crewkerne. *See English Martyrs, Chard*.

St. Peter's School, Gloucester. *Like a grain of mustard seed. [history] 1864–1964*. (1965)

St. Peter and Paul, Coombe Down. *A short history*.

St. Thomas More, Cheltenham. *The first 21 years*. Nd.

St. Thomas of Canterbury, Fairford. *A short history*. Nd.

Scott, G. The early career of Bishop Charles Walmesley O.S.B., F.R.S. 1722–97. *Downside Review*, October, 1997.

Stevens, L. L. *A history of St. Joseph's Church, Fishponds*. (1975)

Storer, P. *St. George's Catholic Church, Taunton*. (1990)

Tisbury and Wardour. *A history of the parish*. (1998)

Vose, J. *Cirencester: post Reformation Catholicism and St. Peter's Church*. (1995)

Williams, J. A. *Bath and Rome: the living link*. (1993)

Williams, J. A. *Catholic recusancy in Wiltshire 1660–1791*. (1968)

Williams, J. A. *Catholicism in Bath*. (1975)

Williams, J. A. Bishops Gifford and Ellis and the Western Vicariate. *Journal of Ecclesiastical History*, 15. (1964)

Unpublished Theses

Appleby, C. The English Catholic community: Catholics in the West of England. MA, Bristol. (1978)

Cashman, J. Bishop Baines and the tensions in the Western District ... M. Litt. Bristol. (1989)

— The 1902 Education Act and Roman Catholic Schools. Ph.D. Keele. (1985)

Gilbert, P. J. In the midst of a Protestant people: the development of a Catholic community in Bristol in the nineteenth century. Ph.D. Bristol. (1995)

Hankins, K. The contentions of power: the role of the Jesuits in the Catholic ,
of Bristol 1700–1830. Ph.D. Bristol. (1998)

Harding, J. A. The rebirth of the Roman Catholic community in Frome, 1850
1927 M. Litt. Bristol. (1986)

— Dr. William Clifford, Third Bishop of Clifton 1857–1893: his influence at the
First Vatican Council and on the English Catholic Church. Ph.D. London.
(1991)

Heiman, M. E. English Catholic devotion 1850–1914. D. Phil. Oxford. (1992)

Hickman, M. A study of the incorporation of the Irish in Britain with special
reference to Catholic state education. Ph.D. London. (1990)

Nelson, G. L. Charles Walmesley and the episcopal opposition to English Catholic
Cisalpinism 1782–1797. Ph.D. Tulane [USA] (1987)

Quinn, D. A. English Roman Catholics and politics in the second half of the nineteenth century. D. Phil. Oxford. (1985)

For Further Reading

The origins and development of the Clifton diocese took place within the
wider social and political context of Catholicism in England and Wales.
Therefore we are indebted to many of the standard works on the history
of British Catholicism. We include a select bibliography of published
sources of information for general reading or systematic study.

Anson, P. *The religious orders of Great Britain and Ireland.* London, 1949.

Aveling, J. C. H. *The handle and the axe: the Catholic recusants from the Reformation to
Emancipation.* London, 1967.

Basset, B. *The English Jesuits from Campion to Martindale.* London, 1962.

Bayne, C. G. *Anglo-Roman relations 1558–1565.* London, 1913.

Beales, A. C. F. *Education under penalty: English Catholic education from the Reformation
to the Fall of James II.* London, 1962.

Beck, G. A. *The English Catholics 1850–1950.* London, (1950)

Bellenger, D. A. *The French exiled clergy in the British Isles after 1789.* Downside,
(1986)

Bellenger, D. A. (Ed.) *The English and Welsh priests 1588–1800.* Downside, (1984)

Bence-Jones, M. *The Catholic families.* London, (1992)

Berrington, J. *The state and behaviour of English Catholics from the Reformation to the year
1780.* Birmingham, (1780)

Butler, C. *The life and times of Bishop Ullathorne.* 2 vols. London, (1926)

Caraman, P. *The years of siege: Catholic life from James I to Cromwell.* London (1966)

Caraman, P. *The Western Rising.* London, (1984)

Chadwick, O. *The Reformation.* Harmondsworth, (1966)

Chinnichi, J. P. *The English Catholic Enlightenment.* London, (1980)

Connell, J. *The Roman Catholic Church in England 1780–1850: a study in international
politics.* Philadelphia, (USA) (1984)

Dickens, A. G. *The English Reformation.* London, (1972)

ımm, W. *The Old Palace: the Catholic chaplaincy at Oxford*. Oxford, (1991)

ıffy, E. *The stripping of the altars: traditional religion in England 1400–1550*. New Haven, (1982)

)uffy, E. (Ed.) *Challoner and his church: a Catholic bishop in Georgian England*, London. (1982)

Evennett, H. O. *The Catholic schools of England*. Cambridge, (1944)

Fielding, S. *Class and ethnicity: Irish Catholics in England 1880–1939*. London. (1993)

Fitzgerald-Lombard, M. C. *English and Welsh priests 1801–1914*. Downside, (1993)

Gillow, J. *A literary biographical history or bibliographical dictionary of the English Catholics*. 1885. [Index vol. J. Bevan 1985] Reprinted, 1999. 5 vols.

Haigh, C. *Reformation and resistance in Tudor Lancashire*. Cambridge, (1975)

Hartigan, M. & Hickman, M. J. *A history of the Irish in Britain: a bibliography*. London, (1986)

Havran, M. J. *Catholics in Caroline England*. London, (1962)

Haydon, C. *Anti-Catholicism in eighteenth-century England: a political and social study*. London, (1995)

Hemphill, B. *The early Vicars Apostolic of England*, London, (1954)

Holmes, J. D. *More Roman than Rome: English Catholicism in the nineteenth century*. London, (1978)

Holmes, J. D. & Bickers, B. *A short history of the Catholic Church*. London, (1993)

Johnstone, T. & Hagerty, J. *The Cross and the sword: Catholic chaplains in the forces*. London, (1996)

Kenyon, J. P. *The Popish Plot*. London, (1972)

Leys, M. D. R. *Catholics in England: 1558–1829: a social history*. London, (1961)

Little, B. *Catholic churches since 1623*. London, (1961)

McClelland, V. A. *English Roman Catholics and higher education. 1830–1903*. Oxford, Clarendon, (1974)

McCoog, T. *The reckoned expense: Edmund Campion and the English Jesuits*. Woodbridge, (1996)

McGrath, P. *Papists and Puritans in Elizabethan England*. London, (1967)

Machin, G. I. T. *The Catholic question in English politics 1820–1830*. Oxford, (1964)

Mathew, D. *Catholicism in England 1535–1935*. London, (1935)

Moloney, J. *Westminster, Whitehall, The Vatican: the role of Cardinal Hinsley 1935–43*. London, (1985)

Murphy, J. *The religious problem in English education*. Liverpool, (1959)

Norman, E. R. *The English Catholic Church in the nineteenth century*. Oxford, (1984)

Norman, E. R. *Roman Catholicism in England from the Elizabethan Settlement to the Second Vatican Council*. Oxford, (1985)

Pawley, M. *Faith and family: the life and circle of Ambrose de Lisle*. London, (1993)

PaPaz, D. G. *Popular anti-Catholicism in Victorian England*. Stanford (USA), (1992)

Perceval, J. *The Great Famine: Ireland's potato famine 1845–51*. London, (1995)

Questier, M. *Conversion, politics and religion in England 1580–1625*. Cambridge, (1996)

Scott, G. *Gothic rage undone: English monks in the Age of Enlightenment*. Bath, (1992)

Shorney, D. *Protestant non-conformity and Roman Catholicism: a guide to sources in the Public Record Office*. London, (1996)

Scarisbrick, J. *The Reformation and the English people*. Oxford, (1984)

Swanson, D. *Catholic England before the Reformation*. Manchester, (1993)

Swift, R. & Gilley, S. (Eds.) *The Irish in the Victorian city*. Durham, (1989)

Trimble, W. R. *The Catholic laity in Elizabethan England*. Cambridge (Mass.), (1964

Turner, D. H. *The Benedictines in Britain*. London, (1980)

Ullathorne, W. B. *The Devil is a jackass: the autobiography of William Bernard Ullathorne;
    edited by L. Madigan*. Downside, (1996)

Ward, B. *The dawn of the Catholic revival in England: 1781–1803*. 2 vols. London,
    (1909)

Ward, B. *The sequel to Catholic Emancipation*. 2 vols. London, (1915)

Walsham, A. *Church papists: Catholic conformity and professional polemic in early modern
    England*. Oxford, (1993)

Watkin, E. *Roman Catholicism in England from the Reformation to 1950*. London, (1957)

Williams, G. *Wales and the Reformation*. Cardiff, (1997)

Williams, J. Ll. *Welsh Catholics on the Continent*. London, (1903)

Woodward, G. W. *The dissolution of the monasteries*. London, (1966)

Wolffe, F. E. *The Protestant crusade in Great Britain 1829–1860*. London, (1991)